JUSTICE AND REMEMBRANCE

Dedicated to
Seyyed Hossein Nasr

JUSTICE AND REMEMBRANCE

Introducing the Spirituality of Imam ʿAlī

Reza Shah-Kazemi

I.B.Tauris *Publishers*
LONDON • NEW YORK
in association with
The Institute of Ismaili Studies
LONDON

Paperback edition published in 2007
First published in hardback in 2006 by I.B.Tauris & Co Ltd
6 Salem Rd, London W2 4BU
175 Fifth Avenue, New York NY 10010
www.ibtauris.com

in association with The Institute of Ismaili Studies
42–44 Grosvenor Gardens, London SW1W 0EB
www.iis.ac.uk

In the United States of America and in Canada distributed by
St Martin's Press, 175 Fifth Avenue, New York NY 10010

ISBN 978 1 84511 526 5

A full CIP record for this book is available from the British Library
A full CIP record for this book is available from the Library of Congress

Library of Congress catalog card: available

Typeset in Minion Tra for The Institute of Ismaili Studies

Printed and bound in Great Britain by TJ International Ltd, Padstow, Cornwall

The Institute of Ismaili Studies

The Institute of Ismaili Studies was established in 1977 with the object of promoting scholarship and learning on Islam, in the historical as well as contemporary contexts, and a better understanding of its relationship with other societies and faiths.

The Institute's programmes encourage a perspective which is not confined to the theological and religious heritage of Islam, but seeks to explore the relationship of religious ideas to broader dimensions of society and culture. The programmes thus encourage an interdisciplinary approach to the materials of Islamic history and thought. Particular attention is also given to issues of modernity that arise as Muslims seek to relate their heritage to the contemporary situation.

Within the Islamic tradition, the Institute's programmes promote research on those areas which have, to date, received relatively little attention from scholars. These include the intellectual and literary expressions of Shiʿism in general, and Ismailism in particular.

In the context of Islamic societies, the Institute's programmes are informed by the full range and diversity of cultures in which Islam is practised today, from the Middle East, South and Central Asia, and Africa to the industrialized societies of the West, thus taking into consideration the variety of contexts which shape the ideals, beliefs and practices of the faith.

These objectives are realized through concrete programmes and activities organized and implemented by various departments of the Institute. The Institute also collaborates periodically, on a programme-specific basis, with other institutions of learning in the United Kingdom and abroad.

The Institute's academic publications fall into a number of interrelated categories:

1. Occasional papers or essays addressing broad themes of the relationship between religion and society, with special reference to Islam.
2. Monographs exploring specific aspects of Islamic faith and culture, or the contributions of individual Muslim thinkers or writers.
3. Editions or translations of significant primary or secondary texts.
4. Translations of poetic or literary texts which illustrate the rich heritage of spiritual, devotional and symbolic expressions in Muslim history.
5. Works on Ismaili history and thought, and the relationship of the Ismailis to other traditions, communities and schools of thought in Islam.
6. Proceedings of conferences and seminars sponsored by the Institute.
7. Bibliographical works and catalogues which document manuscripts, printed texts and other source materials.

This book falls into category two listed above.

In facilitating these and other publications, the Institute's sole aim is to encourage original research and analysis of relevant issues. While every effort is made to ensure that the publications are of a high academic standard, there is naturally bound to be a diversity of views, ideas and interpretations. As such, the opinions expressed in these publications must be understood as belonging to their authors alone.

Table of Contents

Acknowledgements ix

Prologue: The Sources of Imam ʿAlī's Intellectual Legacy 1

1. *Introducing Imam ʿAlī and his Spiritual Ethos* 11
   Biographical Sketch 13
   The Spirit of the Intellect 22
   The Discourse to Kumayl 36

2. *A Sacred Conception of Justice in Imam ʿAlī's Letter to Mālik al-Ashtar* 73
   Contemporary Ethics and the *Iḥsānī* Tradition 73
   Justice versus Tyranny 85
   Moral Conscience and Spiritual Consciousness 95
   The Virtue of Worship 114

3. *Realization through Remembrance: Imam ʿAlī and the Mystical Tradition of Islam* 134
   Dhikru'Llāh as a Polish for Hearts 141
   Remembrance as the Quintessence of Worship 156
   The Reality of Remembrance 161

Appendices
I. The First Sermon of *Nahj al-balāgha* 208
II. The Letter of Imam ʿAlī to Mālik al-Ashtar 219

Bibliography 237
General Index 246
Index of Qur'ānic Verses 252

Acknowledgements

First and foremost, I would like to acknowledge the invaluable support I have received from Dr Farhad Daftary, Head of the Department of Academic Research and Publications, and Associate Director of The Institute of Ismaili Studies. It was primarily thanks to him that I was given the time and space to research and write the chapters making up this book. I am also most grateful to Professor Azim Nanji, Director of the IIS, for the constant and stimulating encouragement I have received from him in regard to my approach to Imam ʿAlī; this was of particular value in helping to think of ways of making the Imam's intellectual and spiritual legacy more accessible to a wider audience.

Among my colleagues at the Institute, Mr Muhammad-Reza Jozi, was a continuous source of inspiration for me during my work on the essays that make up this book. His in-depth knowledge and sensitive appreciation of Imam ʿAlī's perspective furnished me with a veritable touchstone; his expertise constantly reminded me of the extent to which I was—and remain—a mere beginner in regard to the monumental teachings of Imam ʿAlī. The vastness of his knowledge in this field has helped me to appreciate more acutely the paucity of mine. I am also deeply grateful to Dr Feras Hamza for his advice on Arabic literature.

As regards the editing of the book, special thanks go to Mr Kutub Kassam, who not only edited the text with great diligence and vigilance, but also engaged deeply with its intellectual content, making several valuable suggestions which, I believe, have resulted in a significantly improved text. I am also grateful to Patricia Salazar and

Nadia Holmes who contributed to the final stages of the production of this book. Julia Kolb and Sorbon Mavlonazarov provided unfailing help on the administrative front, and contributed much to the maintenance of a pleasant, creative and stimulating ambience in the Department of Academic Research and Publications.

I am also grateful to Dr Muhammad-Ja'far Elmi, Director of the Islamic College for Advanced Studies, London, for reading parts of the text and making some useful comments and suggestions.

Chapters 2 and 3 of this book are expanded versions of much shorter essays that were first written as conference papers. Chapter 2 is based upon a paper entitled 'A Sacred Conception of Justice', which was delivered in Tehran in March 2001 at the International Conference on Imam 'Alī, organized by the Institute for Humanities and Cultural Studies. I am grateful to its Director, Professor Mehdi Golshani, for providing the impetus for the conference and encouraging me to expand this paper. It was first published as part of the proceedings of the conference in *Journal of Humanities* (nos. 4 and 5, Tehran, Winter 2000 and Spring 2001). Chapter 3 is based upon a paper entitled 'Imam 'Alī and the Remembrance of God', which was delivered at the conference entitled 'The Ahl al-Bayt in Islam' in Sarajevo, Bosnia, May 2002, organized by the Ibn Sina Foundation, to whose driving force, Mr Saeid Abedpur, I am greatly indebted.

R.S.-K.

PROLOGUE

The Sources of Imam ʿAlī's Intellectual Legacy

One of the reasons why so little has been written by Western scholars on the intellectual content of ʿAlī b. Abī Ṭālib's legacy is the controversial question of the authenticity of the extensive corpus of teachings attributed to him in the Islamic tradition. Before entering into our own reflections on the spiritual teachings within this corpus, therefore, it would be as well to begin this book with a brief look at the controversy.

In large part, the controversy has centred on the status of the *Nahj al-balāgha*,[1] the principal text containing the Imam's sermons, letters and sayings. This text will be the most important of the primary sources referred to in the essays making up the present book. The *Nahj* was compiled by al-Sharīf al-Raḍī (d. 406/1016), a renowned Shiʿi scholar of ʿAbbāsid Baghdad.[2] He compiled the text from all the sources available to him, often travelling great distances in search of material attributed to Imam ʿAlī. He collected whatever he could find in the way of quoted sermons, letters, testaments and short, aphoristic sayings, selecting for the *Nahj* those which he deemed to be the most important in literary terms. The result is a text which is something of a patchwork, with no clear order, either in chronological or thematic terms. Some sermons are clearly fragments of larger discourses that are missing, but which are included nonetheless in the collection. But, as attested by all the greatest authorities on Arabic literature,[3] the style remains the same throughout. An unsurpassable elegance dovetails with profundity of meaning to make this text a veritable model of Arabic *balāgha* (eloquence) down through the ages to the present day.

In the words of possibly the most important of all the commentators of the *Nahj al-balāgha*, Ibn Abi'l-Ḥadīd (d. 655/1257 or 656/1258), the Imam's utterances were regarded as 'below the speech of the Creator but above the speech of creatures (*dūna kalām al-khāliq wa fawqa kalām al-makhlūqīn*)'.[4]

Al-Raḍī's intentions in putting this work together were literary, ethical and spiritual; he did not intend it to be a collection of teachings within the legal and formal disciplines of jurisprudence and *ḥadīth*. Thus, he did not provide *isnāds*, that is, detailed lists of the names of the transmitters of the sayings and sermons, nor did he cite the names of the sources he used, since al-Raḍī's principal aim was to edify and inspire, not to corroborate and authenticate. For well over two centuries after its compilation, the authenticity of the *Nahj al-balāgha* as a text recording Imam ʿAlī's sermons, letters and sayings was not questioned. So many of the sources from which al-Raḍī drew were sufficiently well-known that the absence of the chains of transmitters in the *Nahj* did not seriously affect its credibility.[5] However, with the gradual loss or disappearance of many of these sources, this shortcoming in the 'technical apparatus' of the work became the basis for questioning the authenticity of its attribution to ʿAlī. It was the biographer Ibn Khallikān (d. 681/1283) who first cast doubt on the status of the text, stating, among other things, that it was probably al-Raḍī himself, or his brother, al-Murtaḍā, who was the actual author.[6]

One of the allegations made in this connection was that the sermons were too polished, the rhyming prose far too precise, to have been delivered *ex tempore*, as was claimed. But ʿAlī's ability to speak spontaneously in rhyming prose (*sajʿ*) is corroborated, among other things, by the following report, all the more convincing for having been uttered by a known enemy of the ʿAlids. After the tragedy of Karbalā' (61/680), where Ḥusayn b. ʿAlī and seventy-two of his closest relatives and companions were massacred, Zaynab, sister of Ḥusayn, made a fiery speech of defiance and recrimination at the court of Kūfa before the governor, ʿUbayd Allāh b. Ziyād. Although he was the object of her attack, as one of the key people responsible for the massacre, Ibn Ziyād could not refrain from admiring the power and skill of her oratory. Despite himself, he praised her speech and said, 'She speaks in rhyming prose, even as her father did before her.'[7] Imam

ʿAlī's ability to speak spontaneously in *sajʿ* was thus well known, and this mode of speech made it all the more easy for his listeners to memorize even long sermons.

Over the centuries, Shiʿi scholars have assiduously rebutted the charges made against the authenticity of the *Nahj*; and in recent decades a great deal of erudite labour has been dedicated to proving, firstly, that the material constituting the text cannot possibly be the work of al-Raḍī—the overwhelming bulk of this material being found in sources predating him—and secondly, that most of the material can indeed be traced back, through reliable transmitters, to the Imam himself, even if the sayings do not all attain the highest status in the scale of *ḥadīth* authenticity, that of *mutawātir* (that is, a saying which is transmitted through so many chains constituted by reliable transmitters that its authenticity cannot be seriously doubted). In the recent scholarship that has been devoted to unearthing the sources of all the sermons, letters and aphorisms, two works in particular should be mentioned: *Maṣādir Nahj al-balāgha wa asānīduh* (*The Sources of the Nahj al-balāgha and its* Isnāds), by ʿAbd al-Zahrāʾ al-Ḥusaynī al-Khaṭīb (Beirut, 1988), and *Madārik Nahj al-balāgha* (*Documentary Sources of the Nahj al-balāgha*), by ʿAbd Allāh Niʿma (Beirut, 1972), both of which demonstrate the immense treasury of sources from which al-Sharīf al-Raḍī drew for the *Nahj*, and effectively refute the allegation that he was the actual author.[8]

Summing up his considerable research on this issue, Moktar Djebli states, in his article on the *Nahj al-balāgha* in the *Encyclopedia of Islam* (2nd ed.):

> It is undeniable ... that a large portion of the *Nahdj* (sic) could indeed be attributed to ʿAlī, especially certain historical and panegyrical passages, although it is difficult to ascertain the authenticity of the more apocryphal sections ... Moreover, it has been possible to identify a considerable number of passages, accompanied by complete *isnād*s, dating back to the time of ʿAlī. These texts have been recounted by ancient scholars of repute such as al-Ṭabarī, al-Masʿūdī, al-Jāḥiẓ and many others.[9]

The other principal source in this work is the *Ghurar al-ḥikam wa durar al-kalim* (*Exalted Aphorisms and Pearls of Speech*),[10] a remarkable compilation of short, pithy sayings ascribed to the Imam. The compiler, ʿAbd al-Wāḥid Āmidī (d. 510/1116), was reported to be a student of the great Sufi, Aḥmad al-Ghazālī—brother of the more famous Abū Ḥāmid al-Ghazālī—and one of the teachers of Ibn Shahrāshūb (d. 588/1192), author of the important biographical text on the Shiʿi Imams, *Manāqib āl Abī Ṭālib*; he is thus considered an important authority within Shiʿi scholarly circles.[11] The text—the oldest manuscript of which dates back to 517/1123—consists of over ten thousand short sayings of the Imam, gathered from a variety of sources, including the *Nahj al-balāgha* itself; the *Mi'a kalima* (*One Hundred Sayings*) of the Imam, compiled by the foremost Arabic *litterateur* of the age, Jāḥiẓ (d.255/869);[12] the *Tuḥaf al-ʿuqūl* (*Gracious Gifts of the Intellects*) of Ibn Shuʿba; and the *Dustūr maʿālim al-ḥikam* (*Register of the Characteristic Marks of Wise Sayings*) of the Shāfiʿī jurist, al-Qāḍī Abū ʿAbd Allāh al-Quḍāʿī (d. 454/1062). We shall also refer occasionally to such classical compilations of Shiʿi *ḥadīth* as *al-Uṣūl min al-kāfī* by al-Kulaynī and *al-Tawḥīd* by Ibn Bābawayh al-Ṣadūq.[13]

Whatever the status that can be attributed to these sayings, one can take the following maxim of the Imam as the key for entering into its essential message, which is completely independent of the identity of the author: 'Consider not who said [it], rather, look at what he said.'[14] For any impartial observer and not just the spiritual seeker, the profound content and the pervasive influence of the sayings alone 'proves' their importance, and are thus to be taken seriously, whatever be the degree of historical authenticity ascribed to them. The fact that these teachings have been so significant for an entire spiritual tradition means that they cannot be evaluated solely on the basis of their documented historicity. For those seeking meaning within the tradition, spiritual profundity is clearly far more important a criterion than historical exactitude. The following exchange between ʿAllāma Ṭabāṭabā'ī and Henry Corbin brings out this point well:

> One day in the '60s Corbin asked ʿAllāma Ṭabāṭabā'ī the following question: 'As a leading authority on Shiʿite philosophy and religious thought, what argument would you provide to prove that the *Nahj al-balāgha* was by the first Imam, ʿAlī?' The venerable master of

Islamic philosophy answered, 'For us the person who wrote the *Nahj al-balāgha* is ʿAlī, even if he lived a century ago.'[15]

Even within an academic perspective, the role and impact of the Imam's sayings and teachings cannot be ignored. Rather, they will be accorded a particular significance to the extent that the scholar takes an impartial, phenomenological point of view, that is, a point of view which takes seriously those elements of a given religious tradition which have, in actual fact, configured the matrices within which the quest for meaning and enlightenment takes place. This is the point of view championed by Henry Corbin, to whose penetration and elucidation of the deeper dimensions of Islamic thought all scholars and seekers alike owe an incalculable debt of gratitude. Specifically addressing the issue of the provenance of the *Nahj*, he writes the following, which clearly reveals the influence of the response given to him by ʿAllāma Ṭabāṭabāʾī: 'In order to understand what it contains, it is best to take it phenomenologically, that is to say, according to its explicit intention; whoever holds the pen, it is the Imām who speaks. It is to this that it owes its influence.'[16] This attitude to the *Nahj al-balāgha* expresses well the application of Corbin's general approach to the sources of the Islamic intellectual tradition. These texts have to be read in depth, one has to go from the letter to the spirit, from the form to the essence; and one can only do this effectively by meditating upon the deepest expressions of spirituality within these sources, rather than restricting the scope of one's inquiry to the historical context of the texts.

To repeat: 'Consider not who said [it], rather, look at what he said.' The stress here is placed on the meaning, and the meaning takes priority over the speaker; the 'speaker' stands for the whole gamut of historical factors that generate a 'text'. Simply to locate a text in history—who wrote it, when and with what purpose—is not the same thing as explaining or assimilating its meaning. This is not to deny the importance of history; it is, rather, to deny that universal truths, or spiritual wisdom, can be *substantially* determined by something so contingent as history. The *forms* of their expression may change but truths of the deepest kind, pertaining to what is most profound and immutable in the human spirit, are universal and abiding in human experience. Truths that can change from generation to generation can hardly be called truths; they cannot be said to touch that which makes the human spirit what it is.[17]

One of Corbin's most significant contributions to the understanding of Islamic texts in general lies in his ability to make this tradition at once accessible and challenging. Through his creative meditations and interpretations, he makes the truths of this tradition visible through the veils of time and space. Even if one may not always agree with his interpretations, he succeeds marvellously in galvanizing our awareness of the fecundity of the texts he interprets. As regards the Shiʿi tradition, he succeeds in demonstrating that the texts which lie at the core of this tradition, far from constituting a 'register of conformist opinions',[18] are 'the mirror in which the Shiʿite consciousness has revealed to itself its own aspirations'.[19]

The point of view adopted in this book, however, is not restricted to specifically Shiʿi consciousness. Despite the fact that the *Nahj al-balāgha* is regarded as one of the foundational texts of Shiʿi Islam, after the Qur'ān and the sayings of the Prophet, it should not be seen exclusively as a 'Shiʿi' text.[20] It is simply the case, historically, that the *Nahj* has been most influential and determinative within the Shiʿi tradition, but its role has also been of immense significance in the Sunni tradition, as we hope to show in what follows. The whole of the Imam's corpus of sayings can—and, we believe, should—be viewed from a more universal vantage point. Rather than restricting oneself to its role within the Shiʿi tradition, it is more fruitful to reflect upon this corpus, purely and simply, as a source of wisdom, which is boundless by its very nature.

To make the author's position clear from the outset: The aim in these essays has been to reflect upon the Imam's sayings as an objective observer, but from 'within', that is, out of commitment to the spiritual principles of the Islamic faith. An attempt is made here to evaluate the sayings of the Imam,[21] both as quintessentially Islamic teachings *and* as universal ones, transcending the boundaries that define different religious traditions. There is no contradiction here, for that which is most essential to the spiritual message of Islam has, at the very least, certain 'family resemblances' with the spiritual messages of other faiths; and at the highest level, this message is identical, whatever be the religious form in which it is clothed: 'And We sent no Messenger before thee but We inspired him [saying]: There is no God save Me, so worship Me' (21: 25). It is by dint of this essential identity of the revealed religions that Muslims are enjoined not only to believe in 'God and His angels and His [revealed] scriptures and His messengers', but also to affirm that 'we make no distinction between any of His messengers' (2: 285).[22]

Even if the Imam's sayings so often presuppose knowledge of the specific sources of the Islamic revelation, that is, the Qur'ān and the *Sunna* of the Prophet, one of the most remarkable aspects of the Imam's perspective is the way in which the universal spiritual and ethical content of these sources are brought to light. Our stress on the universality of the Imam's message does not imply the absence of highly specific features; it is intended merely to assert that the essence of the message is not to be reduced to any of the particularities pertaining to later legal or theological schools of thought. It is precisely in the intellectual, ethical and spiritual aspects of this message that the essence is found; it is in these domains, rather than those of law and theology, that Islamic discourse is most universal and intelligible to those who belong to different religious traditions.

To follow the advice given above—to consider what is said and not who said it—one should focus on the teachings of ʿAlī not because he was 'the first Imam' or the 'fourth of the rightly-guided caliphs', but because of their intrinsic worth, their intellectual profundity and spiritual fecundity. This is not to deny ʿAlī's importance as a leader; rather, it is to appreciate that it was because of his wisdom that he was a great leader, or one of the 'true' leaders, as he refers to himself, one of the *a'immat al-ḥaqq*[23]—this, as opposed to the assertion that he must have been wise because he was a leader. He was a spiritual guide irrespective of his political role, and in a deeper sense, remains a guide now, speaking with compelling power across the centuries in a timeless dialect to all those 'who have ears to hear'.

NOTES

1. In this work we shall be referring mainly to the first critical edition of the text of the *Nahj al-balāgha*, which was published by the *Nahj al-balāgha* Foundation in Tehran (edited by Shaykh ʿAzīzullāh al-ʿUtārdī) in 1993. All translations of the Arabic text (including the Appendices) will be by the present writer, unless otherwise stated, and will be referred to hereafter as *Nahj*. In order to provide the reader with the context for all citations, we shall also give references to the best available complete translation of the text in English, that of Sayed Ali Reza, *Peak of Eloquence* (New York, 1996) which will hereafter be referred to as *Peak*.

2. Al-Raḍī's father was the great grandson of Imam Mūsā al-Kāẓim, son of Imam Jaʿfar al-Ṣādiq; and his mother was the great grand-daughter of Imam ʿAlī Zayn al-ʿĀbidīn, son of Ḥusayn b. ʿAlī b. Abī Ṭālib. His elder brother was the famous theologian, al-Sayyid al-Murtaḍā; both brothers were students of the most respected and influential Shiʿi scholar of the age, al-Shaykh al-Mufīd (d.413/1022).

3. For an appraisal of Imam ʿAlī's influence in this domain, see Sayyid Muḥammad Rāstgū, 'Faṣāḥat wa balāghat-i Imām ʿAlī', in ʿAlī-Akbar Rashād, ed., *Dānish-nāmah-i Imām ʿAlī* (Tehran, 2001), vol.11, pp.11–76, which includes a series of sayings from distinguished figures of Arabic literature, such as Jāḥiẓ (d. 254/868) and Ibn Nubāta (d. 374/984–5), on the unsurpassable greatness of ʿAlī as regards rhetoric and eloquence; and Muḥammad ʿAbduh's introduction, reprinted in the Beirut, 1996 edition of the *Nahj al-balāgha*, pp.67–74. See also Muḥammad al-Rayshahrī, ed., *Mawsūʿat al-Imām ʿAlī ibn Abī Ṭālib fi'l-kitāb wa'l-sunna wa'l-ta'rīkh* (Qom, 1421/2000), vol.9, pp.5–102, for a selection of poetry, written by poets of every century from the beginning of the Islamic era to the present, extolling Imam ʿAlī and bearing witness to his influence on them; and vol.10, pp.261–289, for early sources referring to his instrumental role in Arabic literature, including the foundation of such disciplines as grammar.

4. *Sharḥ Nahj al-balāgha li-Ibn Abi'l-Ḥadīd* (Beirut, 1965), vol.1, p.24.

5. See Abu'l-Faḍl Ḥāfiẓiyān Bābulī, '*Nahj al-balāgha*', in A.A. Rashād, ed., *Dānish-nāmah*, vol.12, pp.22–23.

6. Ibid., p.15.

7. Quoted by Jaʿfar Shahīdī on p.*yā' ṭā'* of the introduction to his Persian translation of the *Nahj al-balāgha* (Tehran, 1378 Sh/1999).

8. ʿAbd al-Zahrā' al-Ḥusaynī al-Khaṭīb, *Maṣādir Nahj al-balāgha wa asānīduh* (Beirut, 1988); ʿAbd Allāh Niʿma, *Madārik Nahj al-balāgha* (Beirut, 1972).

9. Moktar Djebli, 'Nahdj al-Balāgha', *EI2*, vol.7, p.904. See also Moktar Djebli, 'Encore à propos de l'authenticité du *Nahj al-balāgha*!' *Studia Islamica*, 75, 1992, pp.33–56.

10. ʿAbd al-Wāḥid Āmidī, *Ghurar al-ḥikam wa durar al-kalim*, 2 vols., given together with the Persian translation, under the title, *Guftār-i Amīr al-mu'minīn ʿAlī*, by Sayyid Ḥusayn Shaykhul-Islāmī (Qom, 2000). We shall also refer occasionally to the one-volume edition *Ghurar al-ḥikam wa durar al-kalim* (Qom, 2001), which appears with the Persian translation of Muḥammad ʿAlī Anṣārī. Whenever references are made to the former, it will appear as *Ghurar*, followed by the volume number; reference to the latter edition will appear as *Ghurar* (Anṣārī).

11. See Nāṣir al-Din Anṣārī Qummī, '*Ghurar al-ḥikam wa durar al-kalim*', in A.A. Rashād ed., *Dānish-nāmah*, vol.12, p.246.

12. It is said that Jāḥiẓ only revealed the existence of this compilation to his disciple, Aḥmad b. Abī Ṭāhir, when he was nearing his death. The latter relates that Jāḥiẓ had said to him on several occasions that there were one hundred sayings of ʿAlī, 'each one of which was equal to a thousand sayings of the scholars of Arabic literature'. See ʿAlī Ṣadrā'ī Khu'ī, '*Mi'a kalima*', in A.A. Rashād, ed., *Dānish-nāmah*, vol.12, p.472. The opening saying of this collection is the famous sentence, 'Were the veil to be removed, I would not increase in certitude (*law kushifa'l-ghiṭā', mā azdadtu yaqīnan*).'

13. Muḥammad b. Yaʿqūb al-Kulaynī, *al-Uṣūl min al-Kāfī* (Tehran, 1418/1997–8); Abū Jaʿfar Muḥammad b. ʿAlī b. Bābawayh al-Ṣadūq, *al-Tawḥīd* (Beirut, 1967).

14. *Lā tanẓur ilā man qāla, wa'nẓur ilā mā qāla. Ghurar*, vol.2, p.1222, no.68.

15. This account was given by Seyyed Hossein Nasr in his 'Reply to Zailan Moris', in *The Philosophy of Seyyed Hossein Nasr*, The Library of Living Philosophers, vol.28, ed. L.E. Hahn, R.E. Auxier, L.W. Stone Jnr. (Carbondale, IL, 2001), p.635. It is noteworthy that Nasr begins the opening essay of this important work, 'An Intellectual Autobiography', with a reference to Imam ʿAlī as the 'representative *par excellence* of Islamic esoterism and metaphysics'. Ibid., p.3.

16. Henry Corbin, *History of Islamic Philosophy*, tr. Philip Sherrard (London, 1993), p.35.

17. 'There is nothing new under the sun.' *Ecclesiastes*, 1: 9.

18. For Corbin, ' ... a Tradition transmits itself as something alive, since it is a ceaselessly renewed inspiration, and not a funeral cortège or a register of conformist opinions. The life and death of spiritual things are our responsibility;

they are not placed "in the past" except through our own omissions, our refusal of the metamorphoses that they demand, if these spiritual things are to be maintained "in the present" for us.' *En Islam iranien* (Paris, 1971), vol.1, p.33. See our essay, 'Tradition as Spiritual Function', *Sacred Web*, no.7, 2001, pp.37–58, for elaboration on this aspect of the meaning of tradition.

19. Corbin, *History of Islamic Philosophy*, p.36.

20. This is demonstrated, apart from other things, by the fact that the most important commentary on the text—in both the Shiʿi and Sunni traditions—is arguably that of the Muʿtazilī Sunni, Ibn Abi'l-Ḥadīd, to whom reference was made above. This is not to deny that various sayings—particularly in Sermon no.3, known as *al-Shiqshiqiyya*—uphold the Shiʿi point of view over the succession to the Prophet. The point is that the text should not be viewed through the prism of historical controversy and political contestation if one's primary concern is with its spiritual message.

21. If in the present work we refer to ʿAlī as 'the Imam' we do so in the most general sense of the term, that of 'leader', which neither excludes the specifically Shiʿi conception of his role as first Imam, nor does it necessarily imply it.

22. See our *The Other in the Light of the One: The Universality of the Qur'ān and Interfaith Dialogue* (Cambridge, 2006), for discussion of this and related themes, based principally upon mystical exegesis of the Qur'ān.

23. These 'true leaders' are described as those who take as sustenance for themselves no more than what the poorest of their subjects take, as will be seen below. *Nahj*, p.244; *Peak*, p.420.

CHAPTER ONE

Introducing Imam ʿAlī and his Spiritual Ethos

I am the city of knowledge and ʿAlī is its gate;
so whoever desires knowledge, let him enter the gate.
(*Anā madīnatu'l-ʿilm wa ʿAlī bābuhā;*
Fa-man arāda'l-ʿilm fal-ya'ti'l-bāb).[1]

To speak of ʿAlī b. Abī Ṭālib—cousin and son-in-law of the Prophet Muḥammad, fourth caliph of Islam and first in the line of Shiʿi Imams—is to speak of the quintessential spirituality of the Islamic tradition. For in this seminal figure of nascent Islam, one finds an integral expression of the two fundamental sources of Islamic spirituality, the Qur'ānic revelation and the inspired *Sunna* of the Prophet.[2] By his *Sunna* we do not mean simply the outward imitation of the Prophet's actions—a reductionism all too prevalent in our times—rather, we mean the spiritual substance of the prophetic perfection to which the Qur'ān itself refers: 'Verily, thou art of a tremendous nature' (68: 4).[3] The Prophet's words and deeds express but do not exhaust this spiritual substance. The inner assimilation of this substance, rather than the merely formal imitation of the words and deeds, is the goal of every spiritually inclined Muslim. There is a profound affinity between the believer's soul and the prophetic nature, a mysterious proximity that goes beyond time and space, as expressed in the verse: 'The Prophet is closer to the believers than they are to themselves' (33: 6). The Prophet, thus, outwardly manifests the perfection which the spiritually sensitive believer intuits, to some degree or another, as determining the very essence of his or her own soul.[4]

It is not surprising, therefore, to find the Prophet saying that 'Alī 'is as my own soul (*ka-nafsī*)',[5] affirming thereby not only the extraordinarily close relationship between 'Alī and himself, but also the affinity—and ultimately, identity—between every sanctified soul and the prophetic nature. More mysteriously, he said to 'Alī, 'You are from me, and I am from you (*anta minnī wa anā minka*).'[6] Likewise, as regards 'Alī's assimilation of the substance of the Qur'ān, we have this prophetic saying: "Alī is with the Qur'ān and the Qur'ān is with 'Alī. They will not separate from each other until they return to me at the [paradisal] pool (*al-ḥawḍ*).'[7] The spirit of the Qur'ān and the soul of the Prophet were thus fully interiorized by 'Alī, and it is this interiorization of the twin sources of the Islamic revelation which constitutes the spiritual path of Islam.

Our principal way of investigating and meditating upon the spirituality of Imam 'Alī is to consider the corpus of teachings attributed to him. Even if not all of the thousands of sayings attributed to him can be confidently ascribed to him, the very magnitude of the corpus testifies to the fact that he must indeed have articulated a very large number of profound teachings. No other companion of the Prophet has anything approaching the corpus attributed to 'Alī. Similarly, even if his foundational role in the development of a whole range of sciences be debatable—sciences such as jurisprudence (*fiqh*), theology (*kalām*), Qur'ānic exegesis (*tafsīr*), rhetoric (*balāgha*), grammar (*naḥw*) and calligraphy (*khaṭṭ*), the mystical knowledge associated with Sufism, as well as such arcane sciences as numerology (*jafr*) and alchemy (*al-kīmiyā'*)[8]—the fact that he is considered by later authorities in these fields as having provided the initial impetus for their sciences bespeaks the far-reaching and penetrating influence of both his formal teachings and personal radiance.

Given that the Islamic intellectual sciences as a whole are so closely identified with 'Alī, the Prophet's definition of 'Alī as the 'gate' to prophetic wisdom, cited as our epigraph, takes on the appearance of both a description of what 'Alī was in relation to the Prophet in their own age, and also a prophecy of the role 'Alī would play in relation to the subsequent unfolding of the sciences of the tradition—all such sciences being understood as so many formal, outward manifestations of the essential, inward spirit of the Islamic revelation, that spirit which was synthetically assimilated and faithfully transmitted by Imam ʿAlī. But before proceeding any further, the main historical outlines of his life should be sketched out.

BIOGRAPHICAL SKETCH

ʿAlī was a 'follower' of the Prophet in the deepest sense of the term. He lived physically in the shadow of the Prophet and absorbed spiritually all that radiated from him. The intimacy of the relationship between them is summed up in the words of one of the Imam's sermons:

> When I was but a child he took me under his wing … I would follow him [the Prophet] as a baby camel follows the footsteps of its mother. Every day he would raise up for me a sign of his noble character, commanding me to follow it. He would go each year into seclusion at [the mountain of] Ḥirāʾ. I saw him and nobody else saw him. At that time no household was brought together for the religion of Islam, except [that comprising] the Messenger of God, Khadīja and myself as the third. I saw the light of the revelation and the message, and I smelt the fragrance of prophecy …[9]

It is ʿAlī as the faithful follower and transmitter of the prophetic norm that we wish to address in this biographical sketch. Thus, we shall take a glance at the early period of his life, from his birth (c. 599 CE) to the death of the Prophet (11/632). Neither the second period of his life, from the death of the Prophet to his own assumption of the caliphate (35/656), nor the third period, consisting of his brief caliphate, dominated by tragic civil wars and culminating with his assassination in 40/661, will be dealt with here, as the issues raised in this part of his biography are fraught with historical and historiographical complexities.[10] Such controversies will deflect us from the primary aim of this book, which is to introduce the spiritual ethos of this extraordinary figure in such a way as to demonstrate its universal relevance, both within Islam itself and also beyond the Islamic tradition. For this ethos transcends formal religious boundaries, just as it rises above the political issues upon which the outward aspect of the Shiʿi-Sunni divergence is based—such issues serving only to distract attention from the essential spiritual message of ʿAlī.

What we wish to draw attention to here, on the contrary, is the unifying force of his spiritual teachings, upon the immense importance and profundity of which all Muslims, whatever their school of thought, are in agreement. In what follows, then, we shall briefly survey the earlier period of ʿAlī's life, that spent with the Prophet, together with the way in which the Prophet described ʿAlī in well-attested sayings, as this constitutes the indispensable background against which his role as gate to prophetic wisdom should be viewed. The second part of this introductory chapter will then address some key principles of his spiritual ethos, with a particular stress on the role of the intellect in that ethos.

According to all Shiʿi authorities and several Sunni sources, ʿAlī had the unique distinction of being born in the Kaʿba in Mecca.[11] His mother was Fāṭima bt. Asad, and his father, Abū Ṭālib, son of ʿAbd al-Muṭṭalib, was a leading member of the clan of the Hashimites. Abū Ṭālib had taken care of the young orphan, Muḥammad, son of his brother ʿAbd Allāh, and was later to be his chief protector when the message of Islam was openly being preached in Mecca. Several years before his mission began, at a time of drought, Muḥammad relieved the pressure on Abū Ṭālib and took his young son ʿAli, then about five years old, into his own household. From this time on ʿAlī was like a son to him, rarely being separated from him.

ʿAlī is regarded as the first male to enter the religion of Islam, though he was but a youth of nine or ten years old. Abū Bakr was the first adult male to enter the new religion, and Khadīja, the Prophet's wife, was the first woman. The immediacy of the young boy's response to the prophetic message and his unflinching loyalty to the Prophet thereafter is of great significance. When, about three years later, the Prophet was instructed by the revelation to 'warn thy nearest kin' (26: 214), he invited the leading members of his clan to a feast, after which he addressed them thus: 'O sons of ʿAbd al-Muṭṭalib, I know of no Arab who hath come to his people with a nobler message than mine. I bring you the best of this world and the next. God hath commanded me to call you unto Him. Which of you, then, will help me in this, and be my brother, mine executor and my successor amongst you?' All remained silent, except for the youthful ʿAlī who spoke up: 'O Prophet of God, I will be thy helper in this.' The Prophet then placed his hand on ʿAlī's neck and said, 'This is my brother, mine executor and my successor amongst you. Hearken unto him and obey him.'[12] Although at the time this was greeted with mockery by the leaders of the clan, it was taken much more seriously as time went on, and the extraordinary character, nobility and intelligence of the Prophet's young cousin became ever more dazzlingly evident.

Also of importance in this early period is the role played by ʿAlī in the migration (*hijra*) from Mecca to Medina (622 CE), the event which marks the beginning of the Muslim calendar. The enemies of the Prophet had planned to assassinate him, and knowing this, ʿAlī risked his own life by pretending to be the Prophet, sleeping in the latter's bed on the night he departed.[13] In Medina, the Prophet adopted ʿAlī as his 'brother' in the pact of brotherhood he established between the 'emigrants' (*al-muhājirūn*), that is, the Muslims who accompanied the Prophet on the *hijra* from Mecca, and the 'helpers' (*al-anṣār*), the tribes of Medina who had embraced the new faith.[14]

In the Medinan period, ʿAlī distinguished himself on the field of battle, as a scribe of the unfolding revelation of the Qur'ān, and as a leading companion of the Prophet. His courage and heroism in the battles fought against the overwhelmingly superior forces of the Meccan Quraysh and their allies was second to none. ʿAlī was at the forefront of nearly all the major battles fought under the Prophet's banner, frequently being appointed as standard-bearer. He was undefeated in all the single-combat duels with which the battles normally began—indeed, he was never defeated in any battle in which he fought. Both his indomitable courage and incomparable skill as a warrior became legendary. It is said that during the battle of Uḥud, a heavenly voice was heard proclaiming, 'There is no chivalric knight but ʿAlī, no sword but *dhu'l-faqār* (*lā fatā illā ʿAlī, lā sayf illā dhu'l-faqār*)', the latter being the name of ʿAlī's sword given to him by the Prophet. But the most famous of all battles in establishing ʿAlī's reputation as the pre-eminent—indeed invincible—warrior of Islam was that of Khaybar in 7/629. The Muslims were unable to make any headway against the heavily fortified, apparently impregnable, defences of their opponents. The Prophet then declared that he would give the banner of his army to one who 'loves God and His Messenger and is loved by God and His Messenger', through whom victory would be granted. He sent for ʿAlī, who was absent because of an affliction of the eyes. The Prophet cured him of this ailment by placing some saliva upon his eyes, and ʿAlī proceeded to lead the Muslims to victory. In the thick of battle, having lost his own shield, he is said to have picked up a gate and used it as a shield—a gate which, after the battle, could only be lifted by eight men.[15]

ʿAlī's role as a warrior is but one of many factors making for his unique place in the Islamic tradition. Of much greater significance is his proximity, in all respects, to the Prophet, and the wisdom and sanctity flowing from this proximity. ʿAlī was given the immense honour of marrying the Prophet's daughter, Fāṭima, considered to be the most saintly woman in Islam, along with her mother, the Prophet's first wife, Khadīja. One of the epithets bestowed on Fāṭima in the tradition is *Majmaʿ al-Nūrayn*, 'Confluence of the Two Lights'—the two lights of *nubūwwa* (prophecy) and of *walāya* (sanctity). ʿAlī was thus, after the Prophet, the leader of what was known as the *Ahl al-Bayt*, 'the People of the House', that is, the family of the Prophet.[16]

The Ahl al-Bayt are referred to in an important Qur'ānic verse as being purified of all defilement: 'God only wisheth to remove from you all impurity, O People of the House, and to purify you with a complete purification' (33: 33). According to several of the most important early sources, the Prophet called for Fāṭima, ʿAlī and their two sons, Ḥasan and Ḥusayn, and said, 'This is my Ahl al-Bayt'.[17] On one occasion, according to most sources, the Prophet took these members of his family under his cloak and recited the words of this verse. This event took place when a Christian delegation from Najrān was engaging in religious debate with the Prophet, and a verse was revealed indicating that a challenge of mutual imprecation (*mubāhila*) be made to the Christians. The Prophet brought the four persons mentioned above for this *mubāhila*, but the Christians declined the challenge.[18]

The importance of the Ahl al-Bayt is expressed in another verse in which the Prophet is instructed, 'Say: I ask you for no reward, save love of the near of kin' (42: 23). According to several of the most important commentators of the Qur'ān, the referent of 'near of kin' in this verse is the Prophet's Ahl al-Bayt.[19] Love of the Prophet's family is thus explicitly called for by the revelation, without this excluding the more general import of the verse, love of all those with whom one shares close kinship ties. The extent to which the Prophet's family are to be revered by all Muslims is also indicated in the fact that blessings are to be invoked upon his *āl*, or progeny, as part of the blessings to be invoked upon him. The Qur'ān instructs the believers: 'Truly, God and His angels bless the Prophet. O ye who believe, bless him and greet him with peace' (33: 56). Upon the revelation of this verse, the Prophet was asked how one was to perform this blessing, and he replied that the blessings were to be invoked upon him and his *āl* as follows: 'O God, bless Muḥammad and the progeny of Muḥammad, as Thou hast blessed Abraham and the progeny of Abraham. Truly, Thou art the Praised, the Glorious ...'[20] The importance of this blessing, to be recited during the canonical prayer, together with the necessity of loving the Prophet's family, is well brought out in the following lines of a poem by Imam al-Shāfiʿī, founder of one of the four schools of Sunni jurisprudence:

> Loving you, O family of the household of the Prophet of God,
> is an obligation (*farḍ*) from God in the Qur'ān which He revealed;
> Sufficient to show the grandeur of your dignity
> is that one who blesses you not—no prayer has he.[21]

It is also important to take note of the following Prophetic saying indicating the spiritual importance of the Ahl al-Bayt:

> Truly, I am leaving behind amongst you the two weighty things (*al-thaqalayn*): the Book of God and my Ahl al-Bayt, they will not be parted from each other until they return to me at the [paradisal pool] *al-ḥawḍ*.[22]

In addition to these sayings concerning ʿAlī as the most important member of the Prophet's Ahl al-Bayt, there are sayings of the Prophet concerning ʿAlī specifically, which deserve to be cited in detail, as it is only the basis of these sayings that one can begin to appreciate the immensely important role of ʿAlī in the spiritual dimension of the Islamic faith. These sayings or traditions (*aḥādīth*, sing. *ḥadīth*) will be presented in the form of a list, with minimal comment, this being the way in which they are presented in most standard collections of *aḥādīth*. If one takes prophetic guidance seriously, one cannot but take ʿAlī seriously, and it is largely for this reason that countless Muslims through the centuries have meditated upon these sayings, drawing from them diverse interpretations as well as incalculable inspiration. In a certain sense, these sayings are like the prism through which ʿAlī is viewed by the tradition, and they serve to enhance one's spiritual receptivity to his teachings. The crucial importance of ʿAlī in the spiritual firmament of nascent Islam emerges with greater clarity in the light of these prophetic descriptions of him; they should thus be regarded as a significant aspect of the 'prophetic background' to ʿAlī's seminal contribution to Islamic spiritual and intellectual life, whether in Shiʿi, Sunni or Sufi context.

The traditions given below can be found in any standard Shiʿi collection of *ḥadīth*, but in order to show that they—together with their implications and the devotion generated by them—are certainly not confined to Shiʿi Islam, we cite them here from two of the most authoritative Sunni traditionists, Aḥmad al-Nasāʾī (d. 303/915), author of the *Sunan*, one of the six collections of prophetic traditions in the Sunni corpus deemed to be 'canonical' (*al-kutub al-sitta*);[23] and al-Ḥākim al-Nīsābūrī (d. 405/1014), author of *al-Mustadrak ʿalāʾl-ṣaḥīḥayn* (*Supplement to the Two Sound Collections*).[24] This is a collection of those prophetic traditions that meet the exacting criteria of authenticity established by Bukhārī and Muslim (authors of the *ṣaḥīḥayn*), but all of which were not included by them in their collections. The following sayings pertaining to ʿAlī's distinctions, virtues and merits—all of which are implied in the Arabic word *faḍāʾil* (sing. *faḍīla*)—show why it is that Aḥmad b. Ḥanbal (d. 241/855), another leading Sunni traditionist and founder of one of the four Sunni schools of law, made the following statement: 'No companion of the Prophet has had such *faḍāʾil* ascribed to him as those which have been ascribed to ʿAlī b. Abī Ṭālib.'[25]

'Truly, ʿAlī is from me and I am from him (*inna ʿAlī minnī wa anā minhu*), and he is the *walī* (patron/spiritual master) of every believer after me.'[26]

'ʿAlī is with the Qurʾān and the Qurʾān is with ʿAlī. They will not separate from each other until they return to me at the [paradisal pool] (*al-ḥawḍ*).'[27]

'Three things were revealed to me regarding ʿAlī: he is the leader of the Muslims, the guide of the pious and chief of the radiantly devout (*sayyidu'l-muslimīn, imāmu'l-muttaqīn, wa qā'idu'l-ghurra'l-muḥajjalīn*).'[28]

'Gazing upon ʿAlī is an act of worship (*al-naẓar ilā ʿAlī ʿibāda*).'[29]

'May God have mercy on ʿAlī. O God, make the truth revolve around ʿAlī wherever he turns (*adiri'l-ḥaqq maʿahu ḥaythu dāra*).'[30]

'I am the city of knowledge and ʿAlī is its gate; so whoever desires knowledge, let him enter the gate.'[31]

'O ʿAlī, you are a leader (*sayyid*) in the world and the Hereafter. Your beloved is my beloved, and my beloved is the beloved of God; your enemy is my enemy, and my enemy is the enemy of God. Woe be to those who hate you after me [after I have passed away].'[32]

'Whoever desires to live my life and to die my death and to take his rest in the eternal Garden my Lord has promised me, let him orient himself towards ʿAlī b. Abī Ṭālib, for truly he will never cause you to depart from right guidance, nor cause you to enter into error.'[33]

The Prophet said that ʿAlī was 'as my own soul' (*ka-nafsī*).[34]

He said to ʿAlī, 'You are from me and I am from you (*anta minnī wa anā minka*).'[35]

'... whoever obeys ʿAlī obeys me, and whoever disobeys him disobeys me.'[36]

'You will clarify for my community that over which they will differ after me.' (*anta tubayyinu li-ummatī mā'khtalafū fīhi baʿdī*).[37]

'There is one amongst you who will fight for the *taʾwīl* [spiritual interpretation] of the Qur'ān as I have fought for its *tanzīl* [literal revelation].' Abū Bakr asked, 'Is it I?'. The Prophet said, 'No'. ʿUmar asked, 'Is it I?'. The Prophet said, 'No, it is the one who is mending the sandal.' The Prophet had given ʿAlī his sandal to mend.[38]

'O ʿAlī, there is in you something akin to Jesus, on whom be peace and blessings. The Jews hated him to such an extent that they slandered his mother; and the Christians loved him to such an extent that they ascribed to him a rank he did not possess.'[39]

'O ʿAlī, whoever separates himself from me separates himself from God, and whoever separates himself from you, O ʿAlī, separates himself from me.'[40]

'Whoever curses 'Alī curses me, and whoever curses me curses God.'[41]

The Prophet said to his wife 'Ā'isha, 'Call unto me the leader (*sayyid*) of the Arabs.' She asked, 'O Prophet of God, are you not the leader of the Arabs?' He said, 'I am the leader of the children of Adam, and 'Alī is the leader of the Arabs.'[42]

When Fāṭima was asked by some women why the Prophet had married her to such a poor man as 'Alī, she related this to the Prophet. He said: 'Are you not pleased that God—exalted and glorified be He—conferred upon the people of the world [a benefit] and chose two men, one of them is your father, the other your husband?'[43]

'The first of you to enter the [paradisal] pool (*al-ḥawḍ*) is the first of you who entered Islam, 'Alī b. Abī Ṭālib.'[44]

"Alī is from me and I am from him (*'Alī minnī wa anā minhu*), and nobody can fulfil my duty but myself and 'Alī.'[45]

'Alī himself relates that the Prophet said to him that none but a believer will love him ['Alī], and none but a hypocrite will hate him.[46]

When the Prophet was about to depart for an expedition to Tabūk, he left 'Alī as his deputy in Medina. 'Alī was sad not to be joining him. The Prophet said, 'Are you not happy that you should have in relation to me the rank of Aaron in relation to Moses, except that there is no prophet after me?'[47]

The Prophet prayed to God to bring 'the most beloved of thy creatures' to partake with him in a meal of fowl. Only when 'Alī came did the Prophet ask him to join him.[48]

Among the several verses of the Qur'ān which were commented upon by the Prophet with reference to 'Alī is 13: 7: 'Verily thou art a warner, and for every people there is a guide.' The Prophet said, 'I am the warner … you are the guide, O 'Alī. After me, the rightly-guided shall be guided by you.'[49]

In regard to the revelation of verse 55 of Sūra 5 (*al-Mā'ida*), 'Verily your *walī* is only God and His Messenger and those who believe, establish the prayer and give alms while bowing in prayer,' the commentators relate this to the incident when 'Alī, whilst bowing in prayer, held out his ring for a beggar who had asked for alms. The Prophet recited this verse when told of the incident and added, in what are probably the most well known words of all in regard to 'Alī:

'For whomever I am the *mawlā* [guardian, master, close friend], 'Alī is his *mawlā* (*man kuntu mawlāhu fa-ʿAlī mawlāhu*).'[50]

The last saying was expressed on a number of occasions, the most famous of which was after the Prophet's final pilgrimage to Mecca, in the year 10/632, at a pool midway between Mecca and Medina, known as Ghadīr Khumm. The Prophet assembled all the pilgrims, had a pulpit erected and delivered an address to the thousands assembled. The address culminated in the statement: 'For whomever I am the *mawlā*, ʿAlī is his *mawlā*'. For Shiʿis, this is regarded as a clear designation (*naṣṣ*) of ʿAlī as successor to the Prophet; for Sunnis it indicates the special proximity of ʿAlī to the Prophet, but not his nomination as successor in the political domain. That the reference to ʿAlī as *mawlā* (in some versions, as *walī*) is of the highest spiritual significance, however, is not seriously disputed. 'Umar is reported to have come and said to 'Alī, '*Bakh bakh*', indicating congratulation, 'you have become my *mawlā* and the *mawlā* of every Muslim.'[51] The polemical debate that has exercised countless minds in the past, and which continues to this day, hinges on the political implications of ʿAlī's spiritual authority, his *walāya*.[52]

Although it is not our purpose to enter into a discussion of ʿAlī's role and place within Shiʿi Islam, one should note that his charisma was such that, even in the Prophet's own lifetime, a group was known as the *shīʿa*, or 'partisans' of ʿAlī. Al-Ṭabarī (d.310/923), author of the first voluminous commentary of the Qur'ān, refers to the report that the Prophet interpreted the verse, 'Those who have faith and do righteous deeds, they are the best of created beings' (98: 7), as referring to ʿAlī and his '*shīʿa*'.[53] Four individuals, in particular, were renowned for their devotion to ʿAlī in the lifetime of the Prophet and are referred to as the prototypes of early Shiʿism: Salmān al-Fārisī, Abū Dharr al-Ghifārī, ʿAmmār b. Yāsir and Miqdād b. ʿAmr.[54] Although this early manifestation of love for ʿAlī should not be identified with the theological doctrines that were later to be elaborated in what came to be known as the Shiʿi branch of Islam in the following generations, it is worth pointing out that, at the core of Shiʿism—in all its different expressions—lies the notion of fidelity to ʿAlī.[55] This fidelity, loyalty or love constitutes one aspect of *walāya*; the other, complementary aspect being the spiritual authority or sanctity of ʿAlī.[56] It is also important to stress that neither devotion to ʿAlī nor the spiritual orientation towards the *walāya* he embodies, is to be associated only with Shiʿism—rather, it extends to the whole of the Islamic faith, for devotion to ʿAlī as head of the Ahl al-Bayt of the Prophet is found throughout the length and breadth of the Muslim world, and is particularly deep wherever Sufism flourishes. As will be discussed in Chapter 3, Imam ʿAlī is regarded as the first spiritual 'pole' (*quṭb*) of Sufism after the Prophet himself, and is situated at the summit of all the spiritual chains (*salāsil*, sing. *silsila*) by which the Sufi orders link their masters to the Prophet.[57] To speak of ʿAlī is to speak not of exclusivist sectarianism but of universal spirituality.

THE SPIRIT OF THE INTELLECT

What we propose to do in this section is adumbrate some of the key dimensions of the spiritual ethos of Imam ʿAlī, with particular stress on its intellectual aspects. In addition to demonstrating the pivotal role played by the intellect (*al-ʿaql*) in the elaboration and assimilation of the Imam's spiritual teachings, this exercise should help to ground more firmly the explorations of the ethos given in the following chapters. In this section, then, one of the key aims is to show something of the 'spirit of the intellect' in the worldview of the Imam, a spirit that surpasses, while comprising, the activities of the rational mind, as well as encompassing domains not nowadays associated with the intellect, domains such as moral comportment and aesthetic sensibility. We also hope to demonstrate the manner in which this spiritual view of the intellect is directly related to the Qur'ānic conception of the spirit (*al-rūḥ*), and to explore some of the concomitants or fruits of engaging deeply with this unifying spirit proper to the intellect.

It may be useful at the outset to clarify our preference for the English word 'intellect' rather than 'reason' to translate *ʿaql*. What we wish to evoke here is the original meaning of *intellectus* in Latin Christendom, a meaning which is practically identical to that of *nous* in the Patristic Greek tradition: *intellectus/nous* is that which is capable of a direct contemplative vision of transcendent realities, whereas reason—the translation of the Latin *ratio* and the Greek *dianoia*—is of an indirect, discursive nature; it works with logic and arrives at mental concepts, only, of those realities. With the intellect, then, one is able to contemplate or 'see' the Absolute; with the reason, one can only think about it.[58]

This preliminary exploration of the spirit of the intellect in the Imam's ethos will be sketched chiefly by some reflections on a short discourse of the utmost importance in the *Nahj al-balāgha*, that given by the Imam to one of his closest disciples, Kumayl b. Ziyād.[59] In this series of reflections the same *modus operandi* will be employed as that used in the following two chapters, namely, an interpretive commentary on the Imam's words that engages not only other sayings of the Imam on the theme in question, but also concordant Qurʾānic verses and, occasionally, traditions of the Prophet that either help reveal aspects of the meaning of the Imam's saying being considered, or conversely, are themselves elucidated by the saying in question.

Before looking at this dialogue, however, it is important to stress three factors which are inherent to the spirit of the intellectual perspective being considered here, namely, the centrality of revelation, the harmony between revelation and the intellect, and the distinction between the intellect, conceived as the principle of the articulation of consciousness, and reason, understood as *one* of the expressions of this principle.[60] To begin with the first, one must assert at the outset that everything about the Imam's life and his teachings is centred on the Qurʾānic revelation and its embodiment in the Prophet's conduct. Indeed, both the thought and life of the Imam can be read as a kind of spiritual commentary, a *taʾwīl*, on the sacred text. On the doctrinal plane, it can be asserted with confidence that ʿAlī was one who had an 'innate aptitude' for performing the task of *taʾwīl*.[61] On the existential plane also, his life, from his birth in the most holy shrine of the Kaʿba to his martyrdom in the mosque of Kūfa, can be read as a dramatic unfolding of the inner meaning of the revealed text. ʿAlī's refusal to stop short at the superficial surface of things—religious, ethical, political—manifested an unflinching fidelity to the sacred substance of the religion, a fidelity which entailed not only intellectual penetration inwardly but also combative resistance outwardly. The saying of the Prophet, cited earlier, is of considerable importance in this connection: ʿAlī would fight for the *ta'wīl* of the Qur'ān as he, the Prophet, had fought for its *tanzīl*.[62]

As mentioned earlier, ʿAlī's short caliphate was dominated by bloody civil wars. It can well be argued that all three of these wars were indeed fought for the sake of the correct interpretation and application of the Qur'ān, the clarification of its fundamental message, that of *tawḥīd*, and the realization of this oneness on all levels, spiritual and social. This claim is substantiated in a graphic manner by the Imam's response to a bedouin who, just as the battle of the Camel (al-Jamal)[63] was about to begin, came to the Imam and said, 'O Commander of the Faithful! Do you say that God is one?' Those present remonstrated with the bedouin, telling him that this was neither the time nor the place for such questions. The Imam, however, intervened: 'Leave him, for surely what the bedouin wishes is what we wish for the people.'

We can begin our reflections on the spirituality of Imam ʿAlī by considering his response to the bedouin, a response which relates to the principle of right intention taking priority over outward action, whatever that action be. For the Imam, the most fundamental intention motivating every action, whether religious in the ordinary sense or military as in the present context, is knowledge of the true nature of ultimate reality. What the Imam 'wishes for the people' then, is this knowledge, which must lie at the very heart of all concerns, motivations and actions, whether on the battlefield or the prayer-rug. Thus, there is no time or place where this question—'What do you mean by saying God is one?'—is irrelevant or out of place. It was for the sake of the correct knowledge of the divine—and all its concomitants and repercussions in society—that the Imam was fighting, in fulfilment of the prophecy of the Prophet just mentioned. On the very field of battle, then, the Imam gives a discourse on the meaning of divine oneness.[64] The very first part of the Imam's reply contains a key to the understanding of his whole spiritual ethos. He refutes the notion of God's oneness being in any way a 'numerical' or 'countable' oneness. He tells the bedouin that it is not permissible to say 'one', while having in mind any numerical conception, for 'that which has no second does not enter into the category of numbers'.[65]

'That which has no second'[66] is not just a divinity to which no other partner can be ascribed, as the theologian would have it, but that reality which has no 'otherness', the Real, *al-Ḥaqq*,[67] which is both transcendent and immanent, beyond all 'things' and manifested by all 'things', at once inaccessible and inalienable. In these few words the Imam effects—for those who have 'ears to hear'—a shift of consciousness from the dogmatic notion of one God versus many gods to the mystical apprehension of the one and only Reality, in the face of which everything else is but an appearance. All things become apprehended as so many outward phenomena which call out to be deciphered, so many signs (*āyāt*) pointing to That of which they are manifestations. Retracing these appearances back to their source and origin is the literal meaning of *ta'wīl*: going back to the *awwal*, 'the First'. On one hand, the Real is described as being the beginning and end of all things, the apparent and the hidden; there is nothing in being but this one Reality: 'He is the First and the Last, the Outward and the Inward' (57: 3). On the other hand, apparent multiplicity is to be 'brought back' to real oneness: 'We shall show them Our signs (*sa-nurīhim āyātinā*) on the horizons and in their own souls, so that it be clear to them that He is the Real' (41: 53).

In one saying attributed to ʿAlī, there is a reference to the Prophet as the first of those who were taught by God the science of *ta'wīl*, and that he, the Prophet, in turn taught ʿAlī the same. According to the Prophet, as noted earlier, 'Truly, ʿAlī is with the Qurʾān, and the Qurʾān is with ʿAlī.' In another famous saying, often quoted by Sufi commentators, ʿAlī claimed to be able to load seventy camels with the pages of the commentary he could give on the opening chapter of the Qurʾān, the *Fātiḥa*. It should be noted also that ʿAlī's cousin, Ibn ʿAbbās, often referred to as the 'first commentator', claims to have learnt the science of interpretation from ʿAlī.[68]

In this connection, the following saying of the Imam is of fundamental importance, as one of the many which help explain why it is that in the discipline of Qurʾānic exegesis, *tafsīr*, he is held in the highest esteem: 'The Qurʾān consists of a book inscribed, between two covers; it speaks not with a tongue, it cannot do without an interpreter (*lā budda lahu min tarjumān*).'[69] The reciprocity between revelation and the intellect is further underlined in the saying, 'The prophet of a man is the interpreter of his intellect (*rasūl al-rajul tarjumān 'aqlihi*).'[70] Elsewhere we find an explicit correspondence between the intellect and the 'inner' messenger: the intellect is 'the messenger of the Real'.[71]

Thus, the Imam's teachings, which express his spiritual ethos, should be read essentially as creative interpretations of the Qur'ānic revelation. They initiate a movement from the letter of the revelation to its spirit, and from the spirit of the revelation to the spirit of the Revealer—a process of 'retracing', of going back to the source, the origin, the beginning, *al-awwal*, which will be accomplished in the measure that the spirit of the intellect is enlivened within the interpreter. But the Revealer remains perforce concealed at the very same time as being revealed through the revelation, concealed because the essence of what is revealed—the divine Reality in itself—is ineffable and inexpressible; only the forms of its manifestations are susceptible to revelation. The dialectical interplay between the form and the formless, the evident and the hidden, the revealed and the concealed—such antinomies lie at the root of the paradoxical mode of expression for which the Imam is renowned, and which we will encounter throughout this book. The relationship which especially concerns us at present is the second of the factors mentioned above, that between revelation and 'intellection', by which term we mean the creative use of the intellect. This relationship takes on particular salience in a context substantially defined by fidelity to revelation. Whereas intellect and revelation are regarded as mutually exclusive by rationalists in the strict sense,[72] they are seen in this perspective as perfectly harmonious, subsisting in a state of creative reciprocity, each requiring the other[73] for completeness, integrity, the 'making one' that is the very essence of *tawḥīd*.

Indeed, one of the most striking aspects of the Imam's perspective is the way in which it reveals the hollowness of many of the false or excessively polarized dichotomies that later came to characterize, or be imposed upon, Islamic thought. This is due to the highly synthetic style of the Imam's discourses, viewed as 'pre-philosophical' by some academics,[74] and as 'supra-philosophical', inspired and evocative by those within the Islamic spiritual tradition. The apparently insuperable dichotomy between intellect and revelation is found in various polarized ramifications, such as reason versus faith, convention (*sunna*) versus nature (*tabīʿa*), imitation (*taqlīd*) versus verification (*taḥqīq*), piety versus inquiry, and so on.[75] However in Imam ʿAlī's ethos, intellect and revelation, rather than being regarded as mutually exclusive, are complementary and, at the highest level, indeed inseparable, truth being one. While it is clear that the human intellect cannot in any way be equated with divine revelation, the spirit animating the intellect is not, in the final analysis, restricted by human limitations, as we shall see. It is this spirit which perceives and grasps the divine quality of revelation.

The divine spirit articulating the form and infusing the content of revelation must be fathomable to some degree by human consciousness, failing which the revelation would be nothing more than so many rules and regulations for the will, rather than a source of creative inspiration for the intelligence. It cannot be too heavily stressed that divine revelation, far from cutting short the operations of reason and imposing some unintelligible *diktat*, on the contrary presupposes a creative engagement with all the resources of the intelligence, in particular those processes of reflection and meditation for which the Imam is himself renowned, and which the Qurʾān itself repeatedly calls for.[76]

The revealed text is silent and 'speaks' only through the 'interpreter', the intellect. This view of the relationship between intellect and revelation rigorously excludes all literalism and superficiality, all attempts to confine meaning within a flat, unilateral reading. On the contrary, such a view seeks the very opposite: rather than 'enclose' meaning, the tendency generated here helps to 'dis-close' it, to open up the inner horizons of multiple levels of meaning hidden in the text. This polyvalent signification is plumbed in accordance with the depth and penetration of the intellect of the 'interpreter'. At its most profound, this 'prophetic' intellect rejoins the source of revelation itself. For it is this 'inner prophet', or inmost degree of consciousness, which is the ultimate basis on which one is able to confirm as true the verses of the outer revelation—to 'validate' them experientially and not just affirm them dogmatically. It is thus that the Imam says, in the first sermon of the *Nahj*, that one of the purposes of revelation, of the 'sending forth of prophets' by God to mankind, was 'to unearth for them the buried treasures of the intellects (*dafā'in al-'uqūl*)'.[77]

This saying constitutes one of the keys of the spiritual ethos being considered here, and we shall have occasion to return to it repeatedly throughout these essays. The intellect is not stifled by revelation; rather, it is enlivened by it. Revelation is a clarion call to the spiritual depths of the intellect; it cultivates and brings to fruition the seeds of consciousness planted therein by God. The spirit of one's intellect, then, cannot be alien to that which descends as revelation from on high; on the contrary, it must be fundamentally akin to it. It is for this reason, precisely, that one can have absolute certainty that the revelation indeed comes from the Absolute. It is not so much a question of setting up a dichotomy between intellect or revelation, but of seeing the intellect *as* revelation, or at least as one mode of revelation, the God-given means by which the individual comes to discern, affirm and plumb the divine 'revelations' outside himself: both those of scripture and those constituted by the 'signs' (*āyāt*) of the natural world. If the human intellect can perceive and recognize revelation, it is on account of the fact that both are rooted in the same ultimate source. Prophetic revelation awakens and quickens the depths of human intellect. It does not replace or displace the intellect. From this perspective, the revealed text is not to be seen as some extraneous source opposed to the intelligence, but as the objective, outward expression of the very principles that the intellect itself yields to the 'inner prophet'—understanding by 'intellect' not simply the faculty of reasoning but the source of consciousness articulating the human spirit.

The intellect contains unsuspected depths—'buried treasures'—and is thus far from being exhausted by its surface operations, the cognitions and reasonings proper to its purely mental dimension. These considerations take us to the third of the factors mentioned above, the relationship between intellect and reason. Just as there can be no contradiction whatsoever between revelation and intellection, likewise one must avoid setting up a false dichotomy between reason and intellect. Instead, reason should be perceived as one of the modes of the intellect; reason no more contradicts intellect than intellect contradicts revelation. Reason is a mode of the intellect but is not to be equated with it *grosso modo*; similarly, one cannot reduce the universal objectivity of revelation to the subjective specificities of any one individual's intellection, to his or her own 'private' revelation. To equate reason with intellect would be tantamount to denying the existence of the 'buried treasures' of the intellect, those supra-rational dimensions that are, initially, 'buried' beneath, and thus hidden from, the rational surface of the intellect. The revelation constituted by the intellect is embedded within the creation of the human being, the intellect being that which most critically defines the human being as such.

Far from pitting the intellect against revelation, then, each is to be seen in the light of the other. The substance of revelation cannot be engaged except through the intellect, on one hand, and the 'buried treasures' of the intellect cannot be disclosed except through revelation, on the other. As will be seen below, this understanding of the intellect brings us close to what the Imam refers to as the 'heart', that inmost mode of perception which is capable of 'seeing' God. It is the 'heart' that can 'see' God, not using eyesight but insight, that spiritual insight which is generated by the 'verities of faith' (*ḥaqāʾiq al-īmān*). As the Imam puts it, in response to the questioner asking whether he had 'seen' his Lord, 'Eyes see Him not through sight's observation, but hearts see Him through the verities of faith.'[78] We shall have occasion to return to the 'inner vision' of God through the 'verities of faith'.

To return to the relationship between the intellect and reason, one can say that between the spiritual depths of the intellect and its own rational surface there is both continuity and discontinuity. The aspect of continuity is manifested in the evident fact that all thinking begins with concepts conveying intelligible meaning, thought is initially concerned with ideas that are rationally discernible, and these must bear some relation to the realities they express. But there is also discontinuity between the spiritual and the rational aspects of the intellect, in that reason stops short at the ideas 'de-fined'—the Arabic word for definition, *ḥadd* expresses, like its English equivalent, both the sense of a conceptual definition and that of a limitation, a boundary. To go beyond the limits imposed by the rational act of definition, something more than reason is necessary; and this 'something more' is that which makes the ethos we are considering a spiritual one, not a rationalistic one. It is certainly 'rational' in the sense that the form of the ethos is indeed susceptible to the scrutiny of reason, but it is not 'rationalistic' inasmuch as its essence is not predicated on reason alone.

Now Imam 'Alī frequently hints, in highly allusive terms, at the mysteries and the marvels—the unearthed treasures of the intellect—that he has directly witnessed by the eye of his purified heart. He also indirectly alludes to this supra-rational mode of awareness[79] through the bewildering use of apophatic discourse and paradoxical utterances, all of which are to be found in abundance in the corpus attributed to him. It seems that, in this ethos, the higher the truth, the deeper is the paradox. The incommensurability between the reality in itself and the human conceptions that are made of it is effectively evoked by this creative use of paradox. In modern parlance, each human conception of reality needs to be 'deconstructed'; but then, unlike modern deconstructionism which is so radically destructive that it has nothing left to 'reconstruct', the Imam's apophasis feeds directly into modes of spiritual intuition, contemplation and realization of that which reason, on its own account, is incapable of attaining. It is this intuition and contemplation which 're-members'—or 'reconstructs', if one likes—the spiritual realities that transcend the categories of reason. The value of the paradoxes, antinomies, apophasis and negation is entirely predicated on the eminently positive realities which the intellect can plumb, and thus become aware of its own hidden depths. The resulting consciousness does not negate reason so much as situate it and thereby reveal the limits of the sphere of operation proper to reason; it reveals that reason alone cannot 'comprehend' the higher realities, nor express them fully, however indispensable it may be in initiating the cognitive movement towards those realities.

Thus, when the Imam negates—as he does so often—the possibility of human conceptions encompassing the divine Reality, what is being negated is the limitation which is the inescapable corollary of all such conceptions, and not the positive content, the *ma'nā* or spiritual meaning, of the conception itself; for this conception is a necessary starting point for a process of assimilation that engages a deeper level of awareness than that 'de-fined' by the mind, and which therefore extends far beyond the domain of speculative thought. In this light, the negation of the limitations of human conception should be seen as the prelude to an absolute affirmation: the affirmation of the Absolute, which has no limitation. The spiritual negation of conceptual limitation is of an upward, 'constructive' order, not of a nihilistic deconstructive one. Nowhere is this style of discourse more apparent than in the famous opening lines of the first sermon of the *Nahj al-balāgha*:

> Praise be to God, whose laudation those who speak cannot deliver, whose graces those who count cannot number, whose rightful due those who strive cannot render; He who cannot be grasped by far-reaching aspirations, nor fathomed by profound intuitions; He whose attribute has no binding limitation, no existing description, no time appointed, no term extended.

The divine attribute (*ṣifa*) has no limit in terms of which it can be defined (*laysa li-ṣifatih ḥadd maḥdūd*), and yet it is affirmed as real. It has no 'existing description' and yet it is in some sense described (*mawṣūf*) by the very words of the Qur'ānic revelation. For God is therein described as having such attributes as mercy, compassion, power, and so on. He is the Merciful, the Compassionate, the Almighty, but the Imam affirms that these very attributes cannot be defined, bounded, described. The paradox is further sharpened when the Imam speaks of the perfection of *ikhlāṣ*, the 'rendering sincere' or the purification of one's devotion to, and conception of, God; it is to divest (*nafy*) God of all attributes.[80] On one hand the attributes are affirmed and on the other they are to be negated. The rational mind can only think of God in terms of the attributes given verbal expression in the Qur'ān; and yet here, the Imam appears to negate these same attributes, thereby depriving the mind of any convenient conceptual handle by which to grasp the nature of the divine Reality. The simultaneous affirmation and negation of the attributes raises an apparently irresolvable contradiction, and in so doing, enhances receptivity to a deeper mode of knowing. This style of discourse appears designed to awaken in the listener some latent awareness, inscribed in the heart or the depths of the intellect, and to invite the seeker to dive into those depths, into the knowledge 'buried' in the intellect. The very shock of the apparent contradiction in this apophasis appears intended to precipitate a leap of consciousness from the formal activity of reason to the supra-rational contemplation of the spirit.[81]

Consider the words spoken by the Imam immediately after affirming that his heart had indeed witnessed God, not by means of outward vision but through 'the verities of faith':

> My Lord is not described in terms of dimension (*buʿd*), nor motion (*ḥaraka*), nor rest (*sukūn*) ... nor through coming or going: He is subtle in subtlety but not described by subtlety, magnificent in magnificence but not described by magnificence, great in greatness but not described by greatness ...[82]

The attributes are again affirmed and denied. God possesses these attributes but is not reducible to them. We can begin to think of God in terms of these categories, but He is not reducible to our conceptions. The attributes afford something to the mind by which the divine nature can be understood, but this understanding is fragmentary, never exhaustive, and it needs to be negated as the prelude to a fuller apprehension. The initial conceptual orientation to the divine Reality needs to be both negated and sublimated. It needs to be negated *qua* mental conception, while the positive content of the conception needs to be sublimated through spiritual intuition; only then can the two-dimensional 'portrait' defined by reason be given the third dimension, that of depth. But this third dimension emerges only after the insufficiency of the rational depiction is understood[83]—whence the need for that cognitive shock which paradox produces, a shock intended to reveal the pretension of reason in its effort to disclose the nature of the Absolute, the transcendent source of its own activities.[84]

One sees in the Imam's discourses a repeated combination of affirmation and denial, which mirrors the negation and affirmation found in the first testimony of Islam: *lā ilāha*, 'no god', being the negation (*nafy*); then *illa'Llāh*, 'except God' coming as the affirmation (*ithbāt*). This helps one to see that the negation of the attributes mentioned by the Imam as being the perfection of *ikhlāṣ* is in fact an affirmation of the infinitude of the divine Reality. Thus, each of the attributes is to be 'negated', but only insofar as it is conceived by the mind. Thus negation is necessary because, at the mental level, each attribute excludes other attributes, and also excludes the object of attribution itself, that is, the divine Essence; such an exclusion following inescapably from the very possibility of conceptually distinguishing between the attribute and the object of attribution, that is, between the divine quality and the divine Essence. For any conception to take place in the mind, defined ideas are necessary, and where there are definitions, there are limits and thus exclusions. The reality of the attribute, however, is unlimited, by virtue of its absolute identity with the Essence. The attribute that has been 'negated' is paradoxically affirmed, not in itself but inasmuch as it is nothing but God: *illa'Llāh*. Thus, one can place each of the negated attributes in the place of the *nafy* of the first testimony and arrive at such formulations as *lā raḥmāna illa'Llāh*, 'There is no All-Compassionate except God'; *lā raḥīma illa'Llāh*, 'No All-Merciful except God', etc.

The apparent negation of the attributes becomes, in fact, an affirmation of their true identity, shorn of any restrictive association with the poverty of mental conceptions. The attributes are not superadded to the Essence but absolutely one with it, and differentiable from it only conceptually, not ontologically. The Essence does indeed comprise all the attributes mentioned, such as greatness, subtlety, and so on, but it is also infinitely more than these attributes; and, for their part, the attributes are infinite only within and as the Essence. The Imam's apophasis here can be seen in fact as a commentary of the Qur'ānic refrain, 'Glorified be God above what they describe' (23: 91). The infinitude of God strictly requires, on the human plane, the negation of all that the mind can conceive through reason, but not all that the heart can 'see' through spiritual vision. This very negation on the plane of reason calls out to something deeper, and this, in turn, can only be understood in the light of spiritual praxis, which is always assumed as the reflective, devotional or contemplative context for the hearers of the Imam's sermons and discourses. The heart—symbolic seat of the contemplative intelligence—calls out to be 'polished', and this is precisely what the 'remembrance of God' does, this *dhikr Allāh* being, according to the Imam, the 'most excellent form of worship', as we shall see in Chapter 3 of this book. However, even at this level of praxis there is a further paradox: the 'reality' of the remembrance is not attained until 'you forget yourself in your remembrance'. It is not just the rational mind and the determinate conceptions proportioned thereto that are to be negated or 'deconstructed', but the individual soul itself as the locus of all cognition, rational or supra-rational. This final denouement, or *fanā'*, the ultimate form of apophasis, will be further discussed in Chapter 3.

These considerations have been given in order to try and show the extent to which the spirit of the intellect, in Imam ʿAlī's perspective, transcends the rational faculty. The intellect must be seen, first and foremost, as a spiritual faculty, and the spirit, in turn, must be appreciated as the source of the intellect, as well as the source of life. Without the intellect the spirit is reduced to unconscious existence; conversely, without the spirit, the intellect tends towards lifeless thought. These aspects of the spirit are clearly expressed in the first sermon of the *Nahj*, which can be read as a commentary upon the Qur'ānic verses describing the creation of man in terms of God's 'breathing' of His spirit into man: 'He began the creation of man with clay ... He fashioned him and breathed into him of His spirit' (32: 7–9).[85]

The following lines, from the first sermon, is one of the many passages in which this infusion of the divine spirit into man is commented upon by Imam ʿAlī:

> Then He—glorified be He!—gathered up a quantity of dust, from some hard earth and some soft, some sweet earth and some salty, and poured water onto it until it was pure, then kneaded into it some moisture until it stuck together; then he fashioned from this a form with curves and joints, limbs and parts. He compacted it until it held tightly together, solidified it until it became as sounding clay, assigning to it a measured duration and a known consummation.
>
> Then He breathed into it of His spirit, and it stood up as a human being, endowed with intellectual powers with which to reflect, thoughts by which to conduct himself, limbs to put to service, instruments at his disposal, and knowledge with which to discern between the true and the false ...

In other words, it is the 'in-spiration' (literally, the 'in-breathing' *and* the insertion of the spirit) of the breath of God's spirit that produces consciousness and life. Death, on the contrary, is the 'ex-piration', the departure of the spirit. Life in the absence of 'a-spiration'—the intention to be true to one's spirit—is a kind of death. It is through the spirit that inanimate, unconscious matter is brought to life and to awareness of itself, that is, it not only generates knowledge, but also self-knowledge. This intimate intertwining between the gift of life and the capacity to know—existence which is conscious, and knowledge which is existential—is one of the foundations of any truly 'spiritual' perspective. It is not a question of opposing the spirit to the body, but of realizing that the infusion of the spirit into the body brings the body to life; and it is for this reason that knowledge vivifies, in the very measure that it is spiritual: 'O ye who believe, respond to God and His Messenger when they call you to that which vivifies you' (8: 24). As we have seen, according to the Imam, one of the most important aspects of this 'call' from God to human beings is to 'remind them of the buried treasures of the intellect'.

Existentiation is the bestowal of the spirit, which is consciousness; hence, the *ʿaql* or intellect, the principle of articulation for the spirit, is not merely a mental faculty but is itself constitutive of our true life. The intellect is that of which the mental faculty is one formal expression, one mode of its operation, but by no means the only one. As will be amply demonstrated in the sayings of the Imam below, the *ʿaql* is multi-faceted, comprising aspects that, in our times, are rarely associated with intelligence.

Being true to one's intellect—to the treasures buried deep within it and not just to the rational functions operative on its surface—is tantamount to being 'spiritual'. For Imam ʿAlī, the 'true intellectual' (*al-ʿāqil*) is one who not only *thinks* correctly but also *acts* ethically, and, at the deepest level, one who seeks to *realize* the ultimate Reality. The intellectual is defined as one who 'puts all things in their proper place'.[86] As will be seen in Chapter 2, this is the very definition of justice also; only the true intellectual can, therefore, be fully 'just', for only one who sees things as they truly are is able to put them in their right place. Thought, action and realization are all the concern of the true intellectual, the *ʿāqil*. Correct thinking, impeccable virtue and authentic being are inextricably tied up with the intellect, in the spiritual ethos being considered here. These aspects of the ethos become clearer in the light of the Imam's discourse to Kumayl, to which our attention now turns.

THE DISCOURSE TO KUMAYL

This discourse has been the subject of numerous commentaries through the centuries. Its importance lies, among other things, in its highly esoteric character. The Imam mysteriously takes one of his disciples Kumayl outside Kūfa to a graveyard, to impart the following private counsel.

> O Kumayl ibn Ziyād, truly these hearts are vessels and the best of them are those which hold the most. So retain from me that which I say to you. People are divided into three types: a lordly knower (*ʿālim rabbānī*); one who seeks knowledge (*mutaʿallim*) for the sake of deliverance; and the common folk (*hamaj raʿāʿ*) following just anyone, swaying with every current, not desiring to be illumined by the light of knowledge, nor seeking refuge from any strong support.
>
> O Kumayl, knowledge is better than wealth, for knowledge guards you, while you must guard wealth; and wealth diminishes as it is spent, while knowledge increases as it is disbursed; and the results of wealth disappear with the disappearance of wealth.
>
> O Kumayl ibn Ziyād, the wise apprehension of knowledge (*maʿrifat al-ʿilm*) is a religion by which [God] is worshipped. Through it, man acquires obedience in his life and a good name after his death. And knowledge is a judge, while wealth is judged.
>
> O Kumayl ibn Ziyād, those who hoard wealth perish even while they live, but the knowers endure for as long as time subsists; their [material] forms[87] are absent, but their [spiritual] images in the hearts are present. Ah, what abundant knowledge is here [pointing to his breast]; would that I could find one to bear it. Yes, I found one who was quick to understand, but he could not be trusted with it, exploiting the tools of religion for the sake of worldly gain, empowering himself with the graces of God against His slaves, and with His proofs against His friends. Then there was one who was obedient to the bearers of truth, but lacking heartfelt insight;[88] at the first appearance of obscurity, doubt was kindled in his heart. So alas, neither this one

nor that! Nor one who is greedy for pleasure, submissive to passion, nor one obsessed with acquisition and accumulation—neither of them is a guardian of religion in any respect. They resemble nothing so much as grazing cattle! Thus does knowledge die with the death of its bearers.

But indeed, my God, the earth will never be empty of one who establishes the proof of God, whether overtly with publicity or fearfully in obscurity, lest God's proofs and elucidations come to naught. But such as these—how many are they and where? By God, they may be the smallest in number, but with God they are the greatest in rank. Through them God preserves His proofs and elucidations, so that they entrust them to their compeers and sow them in the hearts of those resembling them.

Through them, knowledge penetrates the reality of insight. They rejoice in their intimacy with the spirit of certainty; they make easy what the extravagant find harsh; they befriend that by which the ignorant are estranged. With their bodies they keep company with the world, while their spirits are tied to the transcendent realm.

They are the vicegerents of God on His earth, summoners to His religion. Ah! how I long to see them! Go now, Kumayl, as you will.[89]

For our purposes here, it suffices to reflect upon the four sentences of the penultimate paragraph, where we are given the description of those who have the title of 'lordly knower' (*ʿālim rabbānī*), those who are fewest in number but greatest in the sight of God and through whom 'His religion' is sustained:—*His* religion, that is, the divine reality of religion, the pure essence of the faith, which is perfect and immutable, in contrast to 'religion' in the ordinary sense, the formal institutions of which are subject to human vicissitudes. It is by means of the knowledge of the true knowers that religion is true to itself, and it is only through such sages that religion truly 'lives' in the world.

'Through them, knowledge penetrates the reality of insight.'

As noted before, knowledge *can* remain merely abstract and far removed from the 'reality of insight'. But it contains a potential that calls out to be realized; it needs to be enlivened in order to 'penetrate' into something deeper than the words and concepts articulating its own form, the immediately intelligible meaning on the surface. Degrees of knowledge are clearly implied here, as is the avoidance of all literalism and superficiality, the making of facile equations between factual information and actual knowledge, let alone wisdom. The shift of consciousness required for the 'penetration' of knowledge is indicated graphically by the Imam's gesture of pointing to his breast.

The word 'penetrate' has been chosen to translate *hajama*, but the primary meaning of this verb is 'to assault', 'to take by storm', 'to charge', etc. In this context, the word helps us to see that there is in conceptual knowledge a latent force—one might almost say an 'explosive' power—deriving from the reality of knowledge, its *ḥaqīqa* or spiritual essence. It is this which calls out to be 'made real', through *taḥaqquq*, that is, realization in depth, not just factual verification on the surface. This *ḥaqīqa* can be indicated, but not captured, by the words and concepts which make up its formal, communicable aspect. By means of this inner force—which its outer conceptual form both hides and evokes—it is capable of effecting a shift of consciousness, from one degree of knowledge to another. An indirect, mental conception of reality thus paves the way for a 'penetrating', existential perception of reality. The 'reality of insight' opens up the intelligence to reality as such, whereas ordinary 'insight', like abstract knowledge, remains only at the superficial level of understanding. The same idea is expressed in a saying of Imam ʿAlī relating to true understanding, which comes to plumb and thus truly 'know' the content of knowledge, its own deeper dimensions or 'buried treasures': 'He who understands, knows the depth of knowledge (*man fahima ʿalima ghawr al-ʿilm*).'[90] The effort required to attain true knowledge, as opposed to the mere accumulation of facts or details, is likewise indicated in this saying: 'Through learning and assimilating knowledge [such that it becomes deeply rooted in one's consciousness], knowledge is attained (*bi'l-taʿallum yunālu'l-ʿilm*).'[91]

The urgency of the need to realize the immanent power within knowledge—to move from the abstract to the concrete, the potential to the actual, the static to the dynamic, the formal to the essential—is effectively evoked by the use of the word *hajama* which is related to a battle. It alerts one to the dangers of taking the initial understanding of an idea for its full comprehension, and its full comprehension, intellectually, for its dynamic interiorization, spiritually. This interiorization is a process of infinite unfolding within, not the simple registering of some fact from without. It thus requires the effective integration of knowledge within being; knowledge from without needs to be transformed into being from within, it needs to be woven into the deepest texture of one's existence. Thus, knowledge demands not just the attention of the mind but the total orientation of the soul.

In this ethos, then, effective integration (*tawḥīd*) of knowledge within being is unattainable without the participation of the whole soul; and this, in turn, requires the elimination of all the vices that flow from egocentricity. Thus, the *ʿāqil*, the true intellectual, is described by the Imam as being constantly engaged in 'struggle against his own soul',[92] against the lower inclinations, the passionate whims and distracting caprices of the ego. All of these vices, far from being confined to the plane of morality, encroach upon the domain of knowledge, and this will be understood in the very measure that knowledge is grasped as a concrete vision of things and not just a notional or conceptual apprehension. The vices are then regarded as so many clouds obscuring the vision proper to the 'reality of insight'. According to the Qur'ān, evil actions become 'rust' that covers over the heart: 'Nay, their hearts have become rusted by that which they have done' (83: 14). The *ʿāqil*, then, is engaged in constant inner struggle against the tendencies which not only sully the soul, they also blind the heart. As a virtuous person, the *ʿāqil* opposes vice on the moral plane because it is contrary to virtue. But vice is also opposed for another reason, one situated on the higher level of spiritual reality: it contradicts the nature of the Real, it obscures the reality of insight, blinding the 'eye' of the heart which alone can 'see' God.

It is not a question here of denying the validity of the moral perspective; rather, the stress is on the deeper motivation propelling the *ʿāqil* towards virtue. This motivation transcends the specifically moral plane, while comprising it; morality emerges here as the fruit or the effect, and spirituality as the seed or the cause. By drawing attention to the intellectual aspect of the *ʿāqil*'s motivation for being rid of vices, the Imam brings out more clearly the way in which immorality is rooted in ignorance. The uprooting of this ignorance, for the true intellectual, is thus tantamount to dissolving the very substance of the vices. This uprooting requires great effort, a relentless battle within, which is, indeed, the most formidable of all battles, *al-jihād al-akbar*, the greatest struggle, as it was defined by the Prophet.[93]

One should take careful note here of the following sayings of Imam ʿAlī on the importance of this inner struggle:

'Struggling against the soul through knowledge—such is the mark of the intellect.'

'The strongest people are those who are strongest against their own souls.'

'Truly, one who fights his own soul, in obedience to God and does not sin against Him, has the rank of the righteous martyr in God's eyes.'

'The ultimate battle is that of a man against his own soul.'

'He who knows his soul fights it.'

'No *jihād* is more excellent than the *jihād* of the soul.'[94]

In another saying, the Imam clarifies what the Prophet meant by defining the greatest *jihād* as that of the soul (*al-nafs*). It is not so much a question of fighting *against* the soul, but the battle *for* the soul itself. This emerges from the metaphor given by the Imam to define the struggle: *al-ʿaql* (the intellect) is the leader of the forces of *al-Raḥmān* (the Compassionate); *al-hawā* (whim, caprice, desire) commands the forces of *al-shayṭān* (the devil); *al-nafs* (the soul) vacillates between them, susceptible to the attraction of both (*mutajādhiba baynahumā*) and enters into 'the domain of whichever of the two will triumph.'[95]

These sayings underline the fact that, for the true intellectual, the soul in its entirety has to be 'conquered' and enlisted on the side of the intellect. It is not a question of destroying the lower soul but of ridding it of the destructive influence of its caprice, its egoistic whims, subjectivism and individualism—all of these notions being connoted by the word *hawā*. The Prophet, we are told in the Qur'ān, speaks not from *hawā*, rather: 'It is naught but a revelation revealed' (53: 3–4). The divine objectivity of revelation is here contrasted with the human subjectivity of passional whim. In the context of the holy war within, an analogous polarity is brought into focus by the Imam's sayings. The objectivity of the intellect must prevail against the subjectivity of individual caprice and egotistic desire. It is the intellect that represents (in the sense of 'makes present') the divine power of *al-Raḥmān*, and which combats the forces of *al-shayṭān*, represented by *al-hawā*.

The word *hawā* is further used in the Qur'ān in the sense of the desires stemming from the ego, by means of which the ego becomes a kind of false god: 'Hast thou seen him who maketh his desire his god?' (25: 43; almost identical at 45: 23). This is the subtle or hidden idolatry (*al-shirk al-khafī*) that the Prophet referred to as being more hidden than a black ant crawling on a dark stone in a moonless night.[96] To eliminate this idolatry of the ego, some force higher than that of the ego has to be engaged, as it is impossible for the ego to be controlled or dominated by something pertaining to the ego itself; and this higher force is the divine Reality, access to which is made possible through the power of the intellect and the graces of faith. This complementarity between the effort to overcome the egoism of *hawā* and the influx of divine grace is well expressed by the following verse of the Qur'ān: 'As for he who fears the station of his Lord, and restraineth his soul from whim (*hawā*), verily, Paradise will be his abode' (79: 40–41).

The soul's fundamental energy is not to be destroyed but converted and redirected, away from the transient objects of individualistic desire, away from the impulses of '*al-shayṭān*', towards the one, true object that is expressed by *al-Raḥmān*. This 'conquest' of the soul involves much more than attaining to some mental conception. For it is not only the mind, the will and the character, but the fundamental disposition of the soul that needs to be integrated into the truth perceived by the intellect, if one is to be rendered capable of perceiving that truth in all its dimensions and ramifications on the different planes of being.

It is important here to stress that, for the Imam, the need to win the soul over in its totality follows naturally from his understanding of *tawḥīd*, the most fundamental principle of Islam. It is important not to lose sight of the fact that *tawḥīd* is a verbal noun: it is often simply translated as oneness or unity, but it literally means 'affirming one' (the affirmation of, and belief in, the oneness of God, which is the outward, theological meaning), or 'realizing one' (the realization that there is but one reality, which is the inner, spiritual meaning). Thus, in the Imam's perspective, the absolutely Real is perceived not only as being one but also as making one, or integrating;[97] the Real is not only unique, it is also unifying. *Tawḥīd* then comes to mean not merely affirming the oneness of God, but also *being* one in order to reflect perfectly the One—to know God is to be 'integrated'. One observes here a link with the etymology of the word *'aql*, whose primary meaning is 'to bind'. But whereas for the later mystical tradition the limitative aspect of the word is stressed—the intellect being that which defines and encloses meaning, as opposed to the heart which intuits and discloses spiritual truth—here one sees that the intellect is that which 'binds together' into an organic unity the disparate elements of the soul. This principle is expressed in the first of the following series of the Imam's sayings, each of which merits deep reflection:

'He who knows God integrates himself (*man 'arafa'Llāh tawaḥḥad*).'

'He who knows his soul disengages himself (*man 'arafa nafsahu tajarrad*).'[98]

'He who knows people isolates himself (*man 'arafa'l-nās tafarrad*).'

'He who knows the world withholds himself (*man 'arafa'l-dunyā tazahhad*).'[99]

Elsewhere this total adherence to the Real is referred to by the Imam as 'sincerity', *ṣidq* or *ikhlāṣ*, terms which denote far more than simply truthfulness, as is already evident from the root of the word *ikhlāṣ*. The verb *khaluṣa* means to be utterly pure, true to one's essence, unadulterated by any extraneous substance. This aspect of the meaning is well expressed in the following saying of the Imam: 'Make purely for God (*akhliṣ li'Llāh*) your action and your knowledge, your love and your hatred, your taking and your leaving, your speech and your silence.'[100]

To be totally sincere, then, means to make oneself 'purely' for God, to have no 'stain' of impurity—here understood as what is other than

God—present in one's devotion, action, intention and even sentiment. One must love and hate only in function of one's relationship with God. Of all the tendencies which insinuate themselves within one's motivations and intentions, the most pernicious is egotism. *Ikhlāṣ*, 'pure sincerity', involves the active effort to be, think and act purely for God, that is, with selflessness, whence the stress placed by the Imam on the holy war within the soul as the 'ultimate battle'. One who succeeds in this battle attains the rank of the 'righteous martyr'. The victor here is the martyr, because he has sacrificed his lower life for the sake of God, with whom is the real life, that which is witnessed by the intellect, the only element within human consciousness capable of objectively looking upon the soul as 'the other'.

To repeat: 'struggling against the soul through knowledge—such is the mark of the intellect'. The intellectual in this battle is also one who bears 'witness' (*al-shahīd*, meaning both martyr and witness, as in the original Greek meaning of 'martyr'). He bears witness to God through the intellect's sacrifice of that which opposes the truth of God, and the key opponent in question is his own egotism, his own 'false life'. To have perfect *ikhlāṣ*, then, is to be rid of all hypocritical self-preoccupation and to install in its place a sincere theocentricity, a mode of being 'centred' upon God, not oneself. Thus, *ikhlāṣ* is to be *for* God, or to *belong* to God, in the sense indicated by the Qur'ānic verse, 'Say: Truly my worship and my sacrifice, and my living and my dying, are for God,[101] Lord of the universes' (6: 162).

The fact that worship is the first thing mentioned in this verse is of particular significance for anyone wishing to appreciate the nature of Imam ʿAlī's spiritual ethos. What must be stressed in the presentation of this ethos is the indispensable role performed by worship and devotion. In our second chapter, this role will become evident in the context of a quest for the fundamental virtue of justice. The ultimate fruits of worship and devotion, of which the quintessence is the remembrance of God, shall be the subject of Chapter 3. One of the key distinguishing features of the Imam's spiritual ethos, indeed, is the stress placed by him on prayer, taking this term in its widest sense, to include all those means—from formal worship and supplication to meditation and reflection, remembrance and contemplation—by which the individual is oriented and attuned to the Real, *al-Ḥaqq*.

Worship is, therefore, an integral aspect of *ikhlāṣ*, in the very measure that worship relates to and sustains a fundamental dimension of the human soul. That within the soul which yearns to worship and is satisfied only by the sustenance given through worship, must be given its due. In a spiritual context, if worship is marginalized, one's sincerity is compromised, for one is not being sincere to God, not being 'just' to God—not rendering God His due. And the spiritual logic of the Imam dictates that if one is not just with God, one cannot be just to His creatures. 'Whoso establishes well-being between himself and God,' he says, 'God establishes well-being between him and mankind.'[102]

One might also quote here the verse of the Qur'ān, 'Worship thy Lord until certainty cometh to thee' (15: 99).[103] The quest for knowledge, then, demands total dedication if it is to yield up its inner riches, and this dedication includes that quasi-alchemical transformation of consciousness wrought by total concentration on the divine Reality—prayer in one of its deepest modes. In this form of prayer, the intensity of 'dedication' is such that there is no room in one's consciousness for anything other than the object to which one is dedicated—the 'remembrance' (*dhikr*) of God strictly implying the forgetting of everything else, including, pre-eminently, oneself. As mentioned above, the spiritual reality of the *dhikr* can only be attained when 'you forget your soul in your remembrance'. Concentration upon the divine Reality as the supreme object of knowledge—rendered present through the Name or Names of God—is thus a mode of prayer, and one which, to be efficacious, requires both presence of mind and a serious engagement with the will; it is far from sufficient to pray absent-mindedly, in mechanical fashion. In this connection, the Imam says, 'He who prays without exertion is like one who shoots [arrows] without a bow.'[104] Likewise, there is certainly nothing passive or easy about the process of acquiring knowledge: 'Knowledge calls out for action; if it is answered [it is of avail], otherwise it departs.'[105]

The same idea is expressed by the Imam more forcefully in this saying: 'When you hear knowledge [being imparted] cleave to it, do not mix it up with jest, lest hearts spew it forth.'[106] Knowledge that is not taken seriously will be of no avail; it remains 'undigested' and refuses to be assimilated by the 'heart', the faculty that has access to the 'reality of insight', and which can thus 'see' God. In fact, it is not the individual who 'assimilates' knowledge to himself, but knowledge—or the reality of being expressed by true knowledge—that assimilates to itself the individual: 'Acquire knowledge, and [true] life will acquire you.'[107] The relationship between life and consciousness, so central to the intrinsic function of the spirit as discussed earlier, is again being stressed in this maxim. At first, knowledge is sought by the individual and consciousness is cultivated; then, life 'seeks' the individual as being makes itself 'real' or realizes itself more fully within the individual. In other words, the individual first makes an active effort to 'integrate' knowledge within his being; but at a certain point, this activity is transformed into passive receptivity—being, 'true life', integrates the individual within itself. To return to the Imam's guidance to Kumayl: '*Through them* knowledge penetrates the reality of insight.' It is not the knowers who penetrate; it is knowledge that penetrates to the reality of insight, doing so through them, and this, in the very measure of their effacement within knowledge, an effacement which is the shadow cast by their effective integration within the life that 'acquires' them.

'They rejoice in their intimacy with the spirit of certainty.'

The next sentence in the discourse to Kumayl is of particular importance in helping us to appreciate the sheer happiness that flows from the 'life of the spirit'. In the Arabic expression '*wa bāsharū rūḥ al-yaqīn*', the primary meaning of the word *bāshara* means having intimate experience of a thing, coming into direct physical contact with it. This form of the verb also relates to joy; hence, the phrase 'rejoice in intimate contact' better conveys something of the meaning of this single word.[108] To touch the 'spirit of certainty' is to come into contact not with some cold, logical fact, the conclusion of a purely mental process; rather, this contact with the spirit of certainty means engaging deeply with the object of certainty, with that of which one is certain—ultimately, this being nothing less than the divine itself. Since this reality is infinitely more beatific than any conceivable paradisal bliss—according to the Qurʾān, the divine *riḍwān* (beatitude, contentment) is 'greater' than Paradise (9: 72)—it cannot but bestow joy upon the soul which effectively opens itself up to that reality. In the words of Imam ʿAlī, 'Learning and reflecting upon knowledge is the delight of the knowers.'[109]

This is what one might call an 'epistemology of joy', for 'the most joyous of mankind is the intellectual (*al-ʿāqil*).'[110] This joyous epistemology—which flies in the face of modern scientistic conceptions of knowledge as dry, cold and abstract—should be considered carefully, as it reveals a crucial dimension of the spiritual knowledge proper to the Imam's perspective, and indeed, to all spiritual traditions worthy of the name. Coming into contact with truths should impart happiness, and this, in the measure that the truths in question are fundamental to one's being or to Being as such.[111] The two modes of being are ultimately identical, given the uniqueness, or the 'one-and-onliness', of Being. That which has no second, no other, cannot enter the category of number; being is indivisible. Hence, the being of the individual cannot be different ultimately from Being as such, however great be the existential disparity—or rather, incommensurability—between the individual and God. True knowledge is knowledge of Being, thus it is perforce a kind of self-discovery, even if knowledge of the Absolute is impossible without absolute self-abandonment. The highest discovery calls for the deepest effacement.

However, in the initial stages of this process, true knowledge, acquired by the intellectual is a kind of self-discovery that imparts the happiness of a homecoming, a return from the exile of ignorance. This follows because 'the most intellectual of people' is 'the one who is closest to God',[112] and 'the one who is most alive.'[113] To be close to God is to be fully alive, and this true life gives profound joy, the *joie de vivre*, the sheer joy of living. This is a joy proper to existence as such and, as will be seen below, it is independent of particular experiences that may or may not be pleasurable.

Here again we see the crucial relationship between life and consciousness: the fruits of the 'in-spiration' of the spirit of God on one hand, and between this life of spiritual consciousness and joy on the other: those who are true to the spirit of God within them truly possess joy. It is also by reason of the intimate and unshakeable certainty of the divine goodness and compassion that the true *faqīh*—not so much 'the jurist' as 'one who truly understands'—is defined by the

Imam as 'he who does not make people despair of the mercy of God, and does not make them lose hope in the gracious spirit of God (*rawḥ Allāh*).'[114] Such is the sage's state of immersion in the joyous certainty of God's mercy that there is no place for any despair. It is a sign of disbelief to despair of this mercy: '... and who despaireth of the mercy of his Lord except those who stray in error?' (15: 56). The divine assurances of mercy in the Qur'ān, such as 'My mercy encompasseth all things' (7: 156) and 'thy Lord has prescribed for Himself mercy' (6: 54), are brought to life fully in the souls that have profound and not just notional knowledge of the beatific nature of the divine Reality; they are the ones who truly 'understand', the true *fuqahā'*.

This opening to joy through intimate knowledge of the mercy of God is inseparable from beauty, the perception of which is another unexpected concomitant of the intellect in the Imam's perspective. The appreciation of beauty is not merely a question of subjective aesthetics; it is an objective aspect of the function of the intellect. Beauty also takes one to the heart of ethics. The Arabic *iḥsān* is often simply translated as 'virtue' or 'excellence', but one of its key literal meanings is 'making beautiful'—*ḥusn* means 'beauty'. Virtue, *iḥsān*, can thus be understood as that which 'makes the soul beautiful'. In this light, the relationship between the intellect, ethics and aesthetics is more clearly discerned: 'The excellence of the intellect', says Imam 'Alī, 'is in the beauty of things outward and inward (*jamāl al-ẓawāhir wa'l-bawāṭin*).'[115] The outward beauty of forms and actions must be complemented by inward beauty, that is, beauty of soul, or virtue in the most integral and penetrating sense of the word. All of this follows naturally from two sayings attributed to the Prophet: 'Truly God is beautiful and He loves beauty,'[116] and: 'Assume the character traits of God.'[117]

This cultivation of 'beautiful traits' within oneself makes one lovable to God, since He 'loves beauty'. This process of making oneself lovable to God is inseparable from the emulation of the virtues brought to perfection in the soul of the Prophet. 'Say: O ye who believe, if ye love God, follow me [the Prophet]; God will love you' (3: 31). This attraction of God's love through making oneself beautiful in the fullest sense is alluded to in another saying of the Imam: 'The foundation of the intellect is the assimilation of love (*awwal al-ʿaql al-tawaddud*).'[118] Rather than simply referring to love as such (*wudd/mawadda*), the Imam draws attention to the need to make oneself lovable to God by using the form *tawaddud*, alluding thereby to the process of integrating or realizing the principle of love within oneself, as well as expressing outwardly the love that is experienced inwardly, love being thus appreciated both as outward radiance and inner attraction.[119]

To 'follow' the Prophet and thus make oneself receptive to the divine influx of love means, among other things, cultivating the 'prophetic' virtues. These virtues are prophetic not in the sense that they belong exclusively to the Prophet, but because he is deemed to have realized virtue in all its plenitude, and is thus the exemplar, *par excellence*, of virtue as such. It is thus not surprising to find that it is not only beauty and love that articulate the receptivity of the intellect to the divine Reality, but also such qualities as kindness and contentment,[120] courtesy,[121] generosity and modesty,[122] wise forbearance (*ḥilm*).[123] None of these moral qualities are absent from the soul of the true intellectual. There can no wisdom or intellect in the fullest sense if the soul lacks these fundamental qualities.[124] It is thanks to the presence of these virtues that the intellect is able to develop those dimensions of depth and breadth without which it remains confined to the flat, horizontal plane of its own operations—confined, that is, to the activity of reason alone, which is, until touched by faith and deepened by grace, unaware of what lies beneath the surface of its own field of activity, oblivious of the 'hidden treasures' of the intellect, blind to the need to 'integrate' the whole of the soul within the mould of that 'integral', or 'unifying' virtue which bestows integrity upon the intelligence. Such integration, or 'making one', is absolutely fundamental to *tawḥīd*, this now being grasped as a dynamic process of spiritual unification that is demanded by the idea of the oneness of God. It is clearly necessary that truth must inspire the soul, but it is equally necessary that, conversely, virtue 'aerate' the intelligence, provide it with the 'leaven' which allows it to expand to its full dimensions.

Sinful, immoral qualities are grasped in this perspective not only as vices but also as so many blind spots or intellectual dysfunctions. The heart is 'diseased' by vice, its 'eye' blinded by them and thus unable to 'see' the Real. As is said in the Qur'ān, 'In their hearts is a disease and God increased them in disease' (2: 10), and 'It is not the sights that are blind, but blind are the hearts' (22: 46).

As noted above, the vices are all comprised within egotism and this, in turn, is often described simply as 'caprice' (*hawā*). In one saying, the Imam refers to this conquest over caprice as being tantamount to salvation: 'He attains deliverance whose intellect dominates his caprice.'[125] Deliverance—*falāḥ*, which comprises the sense both of salvation and beatitude—is thus to some degree accessible here and now; it is not only a grace granted posthumously. This deliverance involves tasting the joy which emanates from certainty, from intimate contact with the spirit of this certainty. As to the means of cultivating receptivity to this spirit of certainty, what is required—over and above obedience to the rules and regulations of the revealed Law—is that combination of purity of intention and sincerity of devotion which is expressed by the word *ikhlāṣ*. Without this sincerity or purity, complying with those formal rules is nothing but hypocrisy (*nifāq*) and pretension (*riyā'*) which, in turn is defined by the Imam as the gravest of all sins, *shirk*, or polytheism, the attribution of 'partners' to God: 'Know that the slightest pretension (*riyā'*) is polytheism.'[126] This sentence can be taken as a comment upon one of the most important condemnations of hypocrisy found in the Qur'ān. The verses in question refer to those who deny the essence of the faith, even while outwardly conforming to it:

> Hast thou seen the one who belieth religion? He is the one who repelleth the orphan and urgeth not the feeding of the poor. So woe be to those who pray, those who are heedless of their prayer, who want only to be seen, and withhold small kindnesses (107: 1–7).

This short *sūra* makes it clear that to be 'religious' in one's formal acts of devotion has no value whatsoever unless these acts be integrated into a life of virtue, and unless one is performing one's devotion with the right intention, that is, with *ikhlāṣ*. It also helps us to see the reason for not referring to the Imam's ethos as simply 'religious' but as 'spiritual', taking the ideals of religion to their most profound application. Without this dimension of depth, religion is meaningless. 'There is no religion for one who has no intellect,'[127] says the Imam. Likewise, 'Action without knowledge is error.'[128] The intention motivating action is what counts, for 'action—all action—is dust, except what is purified [accomplished sincerely] within it.'[129] This detachment from action as such and the orientation instead towards an inner state of being, one from which good actions cannot but emerge, clearly reflects what is found in the Qur'ān: 'It is not their [sacrificed] flesh nor their blood that reacheth God, but it is piety from you that reacheth Him' (22: 37).

'There is no religion for one who has no intellect'. One might argue that no group better epitomized the principle expressed in this saying than the Khārijites. Among this group that rebelled against the Imam were numerous 'readers' (*qurrā'*, sing. *qāri'*) of the Qur'ān, people who possessed considerable religious prestige on account of their knowledge of the Qur'ān and their intense worship. Their piety, however, was more apparent than real; it was in fact a 'zeal of bitterness', a caricature of true piety.[130] When his supporters made mention of the long night vigils performed by members of this group, the Imam gave this sharp reply: 'Sleeping with certainty is better than praying with doubt'.[131] Certainty, as we have seen, imparts peace and joy; thus, sleep, for one who is immersed in what the Imam calls 'the spirit of certainty', is a bodily repose which further deepens the happiness that flows from a good conscience and spiritual certitude, the latter understood as a kind of permanent 'wakefulness', in the sense of being awake to the higher realities. Thus, bodily sleep does not contradict spiritual wakefulness. As the *ḥadīth* of the Prophet has it, 'My eyes sleep, but my heart sleeps not.'[132]

In relation to formal worship, the true intellectual is one who is obedient to the divine injunction to pray; but rather than praying in mechanical fashion and believing that the action alone suffices, the *'āqil* knows that such obedience is a necessary but not sufficient condition for achieving receptivity to grace. There must be consciousness of what one is doing, why one is doing it, and it is this awareness, together with virtue, or 'inward beauty', that attracts the divine acceptance. 'The most worthy knowledge for you' says the Imam, 'is that by virtue of whose presence action is accepted by God.'[133]

'They make easy what the extravagant find harsh; they befriend that by which the ignorant are estranged.'

This sentence now takes us, among other things, to the impact made on the soul of the true sages by recollection of the inevitability of death in this world and the consequent necessity of renunciation within it. In the first place, that which is found to be 'harsh' by those who are extravagant—the avid, worldly types—is outward adversity, difficulty, deprivation. These are all circumstances which, in the Qur'ān, are viewed as the trials which inevitably accompany life in this world:

> And We shall try you with something of fear and hunger and loss of property and life and fruits; but give glad tidings to the patient—those who, when struck by affliction say: 'Verily, we belong to God and verily unto Him we are ever-returning.' These are the ones upon whom there are blessings from their Lord, and mercy; and these are the ones who are rightly guided. (2: 155–157)

The wise, the rightly-guided (*al-muhtadūn*), perceive the 'blessings' that are showered down upon those who are patient in the face of afflictions, this patience being a concomitant of their knowledge of the truth: 'By the Age, truly man is in a state of loss—except those who believe and do virtuous deeds and exhort one another to truth and exhort one another to patience' (103: 1–3). These are the believers who remain steadfast in the face of trials, being firmly rooted in their awareness of their origin and end, and the fact that 'unto Him we are ever-returning'. For this reason, they can 'make easy' the trials and difficulties of life, whereas the 'extravagant' experience them solely in their aspect of harshness and bitterness. The 'ease' that inheres in all difficulty is hidden from the ignorant but discerned by the wise: 'Verily, with hardship cometh ease; verily with hardship cometh ease' (94: 5–6). The wise go even further than just anticipating 'ease' as the inevitable fruit of hardship; they taste this fruit already as the seed hidden within hardship itself, for they actually 'befriend that by which the ignorant are estranged'.

We can understand one level of meaning here with the help of this saying of Imam ʿAlī: 'Death is more intimate to me than the breast of the mother is to the suckling babe.'[134] For, in the verse cited above, the mention of trials and difficulties is preceded by a reminder that those who are slain 'in the path of God' are not really dead, 'nay, they are alive but ye perceive not.' We have here not simply an affirmation of the life hereafter, but also an allusion to the esoteric meaning of being 'slain' for God, *al-fanā' fi'Llāh*, 'extinction in God'. The intimacy with death mentioned by the Imam can be seen to relate to this 'death' while still alive, which he also alludes to in another saying: 'I am the death of the dead.'[135] It is because life in the world itself is a kind of death—a limitation, hence privation in contrast to the infinite plenitude of the divine realms—that dying to this death is tantamount to true life. 'And the life of this world is nothing but sport and play' says the Qur'ān, 'and verily, the abode of the Hereafter—that is [true] life, did they but know' (29: 64).

However, it is important to stress that it is not the physical world as such that is to be negated, rather it is worldliness—egotistic attachment to the world—that must be overcome. Here, we need to dwell a little on one of the key principles of the Imam's perspective, one which is stressed repeatedly throughout the *Nahj al-balāgha*: this is the principle of *zuhd*, which cannot be translated by any single word in English; it comprises several meanings, such as asceticism, austerity, abstention, detachment, 'doing without' and 'making little of'. The following passage from the *Nahj* expresses well the attitude of the *zāhid* toward this world:

> The world is an abode for which annihilation is ordained, and for its people departure from it is decreed. It is sweet and green, and it hastens to one who seeks [it], and confounds the heart that gazes upon it. So set out from it with the best of the provision available to you, and ask not from it above what suffices and seek not from it more than what can be attained.[136]

What is this 'best of provision' (*zād*)? In many places in the *Nahj* it is described as *taqwā*, another word which is difficult to translate, the meaning being piety, fear of God, awe, God-consciousness: 'I exhort you, O slaves of God, to *taqwā*, which is the provision,'[137] says the Imam. This provision for the next world is only attained, however, in the measure of one's detachment from the perishable aspects of the 'life of this world', for 'whoso desireth that [life of the world] which hasteneth away, in that [life] We hasten for him what We will … (17: 18).'

The despicable aspect of the world is described in vivid terms by the Imam: 'By God, this world of yours is more contemptible in my eyes than a [chewed-up] bone of a pig in the hand of a leper';[138] 'an image of the world is the snake—soft to touch, but virulent poison within';[139] the world is 'as worthless to me as that which drips from the nose of a goat'.[140] It is the grandeur and beauty of God that render the world insignificant and distasteful; it is only in the light of the Absolute that the pleasures and attractions of the world appear fleeting and illusory: 'The greatness of the Creator for you belittles creatures in your view.'[141] In similar vein, the Imam refers to a 'brother in God': 'What made him great in my eyes was the smallness of the world in his (*kāna yuʿaẓẓimuhu fī ʿaynī ṣighar al-dunyā fī ʿaynihi*).'[142]

This, according to the Qur'ānic usage of *zāhid*, is the real meaning of *zuhd*. In the Sūra named after Joseph (Yūsuf), the brothers of Yūsuf 'deemed him of little value' in selling him for a small price (12: 20); they were described as being, in relation to him, '*zāhidīn*'. The world, in the Imam's perspective, is likewise deemed of little value—not that it is altogether valueless, but that, in relation to the Hereafter, to eternity, to the ultimate reality, it is rendered all but insignificant. All created things are reduced to infinitesimal, fleeting shadows destined for annihilation: 'Everything perishes except His Face' (28: 88). However, the world is not deprived of all value; indeed, its significance lies precisely in what it signifies and cannot but signify: 'And there is nothing that does not hymn His glory with praise' (17: 44). Everything in the world, all the creatures in existence, thus proclaim the infinite creativity of the Creator; and to help us imaginatively fathom the mystery of this universal praise, the Qur'ān tells us: 'And the birds in flight—each one knoweth its prayer and glorification' (24: 41).

It is thus not at all contradictory for the Imam to both despise the world and yet wax lyrical in his description of the beauties of virgin nature, including that unsurpassable marvel, the peacock.[143] This comes in a sermon which includes descriptions of birds in general, mentioning also ants, serpents and elephants. It is noteworthy that the sermon concludes with a galvanizing description of Paradise, juxtaposing the marvels of this world with the delights of the next; in the light of the latter, all terrestrial phenomena pale into insignificance. For once the 'eye of the heart' is directed to Paradise, 'your soul would become averse to the marvels of this world—its passions, its pleasures and its embellished scenery'.[144]

It might seem contradictory to bring together such apparently opposed qualities as joy in certainty, discussed above, and the 'befriending' of hardship. But the latter is in fact the fruit of the former. All difficulties without exception are endured thanks to the spiritual resources that are made available by faith combined with intellectual assimilation, or rather: in the measure that faith is intellectually assimilated, and thus becomes *maʿrifa* or gnosis, comprising a certainty which is so deep and so complete that 'even if the veil be lifted' it cannot increase, according to the famous saying noted earlier. It is possible to believe, at one level of the mind, that 'there is no god but God'. The Imam, however, draws attention to what this apparently simple belief should imply when it is 'sincere' or 'pure': 'I bear witness that there is no god but God alone Who has no partner—a testimony whose sincerity has been tested and whose essence has been assimilated with conviction (*muʿtaqadan muṣāṣahā*).'[145]

The word *muṣāṣ* refers to the choicest and purest part of any substance, that which constitutes its essence. The root of the word *maṣṣa* means 'to suck', the idea here being that the liquid or juice of a substance or fruit contains its essence, that which is 'sucked' out of it. In the present context, the Imam is stressing the spiritual substance of the testimony, as opposed to the merely verbal affirmation or mental comprehension of the words. That is, he affirms a heartfelt connection with that to which the testimony bears witness; the words defining the testimony being as an echo of the reality they convey. The words are not to be confused with that reality itself. He continues: 'We cling to it always, for as long as we endure, storing it up [as protection] against the terrors that will befall us. For truly, it renders faith resolute, opens up spiritual virtue, pleases *al-Raḥmān* (the All-Compassionate), repels *al-shayṭān* (the devil).'[146]

Going back to 'befriending' that by which the ignorant are estranged', one might say that this implies not just the trials of life, which are a source of strength for the wise and repulsion for the ignorant, but also the ineluctability of death. For the wise, this means release, the encounter with God, blissful eternity—in other words, a mode of *tawḥīd*, whereby the soul enjoys ever greater degrees of *integration* within higher principles; for the ignorant, on the contrary, death is perceived as a frightful *disintegration*, the end of their world rather than the beginning of endless life. One should also mention in this connection that prefiguration of death in life already mentioned, that is, *fanāʾ*, 'extinction', 'effacement', the 'perishing' of egoistic consciousness in the face of the Absolute. The ignorant shrink in horror at the prospect of the loss of what is falsely taken to be 'their' life, not realizing that this sacrifice of egoistic and limited self-consciousness is the basis on which infinite consciousness is glimpsed or 'tasted'. One can only 'taste' the ocean of the Real by being drowned in it.

As we shall see in Chapter 3, one could even say that the means to this ultimate attainment is also 'embraced' by the wise and feared by the ignorant, that is, the act of pure prayer, total concentration on the Real. For this concentration strictly precludes all worldly or egotistic preoccupations; the very intensity of the concentration upon the Absolute burns away thoughts of the relative, and for those who ignorantly identify with relativities, both inward and outward, this implies a kind of death. For the wise, on the contrary, this concentration on the Absolute—the unsullied 'remembrance of God'—is a joyous contemplation of reality before which the ego is displaced and all illusions are dispelled. This leads directly to the following sentence of the passage:

> '*With their bodies, they keep company with the world, while their spirits are tied to the transcendent realm.*'

This sentence can be more concretely understood if it is read in the light of another well-known expression of the Imam. He describes himself as belonging to a group whose degree of spirituality is such that 'their hearts are in the Gardens [of Paradise] while their bodies are at work'.[147] The fact of being 'tied' or 'attached' to that realm, consisting of the paradisal abodes, right up to the divine Presence itself, implies then, that they are already 'within' that transcendent realm, more than they are in this earthly one. This helps explain the saying quoted above: God keeps man perpetually in that which his soul desires. Those whose hearts or spirits are 'in' the transcendent domain are those whose consciousness is substantially, and not merely conceptually, determined by the transcendent realities. Those whose consciousness, on the contrary, is determined by worldly matters are 'in' this world, in the sense of being enclosed by its formal limitations; their orientation and imagination are trapped within a worldly framework. Their actions bear the mark of this 'worldliness', whereas the actions of the wise are the fruits of their immersion in a higher reality. One might say that their outward actions in the world belie their inward transcendence of all action; they act, but are not bound by the fruits of their action.[148] As seen earlier, they are aware that 'action—all action—is dust, except what is purified (accomplished sincerely) within it'.

At this point it would be appropriate to dwell briefly on the role played by the notion of the 'Hereafter' within the ethical framework of the Imam. As we saw above, and will see in what follows, the Hereafter is repeatedly invoked or evoked in the discourses of the Imam. Is it a question of offering a heavenly carrot and threatening a hellish stick, in order simply to 'enjoin the good and forbid the evil'? We believe that, even if the answer is affirmative on one level, there is a deeper side to this seemingly simplistic utilization of the ethical import of divine warnings and promises on human action.

The point of view adopted in regard to ethical orientation here is defined essentially by the spiritual reality not just of God but also of the Hereafter, both objectively, in itself, and subjectively, that is, insofar as it is assimilated by the individual. It thus becomes a dynamic dimension—a process, orientation or reflux—within the very soul of the believer, rather than a mere belief or hope. Anticipation of the Hereafter is one thing, and this is what characterizes every believer in principle, but its realization is another, and it is this that characterizes the soul of the 'friend' of God (*walī Allāh*), the saint and the sage. As noted earlier, the Imam says in a famous sentence which bears witness to his state of total immersion within the reality of which he is certain: 'Were the veil to be removed, I would not increase in certitude (*law kushifa'l-ghiṭā', mā azdadtu yaqīnan*).' The anticipation—or better, foretaste—of the Hereafter is deepened, not diminished, in proportion to one's virtue, piety and sanctity; it does not become a merely heuristic tool whose value is restricted to its impact on moral action, and thus rendered superfluous once this impact is achieved. In this connection, the following moving passage from the *Nahj* deserves reflection. What we have here is the description of a blissful vision of the reality of Paradise and not merely a rhetorical flourish in the service of moral exhortation:

> If you were to cast the eye of your heart towards what is described for you of the Garden, your soul would become averse to the marvels of this world—its passions, its pleasures and its embellished scenery. And your soul would be rapt in contemplation of the swaying trees whose roots lie hidden in dunes of musk on the banks of the rivers of the Garden, and the clusters of dazzling pearls hanging down from the branches of its trees ...[149]

It is, of course, true that the highest degree of spirituality transcends the desire for Paradise and the fear of Hell, and the moral conduct proportioned thereto. But this means that when such higher degrees of realization have been attained, the state of the soul is one that can properly be characterized as 'paradisal', that is, as being already so utterly content with the beatific presence of God that it can desire nothing more. This state of soul is called in the Qur'ān *al-nafs al-muṭma'inna* (89: 27), 'the soul at peace in absolute certainty'.

The Imam frequently echoes, implicitly if not explicitly, the Qur'ānic principle that the 'Hereafter is better and more lasting' (87: 17). The Hereafter is not only the 'time' when divine warnings and promises are consummated; it is also the 'space' within which all positive qualities—human, angelic, divine—are manifested in their plenary nature, those qualities that are glimpsed on earth as reflections of the higher realities, and which encompass and subtly penetrate the entire sphere of terrestrial existence. The Qur'ān, perhaps more so than any other scripture, affords to the imagination numerous and complex descriptions of paradisal bliss. One of the key functions of this is alluded to in the Qur'ān itself: 'Assuredly, We purify them with a pure quality—remembrance of the Abode (of the Hereafter)' (38: 46). The mere thought of Paradise is itself a purification of the mind and heart, a means of averting from the soul the ever-present temptation to seek its ultimate happiness and well-being in this world alone. On the contrary, one's well-being in the herebelow, in regard to action lies in the performance of good deeds, and such well-being is proportioned to the depth of one's belief that 'Whatever good ye send before for your souls, ye will find it with God, better and more tremendous as reward' (73: 20).

In other words, a sincere orientation towards the Hereafter is transformed into a perception of heavenly beatitude already in the herebelow, in the form precisely of those acts and attitudes which, being good, are of one and the same nature as that felicity to which they lead. In this light, morally good actions and noble intentions are grasped by one who sees beyond the veil of this world as vivid prefigurations of heavenly realities and not just as ethical prerequisites for salvation. Goodness, in other words, does not just lead to a heavenly reward; it already *is* something of this reward: 'Is the reward of goodness (*iḥsān*) aught but goodness?' (55: 60). The Imam's saying, 'The fruit of good action is like its root',[150] can be seen as echoing this idea that the end is already present in the means leading to it. Finally, let us quote the following verse of the Qur'ān, which is a fitting way to conclude this chapter and introduce the next:

> And give good tidings to those who believe and perform virtuous deeds, that for them are Gardens underneath which rivers flow. Every time they are given to eat from the fruits thereof, they say: 'This is what we were given to eat before'. And they were given the like thereof (2: 25).

The 'fruits' of the paradisal gardens are thus experienced already in the herebelow, in the form of all goodness, beauty and truth, and the diverse modes of happiness flowing therefrom. All such experiences are so many foretastes of the ultimate beatitude in Paradise. On the ethical plane, the performance of good deeds, and even more directly, the realization of intrinsic virtue, *iḥsān*, is thus not simply a prerequisite for posthumous salvation, but is already a kind of deliverance, here and now. It is a deliverance from the imprisonment of sin, on the outward plane, and from the bondage of egocentricity, on the inward plane. This theme of salvation here and now, grounded in unshakeable certitude, is fundamental to the spirit of the Imam's teachings and will be further explored in the rest of this book. In the following chapter, the cardinal virtue of justice will be considered within Imam 'Alī's perspective, rooted as it is in *iḥsān*. This was defined by the Prophet as worshipping God as if one saw him—a vision concretely affirmed by the Imam as real and not just hypothetical, for God is indeed 'seen' by the pure of heart 'through the verities of faith'.

NOTES

1. A saying of the Prophet, cited by al-Ḥākim al-Nīsābūrī, *al-Mustadrak ʿalāʾl-ṣaḥīḥayn* (Beirut, 2002), p.929, no.4694.

2. S.H. Nasr defines succinctly the essence of Islamic spirituality as 'the realization of Unity, as expressed in the Qur'ān, on the basis of the prophetic model, and with the aid of the Prophet'. See his 'Introduction' to *Islamic Spirituality: Foundations*, vol.19 of *World Spirituality: An Encyclopedic History of the Religious Quest*, ed. S.H. Nasr (London, 1987), p.xviii.

3. All translations from the Qur'ān are the author's own, based largely upon those of Marmaduke Pickthall and Yūsuf ʿAlī.

4. The following passage by Rūmī expresses perfectly this reciprocity between ordinary souls and the prophetic substance: 'In the composition of man all sciences were originally commingled so that his spirit might show forth all hidden things, as limpid water shows forth all that is under it ... and all that is above it, reflected in the substance of water. Such is its nature, without treatment or training. But when it was mingled with earth or other colours, that property and that knowledge was parted from it and forgotten by it. Then God Most High sent forth prophets and saints, like a great, limpid water such as delivers out of darkness and accidental colouration every mean and dark water that enters into it ...The prophets and the saints therefore remind him of his former state; they do not implant anything new in his substance. Now every dark water that recognises that great water, saying, "I come from this and I belong to this", mingles with that water ... It was on this account that God declared, "Now there has come to you a Messenger from among yourselves".' (9: 128). *Discourses of Rūmī*, tr. A.J. Arberry (London, 1961), pp.44–45.

5. Cited in Aḥmad b. Shuʿayb al-Nasāʾī, *Khaṣāʾiṣ Amīr al-muʾminīn ʿAlī b. Abī Ṭālib* (Tehran, 1419/1998), p.104.

6. Nīsābūrī, *al-Mustadrak*, p.924, no.4672. One needs Ibn al-ʿArabī's doctrine of the relationship between *walāya* (sanctity) and *nubūwwa* (prophecy) to understand this aright. While the sanctity of a saint is greater—because it is more universal—than the prophecy of a prophet, the sanctity of a prophet is always greater than the sanctity of a saint. Sanctity is deemed higher than prophecy, but both dimensions are realized in all their plenitude within the soul of the prophet. When a saint's sanctity is compared

with a prophet's prophecy, the latter, being determined by the particularities of the message to a given people in a given time and place, will appear to derive from, and thus be subordinated to, the universal principle from which sanctity draws the substance that defines it as such. Thus, 'Alī is 'from' the Prophet inasmuch as his sanctity derives from the sanctity of the Prophet *qua* supreme source of sanctity; but the Prophet can be seen to be 'from' 'Alī, if the latter be seen as symbol of the principle of sanctity, the universal source of the Prophet's sanctity and prophethood alike. For extensive discussion of this theme, see Michel Chodkiewicz, *Seal of the Saints: Prophethood and Sainthood in the Doctrine of Ibn 'Arabī*, tr. Liadain Sherrard (Cambridge, 1993).

7. Nīsābūrī, *Mustadrak*, p.927, no.468.

8. See Rayshahrī, ed., *Mawsū'a*, vol.10, for a wealth of relevant sources dealing with the various disciplines connected with 'Alī.

9. *Nahj*, p.300; *Peak*, p.393.

10. For a comprehensive treatment of the issues and events in question see Wilferd Madelung, *The Succession to Muḥammad: A Study of the Early Caliphate* (Cambridge, 1997); and for a concise overview, see our article, "Alī b. Abī Ṭālib', in *The Encyclopedia of Religion*, 2nd ed., vol.1, pp.256–261. Mohammad Jawad Chirri's *The Brother of the Prophet Mohammad*, 2.vols (Detroit, 1982) is a non-polemical presentation of the life of 'Alī by a contemporary Shi'i religious scholar; it remains the best single biographical source for 'Alī in the English language.

11. See Ahmad Paketchy, *Mawlid Amīr al-mu'minīn: Nuṣūṣ mustakhrija min al-turāth al-Islāmī* (Tehran, 2004), for four early sources—both Shi'i and Sunni, the earliest being that of Abu'l-Bakhtarī (d. 200/815–816), entitled *Mawlid Amīr al-mu'minīn*—that provide compelling evidence for the fact that 'Alī was indeed born within the Ka'ba itself.

12. Martin Lings, *Muḥammad: His Life Based on the Earliest Sources* (London, 1986), p.51. See also A. Guillaume, *The Life of Muhammad: A Translation of Ibn Ishaq's Sirat Rasul Allah* (London, 1955), p.118. The passage in question is taken from the account given by 'Alī himself, as cited in al-Ṭabarī's history.

13. Ibid., pp.222–223.

14. Ibid., p.234.

15. Ibid., p.514.

16. The descendents of the Prophet through 'Alī and Fāṭima, known as the *ashrāf* (sing. *sharīf*) or *sādāt* (sing. *sayyid*), are regarded by all Muslims as constituting a kind of 'spiritual nobility'.

17. See, for example, Nīsābūrī, *Mustadrak*, pp.943, nos. 4759, 4760, 4761, 4762.

18. Guillaume, *Muhammad*, pp.270–277. See also Fakhr al-Din al-Rāzī, *al-Tafsīr al-kabīr* (Beirut, 2001), vol.3, pp.245–250, for an interesting commentary on this verse. It is worth noting that the following *ḥadīth* is cited in one of Rāzī's discussions, and is described (albeit by his opponent in the debate) as one whose authenticity is accepted by both Sunnis and Shiʿis: 'He who wishes to see Adam as regards his knowledge, Noah as regards his obedience, Abraham as regards his friendship [with God], Moses as regards his awe [of God], and Jesus as regards his purity, let him gaze upon ʿAlī b. Abī Ṭālib' (p.248).

19. See Muḥammad Rayshahrī, *Ahl al-bayt dar Qurʾān wa ḥadīth*, tr. Ḥamīd Riḍā Shaykhī and Ḥamīd Riḍā Āzhīr (Qom, 1379 Sh./2000), vol.2, pp.550–552 for specific references to Bukhārī, Tirmidhī, Ibn Ḥanbal, and to various commentaries such as those of Zamakhsharī and Suyūṭī.

20. The Arabic of this is *Allāhumma ṣalli ʿalā Muḥammad wa ʿalā āl-i Muḥammad ka-mā ṣallayta ʿalā Ibrāhīm wa ʿalā āl-i Ibrāhīm, innaka ḥamīdun majīd*. The prayer is then repeated, substituting the words *bārik* and *bārakta* (a synonymous invocation of blessing) for *ṣalli* and *ṣallayta*. See Nīsābūrī, *Mustadrak*, p.943, no.4764.

21. Cited in Rayshahrī, ed., *Mawsūʿa*, vol.9, p.23.

22. Nīsābūrī, *Mustadrak*, p.943, no.4765. The next *ḥadīth* in this collection states that a person who prays and fasts but hates the Prophet's Ahl al-Bayt enters hellfire.

23. Nasāʾī wrote a separate work of traditions composed solely of sayings relating to the distinctions and merits of ʿAlī, entitled *Khaṣāʾiṣ amīr al-muʾminīn ʿAlī b. Abī Ṭālib* (see note 5. above).

24. See note 1 above.

25. Nīsābūrī, *Mustadrak*, p.916, no.4628.

26. Nasāʾī, *Khaṣāʾiṣ*, p.129. In Nīsābūrī's *Mustadrak* (p.19, no.4636), this saying is found without the words 'after me'. It is of interest to note that the Prophet referred to his daughter Fāṭima as 'mother of her father' (*umm abīhā*), which, taking into account her epithet as the 'Confluence of the Two Lights', adds to the mystery of the Prophet's declaration that he is 'from ʿAlī'.

27. Nīsābūrī, *Mustadrak*, p.927, no.4685.

28. Ibid., p.936, no.4723. We translate *ghurraʾl-muḥajjalīn* as 'radiantly devout' on the basis of the Prophetic tradition cited by Lane: 'My community will come on the Day of Judgement as *ghurraʾl-muḥajjalīn*.' The latter are described as those having a whiteness on their foreheads, wrists and ankles from the effects of ablution. See E.W. Lane, *Arabic-English Lexicon* (Cambridge,

1984), vol.1, p.521.

29. Nīsābūrī, *Mustadrak*, p.938, no.4736. A slightly different version of this as one of the sayings of the Prophet transmitted on the authority of Abū Bakr, 'Gazing upon the face of ʿAlī is an act of worship (*al-naẓar ilā wajḥi ʿAlī ʿibāda*),' is given by Jalāl al-Dīn al-Suyūṭī in his *Ta'rīkh al-khulafā'*, tr. H.S. Jarrett, *History of the Caliphs* (Amsterdam, 1970), p.97.

30. Nīsābūrī, *Mustadrak*, p.927, no.4686.

31. Ibid., p.929, no.4694.

32. Ibid., p.929, no.4695.

33. Ibid., p.930, no.4697.

34. Nasā'ī, *Khaṣā'iṣ*, p.104.

35. Nīsābūrī, *Mustadrak*, p.924, no.4672.

36. Ibid., p.925, no.4675.

37. Ibid., p.926, no.4678.

38. Ibid., p.926, no.4679. See also Nasā'i, *Khaṣā'iṣ*, p.217. It is interesting to note that in the Judaic tradition, Enoch (the Muslim Idrīs) is given the epithet of 'the mender of sandals,' as noted by Amir-Moezzi, 'Le combattant du *ta'wīl*. Un poéme de Mollā Ṣadrā sur 'Alī,' in Todd Lawson, ed., *Reason and Inspiration in Islam* (London, 2005), p.449, n.37.

39. Nīsābūrī, *Mustadrak*, p.926, no.4680. This is seen in the tradition as a double prophecy that was fulfilled. On one hand, ʿAlī is to this day seen as God incarnate by some extremist Shiʿi groups; on the other hand, ʿAlī was cursed by official Umayyad decree from all the mosques in its domains, as part of the Friday congregational prayers, a practice instituted by Muʿāwiya and brought to an end by 'Umar II (d.101/720), who replaced the curse with verse 15 of Sūra 59 (*al-Ḥashr*) and verse 90 of Sūra 16 (*al-Naḥl*). All the regions of the Umayyad empire were instructed to curse ʿAlī; the only town that did not was Sīstān. The geographer/historian Yāqūt writes: 'What greater honour than to have refused to curse the brother of the Prophet, even though he was being cursed from the pulpits of Mecca and Medina!' See Yāqūt al-Ḥamawī, *Muʿjam al-buldān* (Beirut, 1388/1968), vol.3, p.191, as cited by Muḥammad Ḥusayn Rajabī, '*Sabb*,' in Rashād, ed., *Dānish-nāmah*, vol.9, p.357.

40. Nīsābūrī, *Mustadrak*, p.927, no.4682.

41. Ibid., p.925, no.4674. It is of note that when Muʿāwiya instituted the cursing of ʿAlī in his domains, as mentioned in the note above, one eminent companion, Saʿd b. Abī Waqqāṣ, refused to comply. Upon being asked why, he referred not to this saying of the Prophet but to these three reasons: ʿAlī was one of the Ahl al-Bayt whom God had 'purified' of all defilement, according to the Qur'ān, 33: 33; 'Alī's rank in relation to him was the same as Aaron in

relation to Moses, according to the Prophet; and it was to ʿAlī that the Prophet gave the banner at the battle of Khaybar. Ibid., saying no.4632.

42. Ibid., p.927, no.4684.

43. Ibid., p.931, no.4700. This adds a further shade of meaning to the epithet of Fāṭima, 'Confluence of the Two Lights.'

44. Ibid., p.935, no.4717.

45. Nasāʾī, *Khaṣāʾiṣ*, p.106. It is worth mentioning here the following incident which illustrates one aspect of this 'duty'. ʿAlī was instructed by the Prophet to recite the newly revealed *Sūrat al-Barāʾa* ('The Immunity'; also known as *al-Tawba* 'Repentance', Sūra no.9) to the pilgrims performing the Ḥajj at Mecca in 631; this, despite the fact that Abū Bakr was leading the pilgrimage that year. When Abū Bakr returned to Medina he was somewhat disconcerted and asked the Prophet whether something had been revealed about him that disqualified him from conveying the new revelation to the assembled pilgrims. The Prophet's reply was, 'No, I was commanded that I or someone from the people of my household should convey it.' Ibid., pp.108–109.

46. Ibid., p.143.

47. Ibid., p.76.

48. Ibid., p.32.

49. See, for example, Suyūṭī's commentary on the Qurʾān, *al-Durr al-manthūr fiʾl-tafsīr biʾl-maʾthūr* (Beirut, 1314/1896), vol.4, p.45.

50. Ibid., vol.2, p.293.

51. Ibn Kathīr, *al-Bidāya waʾl-nihāya* (Beirut, 1974), vol.7, p.350.

52. See the fine article by Hermann Landolt, 'Walāyah', in *The Encyclopedia of Religion*, 1st ed., vol.15, pp.316–323.

53. al-Ṭabarī, Abū Jaʿfar Muḥammad b. Jarīr, *Jāmiʿ al-bayān* (Cairo, n.d.), vol.30, p.320. See also Suyūṭī, *al-Durr al-manthūr*, vol.6, p.379, where he reports the Prophet saying to ʿAlī, after reciting the Qurʾānic verse, 'That is, you and your followers (*shīʿatuk*) on the Day of Judgement, pleased and well-pleasing.' According to Jābir b. ʿAbd Allāh, the Prophet, upon seeing ʿAlī, said, 'By Him in whose hand is my soul, truly he and his Shīʿa are triumphant on the Day of Judgement', and the verse was then revealed. 'So the companions of the Prophet used to say, when meeting ʿAlī, "the best of created beings (*khayr al-bariyya*) has come".' Reported by Ibn Mardawayh in his *Manāqib ʿAlī b. Abī Ṭālib wa mā nazala min al-Qurʾān fī ʿAlī* (Qom, 2001), p.347.

54. There are strongly authenticated sayings of the Prophet indicating the exceptional qualities of these individuals, often in connection with ʿAlī, such as 'Paradise yearns for three [people]: ʿAlī, ʿAmmār and Salmān', cited in Rayshahrī, ed., *Mawsūʿa*, vol.12, p.145, where references are given to

Tirmidhī's *Sunan* and Nīsābūrī's *Mustadrak*. These were the foremost members of the group that believed ʿAlī to be the legitimate successor to the Prophet. 'Historically it cannot be denied ... that these men formed the nucleus of the first ʿAlid party, or the Shīʿa ... ʿAmmār, Miqdād, Abū Dharr and Salmān ... are regarded by all the Shīʿīs as "the Four Pillars" (*al-arkān al-arbaʿa*) who formed the first Shīʿa of ʿAlī.' S. Husain M. Jafri, *Origins and Early Development of Shiʿa Islam* (London—New York, 1979), p.53.

55. One should note here that the term 'Shīʿat ʿAlī' gained currency as a specifically political appellation largely in response to the group known as 'Shīʿat ʿUthmān', those partisans of Muʿāwiya who opposed ʿAlī, ostensibly for the sake of avenging the blood of the slain caliph. See Rasūl Jaʿfariyān, *Tārīkh wa sīrah-i siyāsī-yi amīr al-muʾminīn ʿAlī b. Abī Ṭālib* (Qom, 1380 Sh./2001), pp.130–132.

56. Landolt, 'Walāyah', pp.319–320.

57. It is often asserted that the Naqshabandī order is the exception to this rule, but as will be noted in Chapter 3, even this order has its principal *silsila* pass through Imam ʿAlī.

58. Losing sight of this distinction between the indirect nature of reason and the direct nature of intellectual intuition entails the reduction of the latter—together with all true philosophy (literally, 'love of wisdom') and metaphysics—to the dimensions proper to the ratiocinative faculty alone, whence the reductive and desacralized conception of what constitutes knowledge that has increasingly characterized Western epistemology since the end of the Middle Ages. See S.H. Nasr, *Knowledge and the Sacred* (New York, 1981), for a lucid exposition of the process whereby knowledge has drifted from its original moorings in the sacred, especially Chapter 1, 'Knowledge and its Desacralization', pp.1–60. See also Mehdi Ha'iri Yazdi, *The Principles of Epistemology in Islamic Philosophy* (Albany, NY, 1992), for a good account of traditional Islamic epistemology, in which knowledge is indissolubly wedded to the sacred. Finally, Rūmī's famous line should be noted here, as it brings out well the importance of maintaining the distinction between reason and intellect: 'It is reason *(ʿaql-i juzʾī)* which has destroyed the reputation of the Intellect *(ʿaql-i kullī)*' quoted by Nasr in 'Revelation, Intellect and Reason in the Qurʾān', *Sufi Essays* (London, 1972), p.55.

59. I must express my gratitude to Professor James Morris, whose insights into this dialogue, presented at the annual Imam ʿAlī Seminar, Brunei Gallery, London, November, 2002, drew my attention to the seminal importance of this dialogue.

60. Amir-Moezzi has convincingly demonstrated that the metaphysical

dimension of *ʿilm* and of its instrument *al-ʿaql* was of fundamental importance during the early period of Shiʿism, as attested by numerous sayings of the Imams. Only later, principally with the advent of Shaykh Mufīd in the 5th/11th century, did a more rationalistic view of *ʿaql* develop; correspondingly, a formal conception of the nature of knowledge—determined by its application within law and ethics, in particular—came into prominence. See Muhammad Ali Amir-Moezzi, *The Divine Guide in Early Shiism: The Sources of Esotericism in Islam*, tr. David Streight (New York, 1994), especially the section entitled 'Hiero-Intelligence and Reason', pp.6–13.

61. Corbin asserts that *ta'wīl* is not so much a formal construction as 'a spontaneous act, an innate aptitude'. See *En Islam iranien*, vol.3, p.104, n.137.

62. Cf. note 38 above.

63. The battle of Jamal, in 36/656, was the first of the civil wars of Islam. It was fought between the army of the Imam and the forces led by Ṭalḥa b. 'Ubayd Allāh, Zubayr b. al-Awwām and 'Ā'isha, and it resulted in the death of both Ṭalḥa and Zubayr and the defeat of their forces. After the victory of 'Alī's army, 'Ā'isha was escorted back to Medina with all dignity; in later years she would express profound remorse for having participated in this ill-fated battle, which was allusively foretold by the Prophet. See William Muir, *The Caliphate: Its Rise, Decline and Fall* (Edinburgh, 1924), p.242.

64. This evokes the discourse of Krishna, whose revelation of the *Bhagavad Gita* to Arjuna was given on the battlefield of Kurukshetra just before the battle between the Pandavas and the Kauravas. The Imam combines in fact both roles: Krishna, as divinely inspired sage, and Arjuna, as invincible warrior. It is not difficult to see how and why the Imam, embodying a dazzling array of diverse qualities, should have become the focus of such luxuriant mythological speculation in the Islamic tradition. See for details Matti Moosa, *Extremist Shiites—The Ghulāt Sects* (Syracuse, 1988). For the revelation of the *Gita* in the context of the *Mahabharata*, see *The Bhagavadgītā in the Mahābhārata*, tr. and ed. J.A.B van Buitenen (Chicago, 1981).

65. The Arabic here is *mā lā thānī lahu, lā yadkhul fī bāb al-aʿdād*. This is cited in al-Shaykh al-Ṣadūq, *Kitāb al-tawḥīd* (Beirut, 1967), p.83. See also Rayshahrī, ed., *Mawsūʿa*, vol.10, p.100, for several references in early sources to this text. An English translation of one version of the discourse is given by William Chittick in *A Shiʿite Anthology* (London, 1980), p.37. For further discussion of the theme of divine oneness, see our Chapter 3.

66. It is interesting to note that the phrase 'That which has no second' is found repeatedly as an expression of the essence of the Advaita doctrine of 'non-duality'.

67. God is described as *al-Ḥaqq* in the Qur'ān (41: 53); this term can be translated as 'the Real' or 'the True'. Likewise, Imam 'Alī frequently refers to God by this term, which in itself is an important indication of the intellectual—or supra-dogmatic—way in which the divine is conceived by the Imam. As will be clear in what follows, there is no question of dogmatic coagulation or conceptual reification in regard to the concept of God: the Absolute is not a 'thing' that can be contained or defined within any dogmatic formula. At almost every turn, Imam 'Alī dissolves all such tendencies towards simplification of the inexhaustible mystery of the divine reality.

68. For these four sayings and their sources, see Muḥammad Murādī, '*Rawish-i tafsīr-i Qur'ān*' in Rashād, ed., *Dānish-nāmah*, vol.1, pp.234, 235, 237, 238–239.

69. *Nahj*, Sermon 125, p.144; *Peak*, Sermon 124, p.278.

70. *Ghurar*, vol.1, p.595, no.2. A similar saying found in the *Nahj*, 'Your *rasūl* is the interpreter of your intellect …' (p.469, no.293) underlines the fact that the word *rasūl* in the Imam's saying indicates the properly prophetic aspect of the intellect. The Twelver Imam Mūsā al-Kāẓim refers to the '*aql* as the 'inner proof' (*ḥujja bāṭina*), and the prophets and the imams as the 'outer proof' (*ḥujja ẓāhira*). See Kulaynī, *Uṣūl*, vol.1, p.33. The theme of the intellect as one's 'inner prophet' is thus closely connected with that of the '*imām* of one's own being', so fundamental to Shi'i gnosis. In this connection, one can refer to the statement of an unnamed 'Iranian friend' of Henry Corbin: 'The Imam is for us what the Fravarti was to the ancient Iranians.' Corbin adds: 'Any commentary would weaken this testimony to a lived religion which, in its conciseness, expresses what is perhaps the most original spiritual message that Iran has ever given to mankind.' See Corbin, *Cyclical Time and Ismaili Gnosis* (trs. R. Manheim, J. Morris) (London, 1983), p.128, n.176.

71. *Ghurar*, vol.2, p.954, no.33.

72. By 'rationalist' here is meant those who believe that the rational faculty, alone, explicitly divorced from supra-rational and revealed sources, can attain all truth.

73. The revelation can only be said to 'require' the intellect from the point of view of its assimilation by human beings: as noted above, 'it cannot do without an interpreter'. In itself, and as it were from the divine point of view (*sub specie aeternitatis*), revelation is perfect, complete and requires nothing. According to one of the last verses of the Qur'ān to be revealed: 'This day I have perfected for you your religion, and I have completed My grace upon you, and have chosen the submission (*al-Islām*) for you as religion' (5: 3).

74. That is, those who restrict philosophy to mere ratiocination.

75. See for a useful discussion of these dichotomies, Muhsin S. Mahdi, *Alfarabi and the Foundation of Islamic Political Philosophy* (Chicago—London, 2001), pp.23–24.

76. See, for example, Qur'ān: 2: 73; 2: 242; 3: 191; 4: 82; 6: 151; 7: 176; 16: 44; 23: 68; 38: 29; 47: 24, *et passim*.

77. See Appendix I for our translation of this seminal text.

78. For an English translation of the rest of this dialogue, see William Chittick's *A Shiʿite Anthology*, pp.38–39. Cf. the statement by the Zen master, Hui-jang, in response to his disciple who asked, 'Since the Tao is beyond colour and form, how can it be seen?'. The master replied, 'The Dharma-eye of your interior spirit is capable of perceiving the Tao.' John C.H. Wu, *The Golden Age of Zen: Zen Masters of the T'ang Dynasty* (Bloomington, IN, 2003), p.82. See Chapter 3 for further discussion of the 'vision of the heart'.

79. It is supra-rational but not irrational, it should be stressed; there is nothing irrational in accepting the possibility of modes of intuition and consciousness that transcend the domain within which reason operates.

80. The status of the attributes of God was one of the most oft-discussed themes amongst the various theological schools of Islam. See the article '*Ṣifa*' by D. Gimaret, *EI2*, vol.9, pp.316–323 (part 2).

81. The distinction between 'representational knowledge' (*al-ʿilm al-ḥuṣūlī*) and 'knowledge by presence' (*al-ʿilm al-ḥuḍūrī*), elaborated upon in the later intellectual tradition of 'Irfān, can be seen as implicitly comprised within the intellect as understood by the Imam, the intellect which covers both types of knowledge and is reducible to neither. See Yazdi, *The Principles of Epistemology*, pp.5–57.

82. Ibn Bābawayh, *Kitāb al-Tawḥīd*, pp.305–306. The version here differs slightly from that translated by Chittick in *A Shiʿite Anthology*, pp.38–39, to which reference was made above.

83. Needless to say, the awareness of the insufficiency of reason is a necessary but not sufficient condition for the emergence of deeper modes of knowing.

84. It would not be out of place to note here the clear parallels with the method of *adhyāropa-apavāda* in Advaita Vedanta. The pure Absolute (*Brahma nirguṇa*) is beyond all attributes, but It is falsely endowed with a superimposed attribute, and then this is negated (*apavāda* being cognate with the word 'apophasis'). According to Shankara (Śaṃkara) (c. 788–820), the most important figure in the Advaita tradition, 'That which cannot be expressed is expressed through false attribution and subsequent denial (*adhyāropa-apavāda*).' See *Śaṃkara on the Absolute: A Śaṃkara Source Book*,

tr. A.J. Alston (London, 1981), vol.1, p.147. For a discussion of such themes in comparative context, see our forthcoming publication, *Paths to Transcendence: According to Shankara, Ibn Arabi and Meister Eckhart* (Bloomington, IN, 2006).

85. Cf. Genesis, 2: 7: 'And the Lord God formed man of the dust of the ground, and breathed into his nostrils the breath of life; and man became a living soul.'

86. *Ghurar*, vol.2, p.973, no.12.

87. The word translated here is *a'yān* (sing., *'ayn*), later to be used in a very specific sense in the metaphysics of the school of Ibn al-'Arabī. In this early period, however, the word appears to have meant either simply a personage (*shakhṣ*) or material substance. See Lane, *Lexicon*, vol.2, p.2216.

88. *Lā baṣira lahu fī aḥnā'ihi*: the latter word literally means 'ribs' (*aḥnā'*, sing. *ḥinw*), here meaning heart, breast or bosom.

89. *Nahj*, pp.433–435; *Peak*, pp.600–601. For discussion of this discourse see H. Corbin, *En Islam iranien*, vol.1, pp.112–114; Sayyid Ḥaydar Āmulī, *Jāmi' al-asrār*, ed. H. Corbin and O. Yahya, in *La Philosophie Shi'ite* (Tehran—Paris, 1969), pp.30–32.

90. *Ghurar*, vol.2, p.1167, no.6. The word '*ghaur*' is related to '*ghār*', meaning 'cave'.

91. *Ghurar*, vol.2, p.1027, no.7. It is difficult to avoid interposing words and parentheses to translate this short, powerful Arabic saying, which is all the more potent, in terms of traditional *balāgha*, or rhetoric, by reason of its very conciseness. A literal word-for-word translation such as 'through study, knowledge is attained', would hardly convey the depth of meaning intended.

92. *Ghurar*, vol.2, p.987, no.122.

93. See our article, 'From the Spirituality of Jihad to the Ideology of Jihadism,' in *Seasons: Semiannual Journal of Zaytuna Institute*, vol.2, no.2 (2005), pp.44–68.

94. *Ghurar*, vol.1, pp.208–211, nos. 20, 17, 8, 23, 26, 28.

95. *Ghurar*, vol.2, p.951, no.9. Cf. 'The intellect and passion are opposites. The intellect is strengthened by knowledge, passion by caprice. The soul is between them, pulled by both. Whichever triumphs has the *nafs* on its side.' Ibid., no.10.

96. The saying is found in slightly differing versions in Ibn Ḥanbal, *al-Musnad*, ed. A.M. Shākir (Cairo, 1949), vol.4, p.403; Nīsabūrī, *al-Mustadrak*, vol.1, p.113; and the Qur'ānic commentator Tabarsī in his comment on verse 6: 108. These references are given by the editor of *Al-Muḥīṭ*, vol.1, p.284, n.54.

97. Integration, from the word 'integer'—a whole quantity, the original Latin meaning of the word being 'intact', 'entire', whence the word 'integral', a whole made up of parts constituting a unity; whence also 'integrity', the soul or character being 'all there', knitted together into a harmonious unity.

98. This reminds one of the famous saying of Imam ʿAlī, also attributed to the Prophet: 'He who knows his soul knows his Lord (*man ʿarafa nafsahu ʿarafa rabbahu*).' See the commentary on this saying by Rajab Bursī, one of the most important 'gnostic' interpreters of the spiritual tradition of Shiʿism, in his treatise *Mashāriq anwār al-yaqīn fī ḥaqā'iq asrār amīr al-mu'minīn* ('*The Dawning Places of the Lights of Certainty in the Divine Secrets connected with the Commander of the Faithful*'), as cited in Todd Lawson's article of the same name, in L. Lewisohn, ed., *The Heritage of Persian Sufism* (Oxford, 1999), vol.2, pp.271–273.

99. *Ghurar* (Anṣārī), p.689, nos. 8505–8508.

100. *Ghurar*, vol.1, p.404, no.3.

101. The word *li-* can be translated either as 'for' or as 'belong to'.

102. *Nahj*, p.420, saying no.86; *Peak*, p.589, saying no.89.

103. This verse can also be interpreted as 'Worship thy Lord until the certain [i.e. death] cometh to thee.'

104. *Nahj*, p.475, saying no.330; *Peak*, p.651, saying no.347.

105. *Ghurar*, vol.2, p.993, no.21. The action in question is both with the 'limbs', i.e., outward action, and with the mind and soul, hence inward action, reflection, meditation, contemplation.

106. *Ghurar*, vol.2, p.1001, no.90.

107. Ibid., vol.2, p.994, no.29.

108. See Lane, *Lexicon*, vol.1, p.207 (citing the *Tāj al-ʿarūs*), where this phrase of the Imam enters into the classical lexical definition of one aspect of the meaning of the word *bāshara*.

109. *Ghurar*, vol.2, p.1012, no.175.

110. Ibid., vol.2, p.975, no.29.

111. In our comparative analysis of spiritual realization in Shankara, Ibn Arabi and Meister Eckhart in *Paths to Transcendence*, one of the most striking parallels noted was their conception of the bliss that is inseparable from the consciousness of being. Shankara's elaboration on the formula *Sat-Chit-Ananda* (Being-Consciousness-Bliss) was echoed by Ibn Arabi's *wujūd wijdān al-ḥaqq fi'l-wajd* (being is the awareness of reality in ecstasy) and also by Eckhart's description of the content of the 'birth of the Word in the soul' as immeasurable power, infinite wisdom and infinite sweetness.

112. *Ghurar*, vol.2, p.976, no.35.

113. Ibid., vol.2, p.975, no.30.

114. Ibid., vol.2, p.1156, no.1. One can gauge from this short saying how far many of today's *faqīhs*—experts in jurisprudence—fall short of the merciful disposition of the *faqīh* in the Imam's sense.

115. *Ghurar*, vol.2, p.960, no.80.

116. Cf. A.J. Wensinck et al., *Concordance et indices de la tradition musulmane* (Leiden, 1936–1969), vol.1, p.373, for references to standard Sunni collections of *ḥadīth* which cite this saying, such as those of Ibn Ḥanbal, Muslim and Ibn Māja. In the Shiʿi tradition, this saying is attributed to Imam ʿAlī. See ʿAllāma Muṭahharī, online book, *The Islamic Modest Dress* (http://al-islam.org/modestdress/title.htm) for references to this saying in the compendium of traditions entitled *Wasāʾil al-Shīʿa*. The following saying of Imam Jaʿfar al-Ṣādiq is also noted by Muṭahharī: 'God is beautiful and He loves His creatures to embellish themselves and reflect their beauty.'

117. For discussion of this saying, see al-Ghazālī's *al-Maqṣad al-asnā*, tr. R.J. McCarthy in *Freedom and Fulfillment: An Annotated Translation of al-Ghazālī's al-Munqidh min al-Ḍalāl and other relevant works of al-Ghazālī* (Boston, 1980), pp.340–343.

118. *Ghurar*, vol.2, p.953, no.20.

119. The word *tawaddud* can also mean the manifestation of love, in which case the meaning is that the intellect cannot function properly without being infused with the subtle grace that radiates from the experience of loving that which one knows. Then follows a reciprocal deepening: when one loves what one knows, one can know better, or more fully, that which one loves.

120. *Ghurar*, vol.2, p.969, no.150.

121. Ibid., vol.2, p.961, no.89.

122. Ibid., vol.2, p.956, no.51.

123. Ibid., vol.2, p.969, no.158.

124. Cf. *The Book of Wisdom*: 'For wisdom will not enter into a malicious soul, nor dwell in a body subject to sins' (1: 4).

125. *Ghurar*, vol.2, p.968, no.144. The Arabic of this saying is *man ghalaba ʿaqluhu hawāhu aflaḥa*.

126. *Nahj*, p.83; *Peak*, p.216.

127. *Ghurar*, vol.2, p.970, no.160.

128. Ibid., vol.2, p.1033, no.1.

129. *Al-ʿamal kulluhu habāʾ, illā mā ukhliṣu fīhi*. *Ghurar*, vol.2, p.1040, no.52.

130. In our troubled times of fanaticism assuming the guise of religion, the

Imam's confrontation, both martial and spiritual, with the fanatics of his time takes on added significance, as does his extraordinarily lenient behaviour towards them until the resort to arms was forced upon him. Even when their opposition to him was clear and intense, he never ceased paying them their due from the public treasury, nor did he prevent them from giving vent to their opposition, so long as this was expressed only verbally. The inviolability of 'freedom of speech' is clearly implicit in the key principle defining his attitude as ruler towards the Khārijites: if their opposition was restricted to speech, the Imam's response would be verbal, and only if they resorted to arms would he do so in self-defence. See Ḥasan Yūsufiyān and Aḥmad Ḥusayn Sharīfī, 'Imām ʿAlī wa mukhālifān' ('Imam ʿAlī and [his] Opponents'), in Rashād, ed., *Dānish-nāmah*, vol.6, esp. pp.238–246.

131. *Nahj*, p.422, saying no.93; *Peak*, p.591, saying no.97.

132. *Ṣaḥīḥ al-Bukhārī* (summarized) (Riyad, 1996/1417), *Kitāb al-taḥajjud*, saying no.1155.

133. *Ghurar*, vol.2, p.995, no.39.

134. *Nahj*, p.19; *Peak*, p.120.

135. This enigmatic saying is cited by Rajab Bursī in his treatise, *Mashāriq anwār al-yaqīn*; see Todd Lawson, 'Dawning Places', in Lewisohn ed., *Heritage of Persian Sufism*, vol.2, p.272. One should also note the saying attributed to the Imam, 'People are asleep; when they die, they wake up.' Cited in al-Ghazālī, *The Remembrance of Death and the Afterlife*, tr. and ed. Tim Winter (Cambridge, 1989), p.124; and the saying attributed to the Prophet in Sufi compendia, 'Die before ye die.' These sayings recall the famous Platonic dictum that the philosophers are those who train for death (*Phaedo*, 67cd). Finally, it is worth citing the words of Jesus, 'Whosoever would save his life shall lose it, and whosoever would lose his life for my sake shall find it' (Matthew, 16: 25). See the discussion of this point in Chapter 3.

136. *Nahj*, p.51; *Peak*, p.179.

137. *Nahj*, p.132; *Peak*, p.261.

138. *Nahj*, p.449, saying no.228; *Peak*, p.618, saying no.237.

139. *Nahj*, p.427, saying no.115; *Peak*, p.594, saying no.119.

140. *Nahj*, p.16; *Peak*, p.106.

141. *Nahj*, p.429, saying no.124; *Peak*, p.597, saying no.129.

142. *Nahj*, p.466, saying no.281; *Peak*, p.640, saying no.299.

143. *Nahj*, pp.194–196; *Peak*, pp.334–335.

144. *Nahj*, p.196; *Peak*, p.335.

145. *Nahj*, p.13; *Peak*, p.103.

146. Ibid.

147. *Nahj*, p.302; *Peak*, p.394.

148. This evokes the Hindu concept of *nishkama karma* ('desireless action'), one of the central themes of the Bhagavad Gita.

149. *Nahj*, pp.196–197; *Peak*, p.336.

150. *Ghurar*, vol.2, p.1044, no.80.

CHAPTER TWO

A Sacred Conception of Justice in Imam ʿAlī's Letter to Mālik al-Ashtar

CONTEMPORARY ETHICS AND THE *IḤSĀNĪ* TRADITION

The discussion of justice in this chapter is not intended simply to be an exercise in theoretical speculation on the meaning of justice as expressed in the letter of Imam ʿAlī to Mālik al-Ashtar fourteen centuries ago; rather, the aim is, first and foremost, to situate the discussion of justice in relation to the concept and the reality of the sacred. For, on one hand, the principle of justice possesses a sacred or spiritual dimension, so often overlooked in contemporary discourses; and on the other, a sensitive appreciation of the meaning of the sacred results in a deeper understanding of the roots of justice within the divine nature itself, and a more profound awareness of the necessity of justice in the world and in the soul. To state the basic argument of this essay: In Imam ʿAlī's worldview, the ethical orientation towards justice is immeasurably deepened insofar as it is consciously linked to the spiritual precepts of the Islamic faith. The spirit underlying moral rules and ethical values is strengthened by a commitment to transcendent principles, even though—or precisely because—these principles surpass the realm of action within which those rules and precepts operate. Contemplation and action are seen in this perspective as complementary, not contradictory, as this complementarity goes to the very heart of the Islamic message of *tawḥīd*, of integrating oneness, which is embodied with dazzling evidence in the life of the Imam, as it is in the life of the Prophet. This harmony between the two principles—contemplation and action, being and doing, theory and practice, ideal and reality—pervades the remarkable document which is the subject of this essay.

Secondly, the reflections offered here are intended to be viewed against the background of contemporary ethical discourse and might be seen as a humble contribution, from an Islamic perspective, to the debates on virtue and ethics taking place in scholarly circles. In particular, the essay should be seen in the light of one of the most serious and far-reaching critiques of modern and postmodern notions of virtue in general and justice in particular, that of Alasdair MacIntyre.

Simply put, the thrust of his critique is that, for several centuries, ethical discourse in Western society has drifted far from its moorings in absolute values. He argues compellingly that debates about morality and ethics, together with their philosophical foundations, are no longer grounded in conceptions of 'the good life' or of 'the Good' as such. McIntyre holds that, as a consequence, various shades of relativism, nihilism, utilitarianism and opportunism have emerged, *de facto*, as the shifting bases upon which ethical values are formulated, if they are formulated at all. The practice of virtue on an *ad hoc* basis is not virtue properly speaking—it is a series of pragmatic adaptations to changing circumstances in the absence of any principle of virtue as such. 'We are looking,' writes MacIntyre, 'for a conception of *the* good which will enable us to order other goods, for a conception of *the* good which will enable us to extend our understanding of the purpose and content of the virtues, for a conception of *the* good which will enable us to understand the place of integrity and consistency in life ...'[1]

It is at this level, in particular, that the insights of Imam ʿAlī and other sages of the Islamic tradition have a particular relevance. Not only does MacIntyre's proferred solution to the crisis—the reformulation of an Aristotelian conception of ethics, based on a Thomistic worldview—share much in fact with the Islamic tradition of ethical discourse (*akhlāq*);[2] one can also argue that a careful evaluation of the legacy of the Imam yields much more than a merely theoretical approach to the question of justice, and this in two respects. First, the Imam was himself a paragon of justice and, thus, a living embodiment of this and other fundamental virtues. In his life one observes a perfect, indeed, unflinching adherence to this cardinal virtue. Although in this work we are not entering into many details pertaining to his life and its lessons, we will have occasion to refer to certain incidents and events which help illustrate this point. Secondly, and more importantly for our purposes, in the discourses, letters and sayings attributed to Imam ʿAlī, we are given a rich source of reflection upon the dynamic spirituality which lies at the root of a life of virtue. One is afforded a glimpse into a way of life totally governed by the sacred, one in which a desire for the 'good life' emerges as the fruit of an irresistible attraction towards the Good as such, which is identical to the absolutely Real, *al-Ḥaqq*.

In other words, one is ethically inspired by 'the Good' in the very measure of one's existential orientation to the Real. If moral rules are grounded in ethical perspectives, and if these perspectives are rooted in a conception of the 'good life', this conception of the Good is itself derived from the moral agent's basic understanding of the meaning of life itself. Amyn B. Sajoo, in a recent thoughtful work on Muslim ethics, distinguishes carefully between ethics and morals. He states that ethical discourse is concerned more with conceptions of 'the good', while morals pertain more specifically to rules concerning right and wrong. 'Certainly', he continues, 'the concepts overlap substantially in theory and practice; but it is well to bear in mind the more encompassing sense of reality that typifies ethics.'[3] Placing ethics in the wider framework of spiritual virtue—in the sense of *iḥsān*, as we shall see shortly—expands even further the compass of both ethics and morality, lending the two types of discourse a dimension of existential depth, grounding them in a more organic and all-encompassing framework. Abstract questions of right and wrong come to be rooted in the more definitive principle that emerges in response to the question: what is reality?

One should bear in mind here the discussion in the previous chapter on the deeper meanings of divine unity. In the Imam's spiritual vision of *tawḥīd*, one perceives—according to one's capacity—an ultimate reality which not only 'has no second' but which also has no moral 'opposite'. For the goodness that is proper to God is not the moral opposite of evil, rather, it is situated on a different plane altogether, that of *al-Ḥaqq*, the absolutely Real, the only 'opposite' to which is unreality or nothingness. Thus, while goodness is at one with the pure positivity of the Absolute, evil derives solely from a negative capacity to negate the Real, the Good. In other words, goodness is identified in its essence with the Creator, while evil is a modality of the created. This is strongly implied in the Qur'ānic verse which tells the believer to seek refuge in God from 'the evil of that which He created' (113: 2). This verse is often mistranslated as 'from the evil which He created', which is wrong both theologically and lexically. The expression '*min sharri mā khalaqa*' refers clearly to the evil *deriving from* creation and not the creation as such. In theological terms, God creates morally free agents and it is they who are the authors of the evil in creation. God may be said to 'create' all actions, only in the metaphysical sense that He is the source of all being, and thus of all modalities within being, and actions constitute one such modality; however, God cannot be said to have created evil as such, only the conditions within which evil emerges. Evil is thus the negation of the Good, which is at one with the Real; as such, evil has no ultimate ontological principle.[4]

The verse, then, can be understood to mean seeking refuge in the Real from the unreal, there being no common measure, in terms of being, between goodness and evil. Goodness is opposable only by the *appearance* of evil, an appearance which is grasped as an illusion by the 'eye of the heart', that eye which truly 'sees' God through 'the verities of faith'. This vision of the relative reality of evil, far from engendering indifference towards it, greatly empowers the spiritual resolve to overcome it, for the moral effort to be good is intensified in the measure of the conviction of one's accountability to that goodness. This conviction, in turn, is transported 'inwards' from the mind to the heart by the certainty that goodness is 'more real' than evil; and this certainty itself is nourished by the spiritual vision of the good as the Real. So, the perception of the radical incommensurability between good and evil does not lead to indifference in the face of evil, but to a more existentially compelling orientation to the good.

In the Imam's perspective, the notions of 'right' and 'rightful due' which are comprised within the meaning of *ḥaqq* are infused with an aura of absoluteness; the moral notions of rectitude and propriety are expressions of a principle that transcends morality, a principle which pertains to ultimate reality. One's commitment to fulfilling one's obligations—to giving what is rightfully due to all—becomes infused, likewise, with a strong 'dose' of reality; the resolution to be just is rendered more absolute by the very quality of absoluteness proper to the Real.

This duty to give what is due to each and every being relates to the most explicit definition of justice[5] given by the Imam: 'Justice puts everything in its right place.'[6] One is 'just' insofar as one gives everything its proper due, renders the *ḥaqq* due to each person, indeed to each and every thing in existence; and the ability to be 'just' in this demanding and universal manner is enhanced in the measure that one is attuned to *al-Ḥaqq*, the Real. As should be clear from the discussion in the previous chapter, this spiritual conception of virtue not only encompasses one's duty to all, but also engages all that one is. One has to *be* good before one *does* good; and the only way 'to be', is to be at one with the Real, that which alone 'is'.

The Imam's comment on justice evokes the more famous definition of Plato: '...we have laid down, as a universal principle, that everyone ought to perform the one function in the community for which his nature best suited him ... that principle, or some form of it, is justice.'[7] There are, indeed many remarkable parallels between Plato's *Republic* and the letter of the Imam to Mālik al-Ashtar. In this chapter we shall occasionally refer to some of the more obvious correspondences, and note, at the end of the chapter, the way in which the Imam's explicit spirituality sheds light on what is left implicit in Plato's philosophy, namely, the manner in which one can attain the vision of the Real, which Plato refers to as 'gazing upon the Good'. It is this contemplation of the Good as such that functions as the source of one's ability to act ethically, on all levels, for this vision allows one to take the Good 'as a pattern for the right ordering of the state and of the individual'.[8]

The influence of Platonic and Neoplatonic conceptions of justice on the formulation of ethical discourse in Islam has been amply attested in the sources.[9] Within this discourse, justice is not so much seen as one among several virtues, but as the perfection or sum of the other virtues, especially the three principal Platonic virtues of temperance, courage and wisdom. These must characterize, respectively, the concupiscent, the irascible and the rational dimensions of the soul. When all the dimensions of the soul, 'filled out' by their respective virtues, are in their proper place, then the soul can be qualified as 'just'.[10] However, what has not been given sufficient attention in the sources is the degree to which there is a spiritual correspondence between Plato's chief means of arriving at the vision of the Good, *anamnesis*, and the cardinal role of *dhikr* in Islam, both terms being translatable by the English word 'remembrance'. This underlines the importance of this remembrance, this recollection of ultimate reality, of immutable principles, at different levels of application.[11] It is not a question of learning things anew but of recollecting principles, ones which are inherent in the very substance of the intellect, and by which all things can be understood: principles that are ultimately rooted in the Sovereign Good itself.

Such remembrance should be regarded as the cognitive and philosophical foundation of ethical thought; and the fact that its importance has been ignored is symptomatic of the sundering of ethics and spirituality in modern discourse, treating each discipline as if it were hermetically sealed from the other. Whereas ethics is still taken seriously as a branch of philosophy and as a discipline in its own right, spirituality is all too often regarded as irrelevant to serious scholarly inquiry and relegated to the realm of the imaginary, the woolly and the mythological. This marginalization of spirituality from the field of putatively serious discourse is closely related to the reductive view of knowledge that has increasingly characterized Western thought from the Renaissance onwards, a reduction that goes hand in hand with an emasculation of the sacred dimension of life.[12]

In the Islamic tradition of discourse, the realms of ethics and spirituality are intimately connected. Nowhere is this more apparent than in the Sufi tradition, which is being increasingly and most aptly referred to as the *iḥsānī* tradition—understanding the word *iḥsān* (excellence, virtue, goodness) in the sense imparted to it by the Prophet in a tradition of central importance as regards the three fundamental aspects of the Islamic way. It is known as 'the *ḥadīth* of Gabriel', for the questioner of the Prophet in this exchange, unbeknown to the Companions who were present, was the angel Gabriel, in human guise.

'O Muḥammad, tell me about submission (*al-islām*)', the stranger asked. The Prophet replied, '*Al-islām* is to testify that there is no god but God and Muḥammad is the messenger of God, to perform the prayers, to pay the poor-due (*al-zakāt*), to fast in Ramaḍān, and to make the pilgrimage to the House if you are able to do so.'

The narration continues:

'He [Gabriel] said, 'You have spoken truly', and we [the Companions] were amazed at his asking him and saying that he had spoken truly. He said, 'Then tell me about faith (*al-īmān*).' He [the Prophet] said, 'It is to believe in God, His angels, His books, His messengers, and the Last Day, and to believe in divine destiny, both the good and the evil thereof.' He said, 'You have spoken truly.' He said, 'Then tell me about virtue (*al-iḥsān*).' He said, 'It is to worship God as though you see Him, and if you see Him not, yet truly He sees you.'[13]

The word *iḥsān* can also be literally translated as 'doing what is beautiful', the root of the word being related primarily to beauty, *ḥusn*;[14] virtue and vice are often referred to in Islamic ethical discourse as *ḥusn* and *qubḥ*, literally beauty and ugliness. Ultimately, it is the vision of the divine beauty that inspires virtue, which is beauty of soul. It is thus not surprising to find that, generally speaking, while the specialists in the domain of outward action according to Islam have been the jurists, the *fuqahā'*,[15] and the specialists in the domain of formal belief have been the theologians, it fell to the mystics to be the custodians of the domain of spiritual virtue, of 'making beautiful'. Indeed, it is no coincidence that the overwhelming majority of artists in the Islamic world—calligraphers, painters, poets, musicians, etc., have been practising Sufis.[16]

From the Prophet's definition of *iḥsān* as 'worshipping God as if one could see Him', one sees clearly the crucial relationship between worship and virtue, spirituality and ethics, between devotion to the Creator and goodness to creatures; understanding this relationship takes us to the very heart of the spiritual tradition in Islam. Conversely, it is the denial and subversion of this tradition by some modern Muslims today that—more than any other single factor, we would venture to say—is ultimately responsible for the atrocities currently being committed by Muslims in the name of Islam.[17]

It should be noted here that both the theory and the practice of ethics has always been integral to Sufism.[18] Even some of those who wrote treatises in more philosophical and less spiritual terms, such as al-Fārābī (d.872/950),[19] were known also to be practising Sufis. The most influential figure in whom the domains of spirituality and ethics meet is, of course, al-Ghazālī (d. 505/1111) whose magisterial *Iḥyā' 'ulūm al-dīn* (*Revival of the Sciences of Religion*) is a monument to the impact of the deepest spirit of Islam upon the ethical disposition of the believing soul. He has aptly been referred to as the greatest thinker on ethics in Islam,[20] and given the degree to which his 'thinking' is determined by Sufism, this alone bears testimony to the close relationship between Sufism and ethics. Indeed, it would not be an exaggeration to say that the majority of treatises written by Sufis are, in fact, treatises on 'ethics', if ethics be understood not just as *akhlāq* in the narrow sense of the term, but also as the fruit of *iḥsān* or spiritual virtue. The various spiritual stations (*maqāmāt*) described by the Sufis often bear the names of the different virtues, such as: patience (*ṣabr*), gratitude (*shukr*), contentment (*riḍā'*), generosity (*karam*), etc.[21]

The thread running through all of these 'stations' is the transformative awareness of God, the principle of being and acting 'as if you could see God'—that is, conducting oneself and composing oneself in the consciousness of being constantly in the divine presence, for even if you cannot see Him, 'He sees you'. That is, the imperative of *iḥsān* lies at the very root of a life of virtue in the spiritual universe of Islam. As we shall see in this and the following chapter, Imam 'Alī repeatedly draws the reader back to the 'vision' of God, at whatever degree, as the true basis of a life of virtue; and repeatedly warns of the dangers of the opposite—the engrossing vision of oneself—as being the source of all vice. On one hand, the Imam tells us, 'Know that your every action is dependent upon your prayer,'[22] that is, upon your way of 'gazing upon the Good', to use Platonic terms; and on the other, he warns us to beware of vanity, conceit and lavish praise of oneself by others, as these are 'Satan's most reliable opportunities to efface the virtue (*iḥsān*) of the virtuous (*al-muḥsinīn*).'[23] The true, objective vision of *al-Ḥaqq*, the Real, realized through effacement of oneself in prayer, is here juxtaposed with the distorted, subjective vision of the ego, produced by inflation of oneself through pride. The first leads to justice, putting all things in their proper place, including, pre-eminently, the ego; the second leads to all the injustices that stem from self-aggrandizement, including fanaticism and bigotry, for Satan, epitome of pride and disobedience, is described as 'the leader of the fanatics and the forerunner of the proud (*imām al-mutaʿaṣṣibīn wa salaf al-mustakbirīn*)'.[24] Fanatical bigotry is a particularly intense form of injustice, entailing as it does that pernicious prejudice which subordinates the objective requirements of justice to the putative prerogatives of one's self, whether that 'self' be defined in terms of the individual, family, clan, tribe, nation or religion.

The Letter to Mālik al-Ashtar

The Imam's epistle appointing Mālik al-Ashtar as his governor of Egypt is found as number 52 in most editions of the *Nahj al-balāgha*.[25] In broad historical terms, the letter has been a source of inspiration down through the centuries, being read as an ideal constitution for Islamic governance, complementing—through its relatively detailed description of the duties and rights of the ruler and the various functionaries of the state and the main classes of society—the more general framework of principles enshrined in the famous 'Constitution of Medina' dictated by the Prophet.[26] As will be evident in what follows, however, the advice contained in the letter far exceeds the parameters conventionally set by political or legal texts dealing with governance. Despite being addressed in the first instance to the ruler or governor of the polity, much of the advice pertains, in fact, to universally applicable ethical principles and is, therefore, as relevant to those ruled as to those who rule. It is as much a statement of ethics as of politics—not a discursive 'system' or theory of ethics, to be sure, but an inspiring expression of the spiritual ethos which the Imam embodied and radiated, an ethos that flows directly from the sources of the Islamic revelation, and which therefore discloses the roots of virtue and ethics in a climate governed by the all-embracing principle of revelation.[27] It is possible, therefore, to read this document also as a commentary on that revelation, which in turn encourages the reader to delve more deeply into the meanings enshrined in the revealed texts.

Mālik al-Ashtar was a long-standing and dedicated follower of the Imam, and was referred to as one of his 'right-hand' men. Muʿāwiya, the Imam's main antagonist in the civil war (37–41/657–661) which dominated his caliphate, was one person who referred to Mālik thus, after hearing of the success of his mission to poison Mālik before he was able to take up his post as governor in Egypt. Muʿāwiya is reported by Ṭabarī as remarking, "Alī b. Abī Ṭālib had two right hands. One of them was cut at Ṣiffīn[28] and the other today.'[29] For his part, the Imam's response to the news of Mālik's assassination was as follows: 'Mālik, and what was Mālik! By God, were he a mountain, he would be the solitary one [soaring above the others], and were he a rock, he would have been impenetrably solid. No horse could ascend [such a mountain], no bird could fly up to it.'[30]

Let us return to the Imam's definition of justice noted earlier: 'Justice puts everything in its right place.' What relates this conception of justice to the sacred is the imperative of first putting in its right place one's relationship with God; everything else is derived from this spiritual imperative. The same order of precedence is clearly established in the following important statement in the Imam's letter to Mālik: 'Be just with God and be just with people [giving them what is their due] from yourself.'[31] Being just with God means, among other things, conforming as best one can to His own nature, which is not only the source of justice but *is* justice. 'I bear witness', says the Imam in one of his sermons, 'that He is Justice (*ʿadl*) and He acts justly.'[32]

It might be objected here that, as between the divine reality of justice and the human expression of justice, there is a radical disjuncture. In God, justice means that everything is in its right place, whereas for man justice entails the *effort* to put everything in its right place: an immutable metaphysical quality on the divine side, and a dynamic, volitive effort on the human side. One response to this is as follows: Man's moral effort to act justly in the world here below—where things are not in their right place—is rooted in an innate spiritual predisposition to justice. Just action thus expresses the principle of justice, which, in man as in God, is that immutable principle by which everything is in its right place. Just as divine action in creation, judgement and other realms is an expression of absolute justice, so in man just action is an expression not only of a moral, volitive and intellectual effort to realize justice, but also of a spiritual affinity with the ultimate nature of reality—of things as they truly are in God, and therefore as they ought to be here on earth.

Applied to state and society, one of the most obvious consequences of this conception of justice is the necessity of piety and rectitude on the part of the rulers. As the Imam says in another of his sermons, 'The most momentous of the reciprocal rights that God has made obligatory is the right of the ruler over the subjects, and the right of the subjects over the ruler—a reciprocal obligation which God has ordained for them.'[33] He then makes the following point, which is altogether indispensable for any discourse on good governance in Islam: 'The subjects will not be righteous except through the righteousness of the rulers, and the rulers will not be righteous except through the uprightness of the subjects. So if the subjects render to the ruler his rightful due and he renders them theirs, then will right be honoured amongst them, the ways of religion will be upheld and the banners of justice will be erected.' This stress on the necessity of piety on the part of the ruler is, as one would expect, a central aspect of the Imam's message to his governor; but as will be clear from what follows, it involves much more than a simple exhortation to abide by the formal rules of Islamic law.

The whole of the Imam's life can be seen as a quest for conforming as perfectly as possible to the divine nature and to this quality of justice in particular. There are, therefore, too many aspects of this principle—social, economic, political, juridical—in connection with the Imam's life and teachings to address in the brief compass of this essay.[34] Let us simply refer to one defining moment in the Imam's caliphate which will help illustrate the rigour with which he adhered to justice at all costs.

The revolt of Muʿāwiya, and the resulting civil war into which the fledgling Muslim empire was plunged, can be seen as having started not at Ṣiffīn but in Medina. Upon assuming the caliphate, ʿAlī was advised by his cousin, Ibn al-ʿAbbās, to temporarily confirm in power all of ʿUthmān's governors and, after he had consolidated the new order, to remove them. The Imam's reply to this proposed strategy was reported as follows: 'I do not doubt that this would be best for the sake of reconciliation in this world. But there is my obligation to the Truth (*alladhī yalzamanī min al-ḥaqq*) and my knowledge of ʿUthmān's governors—so, by God, I shall never appoint one of them.'[35]

Thus was the die cast: the Imam dismissed Muʿāwiya, together with all of his predecessor's governors.[36] It was clear to the Imam that Ibn al-ʿAbbās' proposed solution had every chance of success, knowing as he did that all Muʿāwiya wanted was worldly power and would have been content with the prospect of governing Syria, if the Imam had allowed him to do so. While commentators have referred to this incident, which assured the revolt of the governors, as a sign of ʿAlī's lack of political acumen and his intransigence, it ought instead to be seen as the expression of his disdain for worldly ease, if that ease be purchased at the price of essential principles. As he says in one of his aphorisms, 'People renounce no part of their religion for the sake of rectifying their world without God opening them up to something worse than it [i.e., that defect which they were seeking to rectify].'[37]

It is clear that confirming in power those governors whose corruption was beyond both doubt and redemption would be tantamount for the Imam to 'renouncing' a part of his religion, inasmuch as religion without justice is not religion; supporting unjust governors, even for the sake of a tactical manoeuvre, amounted to a compromise on religious principle that was inconceivable for him. The attitude manifested here was embodied in countless actions in the life of the Imam; they show that the principles enshrined in the text of the letter to Mālik al-Ashtar were far from merely theoretical.

In the following sections of this chapter, we turn first to the analysis of a particular dimension of justice, one which is political on the surface, ethical in its outward expression, but spiritual in depth—that is, the justice of the political ruler, justice conceived in relation to its more clearly definable diametrical opposite: injustice, tyranny, oppression and corruption. It will be argued that a deep assimilation of the spirituality embodied by the Imam can bestow an existential power upon the moral effort to live according to just precepts, a power that is lacking when justice is conceived exclusively in terms of individual or horizontal values, that is, according to a secular 'moral philosophy', divorced from religious or spiritual principles. The crucial role played by devotion and worship—formal and supra-formal—is then discussed. It is proposed that contemplation of the divine Reality is the fountainhead from which integral virtue flows spontaneously and ceaselessly. This point will be made clearer by means of a brief comparison with Plato's 'gazing' on the Sovereign Good, source of all virtue.

Our analysis will be based on certain key extracts from Imam ʿAlī's letter to Mālik al-Ashtar, taking into account relevant points from his other letters, sermons and sayings, as well as certain traditions of the Prophet and verses of the Qurʾān which illustrate or elucidate the themes raised in the letter. A full translation of the Imam's letter is given in Appendix II of this work.

JUSTICE VERSUS TYRANNY

The letter is addressed to one of the Imam's closest and most trusted companions; so his warnings as regards injustice and oppression, in addition to expressing a universal theme, ought to be understood also in a very precise way. These warnings are applicable to all those who, while formally subject to Islam and its laws, and possessing, initially, all the right intentions, are nonetheless vulnerable to the temptations offered by political power, taking full cognisance of the unfortunate but proven truth expressed by the maxim, 'power corrupts'; or, in the words of the Imam, 'he who rules, appropriates (*man malaka istaʾthara*)'.[38]

The Imam's approach to justice here expressed clearly transcends the boundaries of its historical context, just as it goes beyond the formal boundaries of the Islamic faith. The letter can be seen as addressing not only those who wish to rule according to just principles, but also all those who, while not having corrupt intentions at the outset, are nonetheless corruptible—this category embracing the overwhelming majority of mankind.

Human virtue and ultimate reality

A note of sombre realism resounds at the very outset of the letter. The potential for evil in man, when left to his own resources and deprived of divine grace, dominates the tone of the preamble—whence the stress on abiding by God's *wājibāt*, the religious obligations binding on every Muslim. Mālik is told to prefer obedience to God over all things, 'to abide by what He has commanded in His Book ... for no one prospers except through abiding by them, and no one is wretched except through repudiating and neglecting them'.[39] The preamble is introductory but by no means perfunctory: obedience to the divine commands is not only to be seen as legally binding, but also as spiritually liberating. This obedience plays a crucial part in liberating one from the tyranny of the 'soul which incites to evil' (*al-nafs al-ammāra bi'l-sū'*), to which the Imam refers, immediately after calling Mālik to obedience: 'For truly, the soul incites to evil, unless God has mercy'.[40] This sentence is almost identical to the words of the Prophet Joseph in the Qur'ān (12: 53), and is of the utmost importance in setting the scene for the ethical injunctions and socio-political instructions to come. For the essential relationship that determines the spiritual substance of the soul, and *a fortiori*, its moral comportment, is the relationship between the human soul and divine grace. Without grace, the soul tends towards evil, but with the assistance of God, the soul is liberated from its own base inclinations and is guided back to its true, primordial nature, its *fiṭra*, to which the Qur'ān refers in the following verse:

> So set thy purpose for religion with unswerving devotion: the nature of God (*fiṭrat Allāh*), according to which He hath created man. There is no altering God's creation. That is the right religion (*al-dīn al-qayyim*), but most men know not. (30: 30)

The actual state of the fallen soul, then, is to give way to the ideal state of original human nature, which is both origin and end of the human condition, but also the true substance of every human soul, and is thus always accessible in principle, even if, for the majority, it remains clouded by fallen human nature in practice.[41] In the quest for the revival of this primordial nature, one returns to the complementary functions of the human intellect and divine revelation. In the first sermon of the *Nahj*, as cited earlier, the Imam tells us that God sent to mankind 'His messengers, dispatching prophets in succession, in order to claim from them [His creatures] the fulfilment of the covenant of His creation; to remind them of His forgotten graces; to remonstrate with them through communication [of His revelation]; to unearth for them the buried treasures of the intellects (*dafā'in al-'uqūl*).'

These 'buried treasures' can be identified with the original, God-given knowledge proper to the *fiṭra*. From this integral human nature, in complete harmony with the divine nature, all the essential virtues flow spontaneously and unhindered. 'Let your most beloved treasure be the treasure of virtuous acts',[42] the Imam writes. Now virtue will indeed be the 'most beloved treasure' for one who reverses the natural inclinations of the egoistic soul and establishes a supernatural orientation towards its own deepest nature, and by that very token, towards the divine Reality that furnishes the ontological foundations of all authentic virtue. For the Real, *al-Ḥaqq*, is not only the deepest foundation of virtue, it is the true substance of every positive quality, and in the last analysis, every single existent entity. As the words in one of the most famous supplications attributed to the Imam put it:

> By Thy tremendousness (*bi-'aẓmatika*), which has filled all things ... by Thy Names which have filled the foundations of all things, by Thy knowledge which encompasses all things, by the light of Thy face, through which all things are illumined...[43]

From this point of view, every virtue can be considered the reflection on the human plane of a divine attribute, that which is denoted as a divine 'Name'. Hence one finds the fundamental theme, in the *iḥsānī* tradition, expressed in the saying: 'Assume the character traits of God (*takhallaqū bi-akhlāqi'Llāh*)'.[44]

The relationship between human virtue and divine reality is altogether indispensable in the Imam's perspective. On one hand—in subjective terms—the practice of virtue attracts the corresponding divine quality; and on the other—in objective terms—the divine quality is the source and, in accordance with true *tawḥīd*, the actual substance of all human virtue. That is to say, every positive quality, both in itself and in its manifestation, pertains to God, the One who 'has no partner', theologically speaking, and who 'has no second' in ontological terms. This mystical assimilation of the principle of *tawḥīd* can be seen as heavily implied in the verse of the Qur'ān, 'And thou threw not when thou didst throw [a handful of dust], but God it was who threw' (8: 17). Not only must the individual be effaced before God in order to be truly virtuous, but he must also participate in and embody the very qualities he wishes God to manifest towards him; and his effort to do so is empowered in the measure that he comprehends these same divine attributes—through intuition and existentially, rather than simply through reason and theoretically. The relationship between intelligence and humility is to be underlined here. The intellectual perception of the divine attributes results in humility, and the effacement of the soul, in its turn, displaces attention from the ego and directs it to the transcendent reality as source of all virtue and truth.

It is worthwhile dwelling a little on the notion of the 'soul which incites to evil', and on the Qur'ānic story of Joseph (Yūsuf) within which this notion arises; for knowledge of this context would have been assumed by the Imam when he composed this letter, and he clearly intended that it be borne in mind by Mālik and, by extension, any other person reading this letter on governance.

Joseph gives this description of man's base inclinations after his innocence of all charges had been proven in the presence of the Egyptian king. He says, though, 'I do not exonerate myself. Truly, the soul incites to evil, unless my Lord has mercy.' Indeed, on the two occasions when he was subjected to the seductive temptations of Zulaykhā, it is made clear in the Qur'ān that his successful resistance to her wiles was due not to his own moral resources but to the grace of God.[45]

This theme of human helplessness in the face of attractive but immoral gratification should be seen as heavily implied in the Imam's repetition of the Qur'ānic notion, 'Truly the soul incites to evil, unless God has mercy'. These, then, are the two poles of attraction for the ordinary soul, that is, the soul not yet 'at peace':[46] its own base inclinations towards negative possibilities within the fleeting world of appearances; and the higher orientation towards the grace of God, attracting the soul back towards the pure positivity of ultimate reality. The very acuteness of the contrast contained within this powerful Qur'ānic sentence galvanizes an awareness of the soul's absolute and unconditional need of God in all circumstances. It is a most fitting way to begin a letter of instruction to one who is being vested with authority over a vast and wealthy country where temptations aplenty lie in wait. It stands as a solemn reminder of the soul's susceptibility to allurement on all planes, gross and subtle, a susceptibility that can be neutralized and overcome, not by the soul itself, but only by the mercy and grace of God. However, going back to the words of Joseph, the 'vision of the evidence' of God implies active discernment and then, by way of moral consequence, resolute self-control. Thus, the human effort to avoid sin does not contradict the necessity of grace for the attainment of virtue, but rather expresses a grace already bestowed, already present within the conscientious soul. The very capacity of the human will to strive for virtue is itself to be seen as a pre-existent 'grace' embedded within the spiritual constitution or *fiṭra*, but it is a grace which must be rendered present, or actualized, through the sincere effort to avail oneself of this God-given power to strive for virtue.

The manner in which this grace is brought into the soul as a determinitive element of moral and spiritual life will be made clearer later on by the Imam in his letter, but for now, the negative side of the question needs further elaboration. For the ever-present temptation, on the part of the ruler, to abuse his power and to perpetrate injustice and tyranny needs to be given more than a passing reference. It might be argued that the question of how to refrain from injustice is much more difficult and subtle a problem than its positive counterpart—how to act with justice. The positive rules of political governance are laid down by the Imam in a direct and straightforward manner,[47] but what is not so straightforward is the actual ability, on the part of any holder of political office, to maintain fidelity to these rules when confronted with the temptations offered by power. One might frame laws for punishing corruption, but what cannot be legislated is the *will or the capacity to remain incorruptible* in the face of the blandishments offered by political authority. This helps explain why the Imam's exhortations take on such a negative quality in the early part of the letter, as for example, in the command to 'break the soul in the face of passionate desires', to 'dominate your inclination', to 'withhold yourself from that which is not lawful for you'.[48] It also explains why the ethical imperative of justice must be placed firmly within the context of a lived spirituality, failing which the injunctions to be fair, just and honest will lack that existential quality that transforms such injunctions from abstract postulates into unquestionable realities, and that transmutes formal obedience to externally imposed rules into spiritual affinity with the source of those rules.

Living according to just precepts no longer takes the form of compliance to something from without, but is the moral concomitant of one's inner being. In other words, an integral approach to justice leads to an *identification* with what is right, with *al-Ḥaqq* as such, and not merely *doing* that which is right. There is a shift of consciousness from doing to being, or from action to contemplation, without this in any way implying that action is weakened or undermined. On the contrary, action comes to reflect, on its own plane, the divine object of contemplation, and thus becomes more, not less, effective. An orientation towards the Real imparts a deeper degree of reality to what one does in the realm of action, and to one's own mode of being. One *does* what is right insofar is one *is* real; this process of realization is expressed in the Islamic spiritual tradition as *taḥqīq*, 'making real': one's ethical comportment is 'made real' through spirituality, and spirituality, for its part, is expressed by, and rendered more concrete through, the practice of virtue.

Overcoming subtle polytheism

The Imam then issues the stern warning, 'Do not set your soul up for war with God.' One might well ask what this means, what kind of actions or attitudes put the soul at war with God. It seems that there is an allusion to something rather deeper than simply disobedience to God, manifested as so many violations of the religious obligations mentioned at the outset of the letter. While this is the most obvious meaning of 'fighting' against God, it does not exclude more subtle modes of opposition to divine reality, that is, attitudes that may accompany outward acts of obedience but which contradict the spirit of those acts. One can take, for example, the cardinal vice of pride (*takabbur*) which the Imam repeatedly warns against. The ruler's pride constitutes a misappropriation of a divine attribute, an arrogation to oneself of a greatness that belongs exclusively to God: He alone has the right to the quality of *takabbur*, and He alone can be called, without insult, *al-Mutakabbir*, 'the Proud'. Vaunting oneself before people is tantamount to inwardly opposing the authority of God and is thus an implicit denial of His unique and incomparable majesty. This denial of a concomitant of God's sovereignty can, in turn, be seen as a kind of 'war' with God. In other words, enmity with the transcendent reality is the invisible substance that pervades all pride and any act of arrogance or oppression by a ruler towards those beneath him.

The paradox here, that only a sense of spiritual values can reveal, is that an attitude of superiority towards those who are 'below' constitutes, in fact, an attitude of rebellion towards that which is 'above'. Hence, an injustice towards creatures not only brings down upon its perpetrator the justice of the Creator, it also manifests, in and of itself, outright opposition to the Creator. Thus, an apparently horizontal vice—'horizontal' in the sense of relating to this world—is in reality a spiritual disorder, the outward immorality of corruption being but the symptom of an inner spiritual malaise, an implicit denial of the absoluteness—and hence uniqueness—of that which is the source of all power and authority, a forgetfulness of the reality expressed by the Qur'ānic verse, 'To whom belongeth the dominion this day? To God, the One, the All-Conquering' (40: 16). The truth expressed by this verse should resound constantly in the ears of all rulers, 'this day' being understood as 'every day' and not just the Day of Judgement.

In the Imam's sermon known as *al-Qāṣi'a*, 'the Abasement', on account of its humiliation of the proud, Iblīs (Satan) is described as being the first of those who 'competed with God' in respect of grandeur, and is thus to be seen as the embodiment of the principle of pride and arrogance. When ordered to prostrate before Adam (38: 71–74), Iblīs refused because 'vehement passion' overcame him; he deemed himself superior to Adam because he was made of fire, whereas Adam was made of clay. Taking pride in this presumed superiority and thus rebelling against God's order, Iblīs is not only the first 'enemy of God' but also, as seen earlier, 'the leader of the bigots and the forerunner of the proud (*imām al-muta'aṣṣibīn wa salaf al-mustakbirīn*)'.[49] The Imam warns his listeners: 'Beware lest he infect you with his disease', through his insinuations, whisperings and machinations. He urges them: 'Be resolute in placing self-abasement over your heads, casting self-glorification beneath your feet, and removing pride from your necks. And take up humility as the fortified watchtower between you and your enemy.'[50]

Humility, then, is the principal weapon in the war against Iblīs, whose key aim, inversely, is to inculcate pride, for pride is not only the worst of vices, but also the poison which infects and destroys all virtue. For virtue itself is converted to vice as soon as it is accompanied by pride. 'The sin that grieves you is better, in the sight of God, than the virtue that makes you proud.'[51] Also, one should recall here what was noted above about the dangers of excessive praise and the conceit it generates, these being among 'Satan's most reliable opportunities to efface the virtue of one who is virtuous'.[52]

It can be observed that, taken together, these statements constitute a commentary upon the Qur'ānic account of Iblīs' disgrace, whereby a simple act of disobedience is grasped at its spiritual root, in a manner that brings home the ever present danger of falling prey to that 'hidden' form of *shirk* (polytheism), to which the Prophet refers in the following words: 'The creeping of *shirk* in my community is more hidden (*akhfā*) than the creeping of a black ant over a hard rock on a dark night.'[53]

The superficial notion of *shirk* as the worship of material idols must be understood more subtly as false gods hidden within one's intentions, attitudes and orientations; and as all elements of hidden pride, vanity, ostentation, pretentiousness. As the Imam says, 'Know that the slightest pretension (*riyā'*) is polytheism.'[54] To act for the sake of earning the praise of others is to act for others and not for God; hence it is an implicit attribution of partners to God: 'Whoso acts for other than God, God entrusts him to those for whose sake he acted.'

In this light, the meaning of Iblīs' act of disobedience can be more deeply plumbed. It is the outward moral consequence of an inner spiritual malaise which arises out of that pride which is tantamount to 'hidden polytheism', and which brings in its wake disgraceful humiliation. Iblīs is disgraced because he disobeyed God and he disobeyed God on account of pride. To be proud is, therefore, in and of itself a disgrace, a state of 'dis-grace', a perversion of the human state that carries within itself the seed of its own inexorable inversion. 'Do you not see how God humiliated him through his pride?'[55] the Imam asks. Being proud is in reality already a form of humiliation, for self-aggrandizement is tantamount to self-destruction.

Returning to the pride of those in power, the Imam expresses succinctly the train of thought that is set in motion within the mind of a ruler who is stepping on the slippery slope towards oppression: 'Do not say, "I have been given authority, I order and am obeyed", for this leads to corruption in the heart and the erosion of religion.'[56] It should be noted that this self-glorification is seen as leading first to inner, spiritual corruption—that of the 'heart'—and then to the destruction of religion, this order of priority highlighting the fact that the outward prescriptions of religion require the right inward attitude if they are to be applied with integrity, and if they are to be maintained with stability. One might restate the Imam's idea thus: When power goes to the head, faith departs from the heart; and conversely, for faith to be properly manifested in the world, it must flow from a heart suffused with humility. This is another aspect of 'putting each thing in its proper place'.

The Imam continues: 'If the authority of your position engenders vanity and arrogance, then look at the grandeur of God's dominion above you ... this will calm your ambition, restrain you from your own vehemence and restore to you what had strayed from your intellect.' The relationship between intellect and humility should be carefully noted here. The part of the intellect that 'strays' when vanity and arrogance enter is precisely the part that is conscious of the absolute reality of God and the relative, derivative and ultimately illusory character of everything else. It is significant that the word for 'arrogance', *makhīla*, is derived from the same root as the word for imagination, *khayāl*, and is thus intimately connected with the realm of the imaginary, the fanciful, the illusory and the unreal. Arrogant pride is, therefore, an intense form of self-delusion, stemming from an intellectual defect; it manifests as a vice, but its cause goes deeper than the level of morality, for it involves not just an over-estimation of oneself, but also and more fundamentally, an under-estimation of the Absolute. In this light, the overt egotism of the tyrant can be seen as an intensification of the congenital egocentricity that accompanies every person who has not realized the truth of the sole reality of God and the ultimately illusory nature of all else. The sage alone assimilates fully the truth expressed by such Qur'ānic verses as: 'Everything is dying away except His countenance' (28: 88); 'Everything that is thereon is perishing, and there subsisteth but the Face of thy Lord, possessor of Glory and Bounty' (55: 26–27); and 'The Truth hath come and falsehood hath passed away; indeed, falsehood is ever passing away' (17: 81). Only the sage draws from this truth the humility that dissolves all individualism and egocentricity—the roots of pride, vanity and arrogance that, in turn, are the life-blood of tyranny and oppression.

One can now better appreciate the Imam's warning: 'Beware of comparing [yourself] with God in greatness and likening [yourself] to Him in might, for God abases every tyrant and disgraces every braggart.'[57] One who does not act with justice towards God and His creatures, and instead tyrannizes them, will find that not only His creatures, but also God Himself will be his opponent: 'He remains at war with God until he desists and repents.' The tyrant will eventually be forced to repent, even if this be only at the point of death and imminent judgement. Even if he appears to have successfully evaded the consequences of his tyranny in this life, he cannot evade them in the Hereafter.

As regards the nature of the tyrant's 'war' against God in this world, prior to repentance or judgement—that is, his implicit opposition to ultimate reality, his violation of the deepest nature of things—this war takes various forms. One form of the war is constituted by the very persistence of tyranny on the part of the tyrant, for the longer the tyranny goes on, the more wretched becomes the soul of the tyrant,[58] the more firmly are the seeds of misery planted in his being, as is implied in the Qur'ānic doctrine of *istidrāj*—the drawing out of punishment by degrees: 'Of those We have created are people who guide with truth and dispense justice therewith. But those who reject Our signs, We will lead them on by degrees [to punishment] from whence they know not' (7: 181–2). The punishment meted out 'by degrees' can take the form of an apparent success in worldly terms, as is clear from the Qur'ānic verse: 'Let not their wealth nor their children please thee. God desireth only to punish them thereby in the world, that their souls shall pass away while they are disbelievers' (9: 85). The tyrant or oppressor can be both a Muslim in the formal sense and at the same time be guilty of a mode of 'disbelief', taking the word *kāfir* in the strictly etymological sense as one who 'covers over' the truth, and its moral concomitants, by his being and by his actions. This is connected with the contrast made in the verses quoted above (7: 181–2), that between those who dispense justice in accordance with the truth, and 'those who reject Our signs'—the oppressors and tyrants, precisely.

MORAL CONSCIENCE AND SPIRITUAL CONSCIOUSNESS

Another form taken by 'enmity with God' is the inner war with one's own conscience. The voice of conscience—the very essence and sum total of secular ethics—can here be grasped in its plenary context, rather than simply as the somewhat hypertrophied foundation of individual morality, to which conscience has been reduced in secular ethical discourse. This fuller context is the supra-individual or metaphysical source of individual conscience, the divine infusion of spiritual discernment within the soul. This infusion or inspiration serves as the basis of ethical discrimination. The divine quality of justice is thus translated, at the level of the morally responsible soul, into the voice of inner conscience: 'And the soul and that which perfected it, inspiring it with [consciousness of] its wickedness and its righteousness' (91: 7–8). The war against one's conscience, even if it be barely acknowledged by the oppressor, is in fact and *a fortiori*, a war against God.

At a deeper level, then, this 'war against God' emerges with clarity as a war against the very reality that defines the soul as such, for the soul not only contains a moral conscience—an intrinsic and inalienable awareness of the difference between good and evil which has been instilled within it by God—it also contains an innate consciousness of the reality of the lordship of the divine, together with the corresponding servitude of the creature. Spiritual consciousness is thus to be seen as the source of moral conscience. The Qur'ān describes the immanence of this spiritual consciousness within each soul in terms which emphasize its supra- or pre-existential nature; it does this by describing the degree of consciousness in question in terms of a 'moment' at the very dawn of creation, a 'moment' or ontological degree, that precedes the human condition as such, but which enters into the creative articulation of the human soul:

> And when thy Lord brought forth from the children of Adam, from their loins, their seed, and made them testify against their souls [saying], 'Am I not your Lord?' They said, 'Yes, verily, we testify.' [This was] lest ye say on the Day of Resurrection, 'Truly, of this we were unaware' (7: 172).

One observes here that the source of morality transcends the human level, even while forming part of the very definition of humanity. From this perspective, that which renders the human soul fully human is, precisely, the element of transcendence that goes infinitely beyond the soul and yet mysteriously furnishes its own deepest being. In this light, the notions of tyranny and oppression take on a much more nuanced meaning, these vices being brought much closer to the lived reality of all souls, rather than being simply restricted to those possessing and abusing political power. The tyrant is he who violates, first and foremost, his own soul, allowing it to be dominated by 'the soul which commands (evil)', *al-nafs al-ammāra*. Thus, the statement given by the Imam as epitomizing the attitude of one on his way to corrupting his own soul and becoming an oppressor—'I order and am obeyed'—is not just to be understood socially but also interpreted microcosmically. It thereby becomes the statement of the evil part of the soul, the *nafs al-ammāra* which, literally 'orders' (*amara*) and is obeyed by the other elements of the soul, the intelligence, imagination, will, sentiment, sensibility, and so on.

The combat against one's own soul (*mujāhadat al-nafs*) is often referred to by the Imam.[59] This necessity of struggling with and overcoming one's own faults is an essential aspect of justice in the sense defined earlier: placing each thing in its proper place means rectifying oneself before presuming to reform or rule over others.

As the Imam says, 'If your aspiration ascends to the reforming of the people, begin with yourself, for your pursuit of the reform of others, when your own soul is corrupt, is the greatest of faults.'[60] In his letter appointing Muḥammad b. Abī Bakr, Mālik's predecessor as governor of Egypt, the Imam makes a strong connection between the bestowal of power and the need to oppose one's soul: 'And be aware, O Muḥammad b. Abī Bakr, that I have appointed you as governor over the most immense of the forces at my disposal, the people of Egypt, *so you are obliged to oppose your soul and protect your religion*'[61] (emphasis added). The relationship between the magnitude of power being placed at one's disposal and the spiritual responsibility resulting from this should be carefully noted. First, it is in relation to one's own soul and its desires, and secondly, in regard to the religion that one must be on guard. The greater the power available, the greater is the obligation to control and restrain oneself; for if the soul yields to its own desires, gratifying them with the power at one's disposal, one ends up corrupting not just oneself but also the religion which one is charged to uphold. Again, one observes the ordering of priorities by an essentially spiritual principle: the outward form and application of religion depends for its integrity on the inward disposition of the soul of the Muslim. This is another expression of the principle of putting each thing in its proper place.

The commanding or ordering soul which arrogates to itself the right of autonomy and dominion is described succinctly by the Qur'ānic verse, 'Truly man is rebellious, in that he deemeth himself independent' (96: 6–7). Insofar as the soul pretends to be self-sufficient and tries to detach itself from its total dependence upon God, it sets itself up as a god in its own right, and herein lies the true description of the tyrant, the one who, as the Qur'ān puts it, 'taketh his own desire as his god' (45: 23). Knowledge of one's nothingness before God, and, consequently, of one's unconditional need of God, might be taken here as the principal means of loosening the grip of the 'soul which commands to evil'. For only that soul which already commands itself to evil commands others to evil, and only the soul which is lowly before God will be humble, compassionate and just in its dealings with people.

This principle emerges clearly from the following words of the Imam: 'Let the most beloved of affairs to you be those most centred upon the right,[62] the most comprehensive in justice, and the most inclusive of popular approval, for the disapproval of the common folk undermines the approval of the elite...'[63] This stress on the importance of the common people is not only sound practical advice for the smooth and fair administration of the state; it can also be seen as reflecting the spiritual imperative of realizing the actual lowliness of man in relation to God, and thus as a way of encouraging the ruler to identify with the poor rather than the rich, in accordance with the principle: 'O mankind, ye are the poor before God, and God, He is the Rich, the absolutely Praiseworthy' (35: 15).

The Imam's own poverty and rigorous austerity was indeed proverbial. That this was far from a simple shunning of the world for its own sake, however, is made clear in the exchange between the Imam and an ascetic, 'Āṣim b. Ziyād, whose family complained to the Imam that he was too abstemious. The Imam tells him to think of his family and not to cut himself from the good things (*al-ṭayyibāt*) that God has permitted. 'Āṣim retorts, 'O Commander of the Faithful, and here you are, in your rough clothes and your coarse food!' The Imam replies, 'Woe to you, I am not like you. God, the exalted, has made it incumbent on true leaders (*a'immat al-ḥaqq*) that they proportion themselves to the weakest among the people (*yaqaddirū anfusahum bi-ḍa'fati'l-nās*), so that the poverty of the poor will not engender covetousness.'[64] Here we have a rigorous expression of the need for the most powerful to identify themselves with the most powerless as regards material wealth. It is difficult to conceive of a more effective way of diminishing worldliness and enhancing spirituality in society than this deliberate lowering of oneself in purely material terms to the level of the weakest people over whom one is ruling. He who could have most chooses to have the least. The Imam is here implying that if a leader is to be among the *a'immat al-ḥaqq*, he must manifest his attachment to *al-Ḥaqq*, the ultimate spiritual reality in the light of which material wealth is of no consequence. Thus, even if the most powerful and the most powerless are poor in material terms, they have access to the treasures of the spiritual domain, and this, in proportion to their realization of the truth expressed in the verse cited: 'O mankind, ye are the poor before God, and God, He is the Rich, the absolutely Praiseworthy'.

It should also be noted that, on the plane of social psychology, the Imam's insistence upon rulers living like the poor, as exemplified in his own life, is an effective way of ensuring that the inevitable inequalities in society will not generate envy among the poor.

The compassion of justice

Identification with the poor also enhances the ruler's awareness of his own perpetual need of God, thus helping him to live more fully on the mercy of God, in hope and trust; and the natural concomitant of such a life is the bestowal of mercy and compassion upon one's fellow human beings. The capacity to act with compassion in no way conflicts with the demands of justice; rather, it is an intrinsic aspect of justice, conceived ontologically, that is, in accordance with the fundamental nature of reality. To act with compassion accords with justice not only in the sense of putting things in their right place—one must extend compassion wherever and whenever it is called for—it also conforms to justice in being at one with the true nature of things, with the intrinsic character of the Real. It is thus that at the head of every chapter of the Qur'ān (except one) the name 'Allāh' is followed by 'the infinitely Compassionate, the ever-Merciful' (*al-Raḥmān, al-Raḥīm*). Put differently, the capacity to act with compassion stems not so much from personal sentiment as from an innate affinity with the very nature of divine reality, that higher reality in which, as the Qur'ān tells us, 'My mercy encompasseth all things' (7: 156); a reality in which 'thy Lord has prescribed for Himself mercy' (6: 54); a reality whose essential character is determined by the principle, 'My mercy takes precedence over My wrath.'[65] One also finds many sayings of Imam 'Alī on the necessity of showing mercy: 'The dispensing of mercy brings down [divine] mercy.'[66] 'As you grant mercy, so will you be granted mercy.'[67] 'I am astounded by the person who hopes for mercy from one above him, while he is not merciful to those beneath him.'[68]

Neither the rigorous side of the nature of things nor the 'wrathful' side of God is being denied here, but they are clearly subordinated to the higher ontological principle of mercy. There is, in other words, no common measure between the relativities that are subject to wrath and punishment, and the realities, intrinsically beatific, to which divine mercy and compassion give access. One is, therefore, more 'real' insofar as one's soul reflects this predominance of mercy, both in respect of spiritual orientation and moral conduct. And in the realm of human society, it is in the very nature of justice, conceived in this sacred manner, to tend towards compassion wherever possible, even though there must also be a place for rigorous application of corrective penalty where this is unavoidable. Indeed, in his letter the Imam goes on to instruct Mālik to inflict corporal punishment upon any executive officer found guilty of misappropriation of public funds.[69] The Imam's counsels and letters are replete with stern warnings of swift and severe retribution to his governors, the severity of his warnings being in the measure of his unflinching fidelity to the requirements of fairness and honesty in the administering of public revenues. For example, he writes to Ziyād b. Abīhi, deputy to the governor of Baṣra, ʿAlī's cousin ʿAbd Allāh b. al-ʿAbbās:

> I swear by God an oath in all sincerity: if news reaches me that you have misappropriated the revenue of the Muslims, whether a small or large amount, I shall inflict a severe punishment upon you, one which will lighten your wealth, burden your back, and degrade your affair.[70]

The Imam was also severe in relation to his own relatives, if there was even a hint of a request for favours that required the abuse of public funds. In one sermon he refers to an incident when his blind brother, ʿAqīl b. Abī Ṭālib, made a request for funds from the treasury which went beyond his due.[71] 'He thought I would sell my religion for him', the Imam said. However, he responded by taking a red-hot piece of iron close to his brother's body. He told his brother that, by making such a request, he was urging him, ʿAlī, to enter into a much more intense fire.[72] Similarly, when informed of the misappropriation of funds by his cousin and long-standing ally, ʿAbd Allāh b. al-ʿAbbās,[73] the Imam's response was a thundering remonstrance. The Imam orders his cousin:

> Fear God and return their property to these people. If you do not, and God gives me authority over you, I excuse myself before God in regard

to you [and your wrongdoing], and I shall indeed strike you with my sword, with which whomever I have struck enters the fire [of Hell]. By God, even if Ḥasan and Ḥusayn had done the like of what you have done, they would not have been granted any leniency by me ...[74]

The mention of the Prophet's grandsons is significant here. However close be the relationship between oneself and a wrongdoer, however exalted their status be, the principle of justice demands absolute impartiality—there are to be no favours for one's favourites. Not only does this attitude express the very opposite of that nepotism that undermined the administration of the Imam's predecessor,[75] it is also precisely what the Qur'ān instructs: 'O ye who believe, be staunch in justice, witnesses of God, even though it be against yourselves, your parents or your near of kin ...' (4: 135).

Returning to the theme of mercy, the following passage is remarkable in placing the necessity of compassion in a universal context, and is one of the most important expressions by the Imam on the unity of the human race and the equality of all human beings. It stands forth as a corrective to all forms of prejudice, particularism and sectarianism that would apply justice or compassion only to members of one's own 'group' however defined:

> Infuse your heart with mercy for the subjects, love for them and kindness towards them. Be not like a ravenous beast of prey above them, seeking to devour them. For they are of two types: either your brother in religion or your like in creation. Mistakes slip from them, defects emerge from them, deliberately or accidentally. So bestow upon them your forgiveness and your pardon, just as you would have God bestow upon you His forgiveness and pardon; for you are above them, and the one who has authority over you is above you, and God is above him who appointed you ... and through them He tests you.[76]

The universal applicability of compassion is here allied to a reminder of the absolute sovereignty of God. No man—whether a governor or the ruler appointing the governor—is anything but a slave of God, utterly dependent upon His mercy. Thus, each person who finds himself in a position of relative superiority over others must constantly remember his own inferiority vis-à-vis the Absolute, and this awareness both leads to compassion on his part towards those beneath him, and attracts to himself the compassion of God above him.

One might cite here also an incident which demonstrates well the Imam's compassionate implementation of justice, and which also serves as an expression of the principle referred to earlier: all people are 'your like in creation'. The Imam came across an old, blind beggar and inquired about him. He was told that the beggar was a Christian. He told those around him, 'You have employed him to the point where he is old and infirm, and now you refuse to help him. Give him maintenance from the public funds (*bayt al-māl*).'[77] In addition, this sentence expresses succinctly the Islamic principle of social welfare (*maṣlaḥa*), based on redistributive justice, and a policy of strict non-discrimination between Muslims and others. Social justice and religious equality flow forth from compassion conceived not as a sentiment, only, but as an intrinsic dimension of the Real, and therefore translates into a fundamental religious duty of all Muslims, rulers and citizens alike.

It should be noted that the final sentence of the passage cited earlier, warning the governor that he should regard his power over his subjects not simply as a privilege, but more as a trial from God, clearly expresses the Imam's own attitude to rulership. In the famous sermon, *al-Shiqshiqiyya*, he says that he accepted power as an unavoidable duty:

> Had God not taken from the learned [a promise] that they would not acquiesce in the rapacity of the tyrant nor in the hunger of the oppressed ... I would truly have flung its reins [that of the caliphate] back upon its withers ... and you would indeed have discovered that this world of yours is as insignificant to me as that which drips from the nose of a goat.[78]

In this, we see a striking exemplification of Plato's ideal attitude to power, that possessed by the true 'philosopher', he who acts as ruler only for the sake of the people, 'not regarding it as a distinction, but as an unavoidable task ... caring only for the right and the honours to be gained from that, and above all, for justice as the one indispensable thing in whose service and maintenance they will reorganize their own state.'[79]

The principle underlying this approach to authority and governance is clearly that of *noblesse oblige*. If one has been granted the grace, the blessing or the privilege of knowledge, together with a clear sense of justice, a correspondingly greater obligation is created. One's duty to God increases in proportion to the graces bestowed. This is expressed as follows in one of the sermons of the Imam, after he had been praised by one of his supporters: 'The blessings of God upon a person do not become immense without the right of God over him becoming immense.'[80]

'A good opinion of God'

We now come to a subtle point in the Imam's letter, one which can all too easily be overlooked, given the extreme conciseness with which it is expressed, and given the fact that its positive concomitant is not explicitly stated by the Imam here. It comes when he is instructing Mālik on the kinds of advisers he should have close to him. He tells him to avoid misers and cowards, adding, 'Truly, miserliness, cowardice and avarice are so many diverse inclinations comprised within a bad opinion of God.'[81] The phrase 'a bad opinion' (*sū' al-ẓann*) evokes the idea of a misunderstanding of the divine nature, arising out of a series of misconceptions of the qualities of God. From this point of view, all human vices arise out of an intellectual dysfunction, which in turn is the consequence of weak faith—or even outright atheism, since disbelief in God is a denial of God's reality, thus, a kind of 'bad opinion' in regard to Him. The converse of this follows logically: a strong and deep faith generates a 'good opinion' (*ḥusn al-ẓann*) of God, an accurate intellectual and contemplative perception of the divine Reality, and this good opinion in turn leads to the soul being 'im-pressed' (and not simply 'impressed') by the divine qualities comprised within that Reality. These qualities must be understood not only as transcendent, being absolutely one with the divine Essence and utterly beyond the purview of the human soul; they are also to be grasped as models, exemplars, patterns or perfections for the soul to emulate, in the measure of its possibilities.[82] This is the very opposite, it should be noted, of 'comparing oneself with God in greatness'. One must be as much 'like' God as possible, but this spiritual development unfolds within the unalterable context of one's servitude to Him. In other words, one must be generous, for God is *al-Karīm*, the Generous, and compassionate because he is *al-Rahmān*, the Compassionate, and so on. But one must also be lowly, humble and effaced, for no amount of virtue or intelligence can diminish the incommensurability between the Absolute and the relative.

All such virtues as humility and effacement are modes of expressing the absolute dependence of man upon God, or as manifesting the transcendence of the Absolute. Thus, as between the human and the divine, there is both positive and inverse analogy: in terms of the first, 'He who shows not mercy will not have mercy shown to him';[83] and in terms of the second, as cited above: 'O mankind, ye are the poor before God, and God, He is the Rich, the absolutely Praiseworthy' (35: 15). There must, therefore, be a synthesis between the active human virtues, as positive reflections of the divine qualities, and the spiritual consciousness of one's nothingness before the divine Reality—the inverted reflection, on the human plane, of the divine transcendence. One is both slave and a representative of God, *'abdu'Llāh* and *khalīfatu'Llāh*. A consciousness of one's servitude ensures that one does not slip from representing God to competing with Him in grandeur, albeit unconsciously; while an active commitment to represent God ensures that this awareness of servitude does not slip into a forgetfulness of the dignity and responsibilities attendant upon the human state, thus engendering spiritual paralysis and the neglect of one's duty towards the world. The equilibrium between these two dimensions of human existence is another aspect of sacred justice, of putting things in their right place; and it also attunes the quality of moral action to the harmony of pure being.

State and society

The Imam then gives in his letter a description of the different classes of people within state and society: the army, the scribes, the judiciary, executive officers, tax-collectors, peasants, merchants, artisans and, finally, the destitute—each class having its particular rights and duties. The instructions that are given in this part of the letter can be regarded as the cutting-edge of justice in actual practice, taking due account of the exigencies of social and political life. The governor is to regard each of the classes under his authority as having rights and obligations, but the essential feature of the governor's relationship to society as a whole is, again, determined by his primary duty to God, for it is God who has 'prescribed to each [class] its share and has ordained—as a binding covenant (*'ahdan*) with us from Him—for each its limits and its duties, according to His Book or the *Sunna* of the Prophet.'[84]

The governor's duty to society, then, is part of the universal covenant between man and God, the *'ahd* that is so frequently encountered in the Qur'ān. Again here, one feels that by using this Qur'ānic term to reinforce the obligation of acting justly towards all classes of society, the Imam knows that the impact of his words would be deepened immeasurably through their resonance with such verses as: 'Is one who knoweth that what is revealed to thee from thy Lord is the truth like one who is blind? But only men of substance take heed, those who abide by the covenant (*'ahd*) of God, and break not the tryst (*mīthāq*)' (13: 19–20); and 'Approach not the wealth of the orphan except with that which is more right, until he attains maturity; and abide by the covenant—truly, the covenant will be asked about' (17: 34).

It is also significant that, immediately prior to the instructions cited above, the Imam advises Mālik to study much with the 'scholars' (*al-'ulamā'*) and to hold much discourse with the 'sages' (*al-ḥukamā'*). This should be done so as to 'consolidate that which brings well-being to your lands, and to further entrench that which has already been established by your predecessors.'[85] The distinction here between scholars and sages is important. It appears to be hinting at the distinction between formal rules as established in the Qur'ān and the Sunna, and the spirit behind them, that is, the spirit of wisdom without which the rules cannot be applied with care and sensitivity.

There follows a passage in which the interdependence of each class or segment of society is succinctly described. It begins with the underpinning of the state by the soldiers and ends with the governor himself as the centre around which the different elements revolve. But this horizontal centre is nothing without the vertical axis that connects it, and thereby the whole of the society, with the Real. The soldiers are described as the 'fortresses' of the subjects; and the governor is told, at the end of this passage, that he cannot accomplish what God requires of him without resolute determination and seeking of assistance from Him (*al-ihtimām* and *al-isti'āna*). This crucial point will be reinforced later in the letter, when the needs of the poor are addressed.

As regards the instructions pertaining to the different categories of state and society, it suffices for our purposes here to draw attention to a few salient points. First, as regards the commander of the troops, Mālik is told to select for this position the person who is 'the most sincere in relation to God, the Prophet and your Imam, the purest of heart, the one most excellent in forbearance (*ḥilm*), who is slow to anger, happy to pardon, kind to the weak, severe with the strong; one who is neither moved by violence, nor held back by weakness.'[86]

This description of the ideal commander, needless to say, reflects the Imam's own character.[87] What is to be noted is the importance placed on kindness, gentleness and forbearance—qualities not usually associated with fighting men. One observes a spiritually refined attitude towards an activity which, left to its own devices, runs riot with the norms of decency and propriety. Again, one cannot help noticing the similarity between the Imam's description of the perfect warrior and Plato's description of the 'guardian', the protector of the ideal state. Plato defines the problem attendant upon the formation of forces for the protection and defence of the city as follows: how to ensure that men whose natural disposition is 'spirited' and courageous are 'to be kept from behaving pugnaciously to one another and to the rest of their countrymen?' For 'they must be gentle to their own people and dangerous only to their enemies.'[88] This echoes the Qur'ānic description of those who are with the Prophet as being 'severe against the disbelievers, compassionate amongst themselves' (48: 29)—whence the Imam's emphasis on the gentle qualities required in a warrior as the essential complement to the martial virtues.

Turning to the next category, the judges, the Imam refers to the following as key virtues that must be present in those who are to dispense legal justice: they must not be confused by complexities or angered by litigants; they must be unflinching in the face of the truth, free from greed, dissatisfied with superficial solutions, consequential in argumentation, steadfast in the search for the truth of all matters, immune to praise and temptations. 'Such people', the Imam adds, 'are indeed rare.'[89] He also recommends that the judge be paid generously, 'so that any deficiency will be removed, thus diminishing the need for help from people'—a key requisite for maintaining the incorruptibility of any judiciary.

As regards the administrators, Mālik is told to test their honesty before employing them, being careful not to allow any partiality or favouritism to intervene in his choice. He is to continue to check and investigate their actions. As noted earlier, stringent punishments are to be administered if there is any evidence of abuse of privilege or mis-appropriation of public funds.

In relation to those tilling the soil, and from whom the land tax is collected, the Imam dispenses this wise maxim: 'Let your concern with the cultivation of the land outweigh your concern with the collection of the tax, for no tax will be collected if there be no cultivation. And whoever exacts the tax, without cultivating the land, ruins the land and destroys the people.'[90] The Imam's further exhortations to be attentive to the needs of the tillers of the soil, and to be fair to all those who seek redress of wrongs, are concluded with the following warning:

> The devastation of the land only comes about through the destitution of its inhabitants; and the destitution of its inhabitants only comes about when the desire to amass wealth rules the souls of the governors, when they have doubts about what endures, and when they profit little from exemplary teachings.[91]

As regards the meaning of the phrase 'having doubts about what endures (*sū᾿ ẓannihim bi'l-baqā᾿*)', according to the commentators this could mean either that the governors think that they will endure forever, forgetting that they will die and be judged in the Hereafter; or that they doubt that their position will endure for long, and hence exploit the opportunities available to them while they can. For our part, the first explanation is the more likely, given the extent to which it echoes the following Qur᾿ānic verses, which can be taken as one such 'exemplary teaching' (*'ibra*) which the Imam mentioned at the very end of the sentence: 'Woe be to every slandering backbiter, who amasseth wealth and counteth it. He thinketh that his wealth will render him immortal. Nay, but he will be flung to the all-consuming Fire' (104: 1–4).

The Imam uses the same word *jamaʿa* for the amassing of wealth that is found in this verse. The lesson is clear: greed is a symptom of spiritual myopia. Forgetfulness of what truly endures leads to differing degrees of greed, understood here as desire for a false material richness instead of a true spiritual plenitude; and this, in turn, engenders exploitation and oppression. Again one observes how, in the Imam's perspective, the vice of injustice not only leads to corruption but is itself also the product of a chain of causes rooted in a basic inversion of spiritual values, a failure to discern the true nature of things.

The advice given as regards the appointment of scribes likewise is sealed with a spiritual message. Mālik is told that he must avoid the temptation to appoint only those persons who have shown their best side to him. The governor must examine their previous record, together with the impression left by them on the common people, and then appoint only those well-known for their trustworthiness. Doing all of this is described as 'proof of your sincerity towards God.'[92]

Merchants and craftsmen are then described by the Imam as being those who bring diverse benefits to society, and must therefore be treated well. On the whole they are peaceable and should be left in peace to do their work, but the vices to which they are prone must be kept in check: hoarding, miserliness and cheating.

The poor: those 'most in need of justice'

The Imam now comes to a point in the letter to which he wants Mālik to pay special attention. He begins the passage with the exclamation, 'Allāh, Allāh' to stress its urgency. The instruction here pertains to those who have no resources at all—the destitute, the crippled, the orphans, the elderly—those who are 'most in need of justice from you' and who should be treated in a manner such that 'God may excuse you on the day you meet Him.'[93] All of these, and others who are in need but refuse to beg, should be helped by the governor, and he should appoint an officer with the specific task of bringing to light the needs of the most destitute and to provide for them. Then he adds the crucial words: 'This is onerous for the governors, and [the fulfilment of] all rights is onerous, but God makes it light for those who aspire to the Hereafter, who restrain their souls in patience, and trust in the truth of that which is promised them by God.'

What needs to be highlighted here is that the spiritual element is what makes practicable an ideal that otherwise would be a heavy 'burden': divine assistance is assured for those whose attention is not confined to this world alone, but whose aspirations extend beyond it to the Hereafter. It is only when this world is seen through to the next, that a fully just attitude towards this world emerges. Those, on the contrary, whose *ṭalab*, or aspiration, does not go beyond this world will be more likely to fall prey to the easy option of neglecting the destitute—for, in the horizontal scales of political evaluation, the costs to the ruler in pursuing a policy of charity towards the poverty-stricken may outweigh the benefits to him. This is where an ethical policy tied to an exclusively this-worldly appraisal, to pragmatic politics or to personal interest, reveals certain inherent flaws. But when the notion of right in regard to the poor is impregnated with firm faith in God's inexorable justice and infinite compassion, and suffused with aspiration for the Hereafter, an attitude of unflinching fidelity to the needs of the destitute in society will be generated and re-generated ever anew.

Such an attitude goes far beyond the conventional notions of charity or generosity. For the person who has realized this attitude to perfection will not be susceptible to any contrary suggestion stemming from self-serving pragmatism or individualism, and still less from indifference or wilfulness. With this attitude firmly in place, the next quality mentioned by the Imam, that of patience, flows naturally. For, in the light of a concrete and not merely notional presentiment of the absolute values in question, patience can be indefinitely extended—no longer dependent on personal will alone, but sustained by the empowering grace that flows from heartfelt faith. The Imam completes the above point with reference to those with the right aspirations having, as a consequence, confidence in the truth of God's promise: if the promise of God's reward, of His unfailing justice and His infinite compassion be true, then the motivation behind the governor's effort to extend mercy to, and to deal justly with, the poor will be immeasurably deepened. The task described by the Imam as 'onerous'—the obligation to help those who are weak and helpless, those from assisting whom no political benefit may be derived—is transformed into an inescapable duty concomitant upon one's spiritual conviction. This conviction is grounded in the certitude that not only is such generosity and compassion good, right and proper, but that such virtues are in harmony with the true and inalienable substance of ultimate reality. These 'moral' implications of spiritual reality—and also, the spiritual repercussions of virtue—are veiled from worldly rulers by their covert prejudices at best, and their overt vices at worst. Such rulers are also oblivious not only to the truth of the divine promise, relating to ultimate felicity, but also to the warnings and threats of retribution for the oppressors, *al-ẓālimūn*. Here, the *ẓālim* can be seen as one who disobeys the divine commandments on justice, and who also, more fundamentally, violates the quality of compassion which lies at the heart of the divine nature.[94]

Realization of intention

These considerations can be elaborated further by bringing in the altogether crucial issue of intention. Even if the effort of the just man to live according to justice is frustrated by the imponderables of worldly life, nonetheless, the right intentions that motivate him—together with his awareness of the immutable divine qualities as models or principles guiding his endeavour—produce a real inward 'taste' of the grace that furnishes the spiritual foundation of his moral life. If God's promise is true and one is absolutely certain of this truth, then the impact of that truth on the soul of the sincere believer transforms a personal ethic into an unconditional imperative, a desirable value into an incontrovertible reality. Morality is thus deepened by (and into) spirituality, an existential and all-encompassing mode of being within which the burden of individual 'duty' is not only lightened immeasurably, it is transformed into an accompaniment of one's 'taste' of spiritual reality. One then acts justly out of a sense of gratitude for what one has already received—the 'joy of spiritual certainty', as seen in Chapter 1—and not only out of hope for something as yet unattained.

For the Qur'ān speaks of the paradisal reward as something already granted to the true believer; the future has already come to pass, for one whose certainty of Paradise is absolute: 'We have given thee [the paradisal fountain of] al-Kawthar; so pray to thy Lord and sacrifice...' (108: 1–2). Worshipping God as a consequence of the certainty of the beatitude to come—and which has thus, in one respect, already come—is well expressed by the following saying of the Imam:

> Indeed there is a group who worship God out of desire [for something not yet attained]; and this is the worship of the merchants. And there is a group who worship God out of fear, and this is the worship of the slaves. And there is a group who worship God out of gratitude, and this is the worship of the free.[95]

Furthermore, the just man is liberated from the material consequences of his actions, this, in the measure of the rectitude and sincerity of his intentions, actions being evaluated in the Islamic perspective not according to consequences but intentions. One's intention is to be just, not for the sake of some earthly reward or some tangible consequence in this world, but purely for the sake of justice itself, and this essence or principle of justice is in turn inseparable from the divine nature. For justice is at one with God not simply because that which God commands is just; rather, God commands just acts precisely *because* they are just and because this justice is one with His own nature,[96] as we noted at the outset: 'I bear witness that He is Justice and He acts justly.' If God acts justly as a result of His very nature, which is pure justice, the spiritual man will act justly out of a desire to conform to God's nature and not simply out of obedience to God's commands, and never out of desire for any earthly reward. As the Qur'ān says:

> The most pious will be far removed from it [the punishment of Hell], he who giveth of his wealth to purify himself. And nobody possesseth, in the sight of such a person, any favour that might be bestowed on him as reward [for his generosity]. [His action is performed] seeking

only the Countenance of his transcendent Lord, and he will be content (92: 17–21).

The same principle is expressed in the description of the righteous, the *abrār*. The commentators of the Qur'ān are agreed that the occasion for the revelation (*sabab al-nuzūl*) of the following verses was when Imam 'Alī and his family went for three consecutive days without food.[97] At the end of each day, just when they were about to break their fast, someone more in need than them asked for food. The Qur'ān relates this as follows: 'They feed, out of love for God, the needy, the orphan and the prisoner, saying, "We feed you only for the sake of God; we desire from you neither reward nor thanks"' (76: 8–9).

In the very measure that good action is performed for the sake of that absolute goodness which God is, the performer of the action is imperturbably content, untouched by the blame or praise of others; and neither deflated by any outward adversity that thwarts his good actions, nor inflated by the successful consequences of his good actions. This view of the relation between action and intention helps us to appreciate the meaning of the Imam's saying, cited above: 'their hearts are in the Gardens [of Paradise] while their bodies are at work.'[98] Again, one observes here the difference between a secular ethic of justice—or one which is devoid of all spiritual or transcendental points of reference—and a spiritual conception of justice. Whereas a secular ethic stands or falls according to the degree of success in realizing outwardly its ideal of justice, a spiritual conception already sees the fulfilment of its ideal in the sincere intention to be just. For the fulfilment of a spiritual ideal of justice essentially requires an unyielding struggle to achieve it, failing which the intention is shown to be lacking sincerity. Without concordant action, aspirations and intentions are lacking in depth and remain purely theoretical. To hold an intention with total sincerity strictly requires striving diligently and ceaselessly in pursuit of its realization. Thus, however formidable the obstacles, however compelling the arguments of political pragmatism may be, however much one's strenuous efforts are brought to nothing due to unavoidable exigencies of outward life, the just man never despairs;[99] he never abandons the effort to achieve justice, *precisely* because the achievement of justice in this world is not the sum total of his aims. The just person knows that the intention is already, in an invisible but spiritually palpable way, its own fulfilment; and he knows, with a sense of sober realism, that the outward realization of all intentions depends upon circumstances beyond his control, and ultimately on the grace of God.

Now, while this may seem on the surface to condone the failure to achieve justice in society and is thus exploitable as a subterfuge by which actual justice is legitimated by appealing to good but thwarted intentions, the very opposite, in fact, is the case. Far from implying any lack of resolve on the part of one motivated by a sacred conception of justice, the efforts of such a person will, on the contrary, be as ceaseless and unyielding as the reward in which one fervently believes is eternal and unfailing. Such efforts will also be sustained by the consciousness of the subtle continuity between just intentions and the divine quality of justice and thereby the divine nature itself. An inalienable sense of the sacred, then, sustains the just man in his pursuit of justice.

One is not arguing that all secular or atheistic conceptions of justice are devoid of all value; only that, in comparison with a sacred conception of justice, they will lack those immeasurable and inexhaustible spiritual resources that are nourished by sincere faith.[100] 'With men this is impossible, but with God all things are possible', as Jesus says, according to the Gospel. Put into the present context, one might formulate this principle as follows: When justice is conceived in isolation from spiritual principles, personal idealism is acutely sensitive to outward contingencies, and all too likely to disintegrate under the pressure of outward difficulties and disappointments; in a sacred conception of justice, by contrast, divine grace supports the incorruptible ideal of justice, which is thus held high above the frailties and vicissitudes to which the human soul and human society are both subject. To the extent that one's ideals are rooted in spiritual knowledge, then, one's susceptibility to disappointment and despair in the face of difficulties is diminished.

The salience of this ideal of justice is clearly to be seen in the Imam's own experience as caliph: a continuous series of bloody conflicts, against foes that professed Islam, prevented him outwardly from putting into effect many of the principles and policies that flowed from his conception of truth and justice—but none of this resulted in dejection, despair or cynicism, or in even a slight diminution in his efforts to achieve justice whenever and wherever possible, as is amply demonstrated in the nature of his own administration, and in the stream of letters and counsels to his officers and governors, including the one now being considered. Such despair is almost inconceivable for one whose inner life is determined by the conviction that 'No act is negligible if it is accompanied by piety.'[101] For such a person, despair is excluded by piety, in the deepest sense of the term, that is, the permanent awareness of divine Reality; for this degree of piety is the *makhraj* or 'way out' from the darkness of all injustices on earth. As the Imam says, 'He who has pious awe towards God, for him God establishes a way out of tribulation, and a light out of darkness (*man yattiqi'Llāh yaj'al lahu makhrajan min al-fitan wa nūran min al-ẓulam*)'.[102]

THE VIRTUE OF WORSHIP

We now come to what is arguably the lynchpin of the entire epistle, the most important means by which the sacred substance of all the virtues is assimilated by the ruler, namely, prayer. We saw at the beginning of the letter how the Imam began with a counsel to observe the obligatory prayers. At this point, after stressing the need to perform all administrative tasks in their appropriate times, the Imam instructs Mālik to set apart the 'most excellent' of his available time for 'what is between you and God',[103] that is, acts of worship and devotion. Mālik is urged to pay special attention to the obligatory prayers as the means by which he 'purifies' his religion for God or renders sincere his devotion to God. Now, this instruction is not to be taken only as an exhortation to perform the formal prayers; it must also, above all, be understood in the light of the deeper meaning of 'purifying one's religion for God', that is, purifying the substance of the relationship between the soul and God, for it is the depth of this relationship that will determine the quality of all human virtue. As the Imam put it, in the saying noted above: 'Know that your every act is dependent upon your prayer.'[104] It is not only the formal, physical and verbal accomplishment of the prayer that matters, but the inward quality that accompanies it and enlivens it from within.[105] The sincerity, intensity and frequency of prayer are essential to its efficacy. The Imam continues: 'Give unto God of your vital energy in your nights and your days, and perform fully that by which you draw near to God, doing so perfectly, without becoming dull or deficient, taking your body to its limits (*bālighan min badanika mā balagha*).'

All the stress here should be on the word *taqarrub*, 'drawing near'. One attains the divine nearness most directly through deep devotion, offered up alone, in the dead of the night, with all one's heart.[106] This nearness being realized, all of one's other actions in the world are imbued with something of the spiritual quality gained through the divine proximity. It is in this manner that all action can be assimilated to 'devotion' in this wider sense, all outward actions being truly governed by the sincere intention to give oneself to God. If one's inner life is dominated by prayer, then prayer comes to penetrate one's outer life also. Hence, as the Imam said, just after telling Mālik to set apart the best of his times for God, 'all times [and actions performed therein] are for God if the intention underlying them is good and if your subjects derive security as a consequence.' In other words, all the actions of the ruler will partake of the sacred, in the measure that his devotion truly enters into the source of the sacred. Then one can envisage an overflow, as it were, from the fountain of obligatory and voluntary prayer, into the outward domain of action. This subtle truth is beautifully expressed in the famous *ḥadīth qudsī* of the Prophet, often referred to as the *ḥadīth* of *taqarrub*:

> My slave draws near to Me through nothing I love more than that which I have made obligatory for him. My slave never ceases to draw near to Me through supererogatory acts until I love him. And when I love him, I am his hearing by which he hears, his sight by which he sees, his hand by which he grasps, and his foot by which he walks.[107]

To 'see' and act through God can be understood, at one level at least, to mean seeing things as they really are, and then acting upon that vision; in other words, it implies perfect justice, putting each thing in its proper place. It is important to note in the above *ḥadīth qudsī* the distinction between the obligatory and the supererogatory acts of devotion—both are means of 'drawing near' but it is primarily through the latter that the slave comes to perceive and act through the divine.

It is also important to note the Imam's phrase, 'taking your body to its limits'. Strenuous effort is called for here, it is far from sufficient to perform the prayers and devotions in a mechanical or perfunctory manner. 'He who prays without making an effort,' says the Imam, 'is like one who shoots arrows without a bow.'[108] As noted earlier, the sincerity (*ikhlāṣ*) demanded by the Imam's conception of the oneness of God calls for the integration of the soul, and it is in prayer that the deepest dimensions of one's soul are expressed, cultivated and integrated. Hence, the prayer must be accomplished not just with one's tongue or one's body, but with all that one is.

Elsewhere, Imam ʿAlī refers to the key (supererogatory) practice by which this spiritual station of 'nearness' is attained. He does this in a commentary upon the following words of a Qurʾānic verse: '... men whom neither commerce nor trade diverts from the remembrance of God' (24: 36).

> Truly God has made the remembrance (*al-dhikr*) a polish for the hearts, by which they hear after suffering from deafness, and see after being blind ... There have always been slaves of God ... with whom He held intimate discourse through their thoughts and spoke with them through the essence of their intellects. They diffused illumination through the awakened light in their hearing and their seeing and their hearts, calling unto the remembrance of the days of God.[109]

The importance of the *dhikr*, both as a principle of awareness of ultimate reality and as a concrete means of attaining this awareness is clearly of the utmost importance in the Imam's perspective. It is necessary to stress here that the Imam implies, by the word *dhikr,* a methodic practice of invoking a divine Name, as well as a principle of permanent awareness of God embracing all modes of worship, meditation and reflection. It is to be understood not only in the sense of being aware of God, or remembering God, but also as an intense mode of prolonged, prayerful meditation on the ultimate reality, represented both symbolically and sacramentally by one or more of the divine Names. (This aspect of the remembrance will be addressed more fully in the following chapter.)

The relationship between the remembrance of God and the cultivation of justice is made clear in this sermon. For the Imam describes those who are illuminated by the *dhikr* as follows:

> Truly there are people who belong to the *dhikr*, they have adopted it in place of the world, such that 'neither commerce nor trade' distracts them from it; they spend the days of their life in it ... they instruct people about justice and themselves are steadfast therein.[110]

It is those souls who truly 'belong to the *dhikr*' that are not only 'steadfast' in justice, but also able to 'instruct people about justice'; putting first things first, they are able to show how to put all things in their proper place. Fervent, lived spirituality is therefore not opposed to dedicated activity in the world, but infuses that activity with an ethical depth that springs from direct contact with the divine, a direct contact articulated by prayer in general and by the *dhikr* in particular.

Just as earlier it was seen that the sincerity of a good intention was proven by the effort to realize it, so it is clear now that, in regard to prayer, its sincerity is likewise proven and rendered efficacious through sustained effort to prolong and intensify it, 'taking your body to its limits'.[111] What this has to do with justice should be clear: if justice is grasped as a quality rooted in the Real (*al-Ḥaqq*), then one's nearness to the Real cannot but draw one nearer to justice and to all positive qualities, spiritual, intellectual and moral. Thus, the relationship between worship and justice must be firmly established if the conception of justice is to be qualified as 'sacred'. From this perspective, justice is both cause and consequence of worship. On one hand, justice requires us to put everything in its place and, thus, God must be given His due, which entails, sacramentally, worship and prayer; on the other hand, justice emerges, ethically, as a consequence of this worship, as do all the virtues, in the measure of the 'nearness' granted by God to His worshipper, and in accordance with the radiant repercussions of that nearness.

Gazing on the Good

We have made occasional references above to some similarities between principles expressed in the Imam's letter and those discussed in Plato's *The Republic*. This chapter can be brought to a close by proposing that what we are given by the Imam in his stress on prayer—together with its essence, the remembrance of God—is a devotional principle which illuminates and, in a sense, sublimates the philosophical position of Plato, and might be seen as rendering explicit in spiritual terms what is implied in Plato's pedagogy. After discussing the question of justice at great length, Socrates comes, in Chapter 23 of *The Republic*, to address the crux of the matter: the nature of the Sovereign Good, which most concerns the ideal ruler, the 'guardian', whose moral and intellectual education is at the heart of the practical dimension of the dialogue:

> '... the highest object of knowledge is the essential nature of the Good, from which everything that is good and right derives its value for us... I need not tell you that, without that knowledge, to know everything else, however well, would be of no value to us ...'[112]

But Socrates does not respond to the entreaties of Glaucon to describe the nature of this Good, offering instead to speak of its 'offspring'. This leads him to make an analogy between the Good and the Sun: what the Sun is to visibility, the Good is to intelligibility and being. He proceeds with the famous allegory of the cave and then describes the educational programme that would turn the attention of his prospective rulers (the guardians) from the world of shadows to the world of real objects, a programme comprising mathematics, arithmetic, geometry, solid geometry, astronomy, harmonics and dialectic. Having successfully passed through all stages of their education, 'when they are fifty, those who have come safely through and proved the best at all points in action and in study must be brought at last to the goal. They must lift up the eye of the soul to gaze on that which sheds light on all things; and when they have seen the Good itself, take it as a pattern for the right ordering of the state and of the individual, themselves included.'[113] But Plato does not anywhere state what this 'gazing' actually means, nor how it is to be achieved, by what means, intellective, contemplative or methodic.

At an important point in *The Republic*, Glaucon presses Socrates on the definition of the Sovereign Good: 'But, Socrates, what is your account of the Good? Is it knowledge, or pleasure, or something else?' Socrates refuses to give an account, saying, after some further discussions, 'I am afraid it is beyond my powers; with the best will in the world I should only disgrace myself and be laughed at.'[114] It is interesting to note in this connection that Dhiʿlib al-Yamānī, very much after the manner of Glaucon, provocatively asked Imam ʿAlī whether he had seen the object of his devotion. To this the Imam replied: 'I would not be worshipping a lord whom I have not seen.' Dhiʿlib then asked, 'O Commander of the Faithful! How did you see Him?' The Imam replied with the important sentence that functions as one of the leitmotifs of our book: 'O Dhiʿlib! Eyes see Him not through sight's observation, but hearts see Him through the verities of faith.'[115]

We are reminded here of the 'polishing' of the heart effected by remembrance, and this very word evokes the essence of Plato's approach to knowledge as 'recollection', *anamnesis*.[116] But, as noted above, Plato does not, in any of his dialogues, make a direct reference to the devotional, methodic or contemplative counterpart to his educational, ethical and intellective endeavour. There is no explicitly postulated link between 'remembrance' as regards the 'forms/ideas' which engender true knowledge, and the 'gazing upon the Good', the contemplation of 'that which sheds light on all things'; in other words, not just knowing/remembering the 'forms', but 'the Bestower of Forms', which in Islam is referred to by the divine Name, *al-Muṣawwir*. There is speculation as to whether there was any spiritual method in Plato's teaching, and if there was, why he did not divulge it.[117] One answer can be gauged from a statement in Plato's famous Seventh Letter, where he denies that any exposition can be given of the true reality of philosophy, and points instead to the 'disciplined way of life' and rigorous 'daily routine' which the subject demands if philosophy in the deepest sense is to be realized. 'No treatise by me concerning it exists or ever will exist. It is not something that can be put into words like other branches of learning; only after long partnership in a common life devoted to this very thing does truth flash upon the soul, like a flame kindled by a leaping spark, and once it is born there, it nourishes itself thereafter.'[118]

This brings us back to the importance of active spirituality for the practice of authentic virtue. If the Real—indefinable in its essence—is the foundation of all good, the means of assimilating the Real existentially—and not just comprehending it mentally—cannot be disdained. Plato's philosophical approach to the Good can be augmented and deepened by an appreciation of Imam 'Alī's means of 'drawing near' to the Real, for in the Imam's perspective, intellectual comprehension and spiritual devotion are inseparable and complementary. Integral, deep-rooted justice emerges as one of the fruits of this 'drawing near', just as, for Plato, gazing on 'that which sheds light on all things ... the Good itself' results in the capacity to take the Good 'as a pattern for the right ordering of the state and of the individual'.

In this chapter we have attempted to sketch the outlines of a spiritual approach to the theme of justice, such as this presents itself in, principally, the letter of the Imam to Mālik al-Ashtar. We are fully aware that we have only skimmed the surface of this important subject, but hope nonetheless to have at least indicated that the Imam's illumination of the principle of justice, although addressed in the first instance to a prospective governor of Egypt in the first century of the Islamic era, is by no means outmoded. Whether one is operating in an avowedly Islamic or an overtly secular environment, whether the rule be autocratic or democratic, whether political institutions be strong or weak: wherever there are individuals vested with power and authority—and by that very token, subject to the temptations offered by power—the approach to justice articulated in the Imam's ethos will not be irrelevant. For this ethos does not presuppose any particular form of government, it engages the universal theme of moral responsibility, but doing so in terms of that which transcends the level of morality, offering us insights derived from a direct vision of the ultimate spiritual realities. The principles which are contemplated thanks to this vision surpass the domain of politics, and, for that very reason, are capable of penetrating deeply and refashioning, from above, the moral substance of political consciousness. So, although the Imam's perspective is particularly pertinent to the interface between spirituality, morality and governance within Islamic discourse and praxis, its relevance extends to all contexts wherein the sense of the sacred plays a part in the articulation of moral sensibility and the cultivation of political responsibility.

We also hope to have demonstrated here that the Imam's letters and discourses are a vast and largely untapped source of inspired ideas that can illuminate the role of spiritual principles in formulating ethical values and determining the quality of political practice. In particular, it should be clear that an integral 'Islamic' approach to politics and society must take into account the requirements and the fruits of 'worship'—understanding this word in its widest sense. Sincere worship transforms the notion of the Absolute into a concrete reality that imparts to the soul an existential impetus and a spiritual resource which buttresses, stabilizes and deepens one's moral life. What is derived from our consciousness of the divine Reality is not so much a philosophy of ethics as a 'spiritual morality', an existential orientation that is both the consequence of a lived spirituality and the cause of continuous, dynamic and ever-deepening realization of spiritual truth, the Real as such, *al-Ḥaqq*. This means that the *ḥaqq* or right due to each person or group will be given, according to the principle of justice, 'putting each thing in its proper place'. Virtue, in such a perspective, is a form of 'ethical realism', understanding by 'realism' here an assimilation of spiritual reality; and morally correct behaviour translates that realism into action on all planes, individual, social and political.

If it be objected that this perspective is hopelessly utopian, the harsh exigencies of politics and the sublime ideals of spirituality being poles apart, we would respond: if no effort is made to comprehend the deeper aspects of Islamic piety and spirituality, the result of any ostensibly 'Islamic' discourse—whether in politics, sociology, ethics or any other field—will be reduced to an outer shell, deprived of the inner life that gives it all its meaning and, more importantly, its transformative power. For Islamic concepts to be grasped aright they must, on pain of abstraction, be assimilated not simply by the mind but by the heart. As the Imam stresses, it is the heart—the inmost point of one's consciousness—that 'sees' the true nature of things. Without this vision of God 'as if one could see Him', there is no *iḥsān* in the ethico-spiritual sense discussed earlier, and without *iḥsān*, the very integrity of the Islamic way of life is fatally undermined, as has been amply proven by a tiny minority of Muslims in our times who betray the highest ideals of the Islamic ethical tradition by resorting to unbridled violence in its name. Without *iḥsān*, religion is reduced to a position of acute vulnerability; it becomes transformed into an ideology, determined by individual passion and subject to political manipulation. It is no surprise to find that those most prone to terrorism in the name of Islam have arisen out of currents most hostile to the *iḥsānī* or mystical tradition.

This leads us back to the devotional practices that are all too often regarded as the preserve of a minority—seen as mystical or misguided, depending on one's standpoint—instead of being grasped as a God-given means of reducing the gap between what one aspires to and what one is; of moving from the actual to the ideal; of making concrete what otherwise would remain abstract; of living that which is thought about; and of rendering existentially galvanizing what otherwise might perhaps only be theoretically compelling. While the principles established here are universal in their import and applicability, it would be wrong to try and 'de-contextualize' the perspective of the Imam, if this means ignoring—as so much unnecessary 'superstructure'—his repeated, insistent and uncompromising emphasis upon the imperative of prayer. The principle of justice requires that all the elements of one's life—devotion, worship, ethics, action—be bound together in a harmonious, indissoluble and interconnected whole, in accordance with the ideal of *tawḥīd*. There can be no question of detaching the domain of the virtues from that of spirituality, for in the Imam's perspective, the only true virtue is one that is rooted in, sustained by and oriented towards the divine Reality. Thus, one must conclude that justice, together with all the other virtues, can only be brought to fruition in a soul—and in a society—that is permeated and penetrated by spirituality, the essence of which is the principle and the practice of the remembrance of God. In other words, it is the remembrance of God that, in the last analysis, determines the quality of human virtue. It is to the spiritual realization intended and cultivated by this remembrance that the following chapter is addressed.

NOTES

1. Alasdair MacIntyre, *After Virtue: A Study in Moral Theory* (London, 1981), p.204.

2. See Majid Fakhry, *Ethical Theories in Islam* (Leiden, 1994), especially Part 3, 'Philosophical Ethics', pp.61–147, for discussion of some of the major figures in the tradition of Islamic ethics, and the influence upon them of Greek ethical thought. For a concise overview of the tradition as a whole, see Azim Nanji, 'The Ethical Tradition in Islam,' in A. Nanji, ed., *The Muslim Almanac* (New York, 1996).

3. Amyn B. Sajoo, *Muslim Ethics: Emerging Vistas* (London, 2004), p.7.

4. For a valuable discussion of key ethical principles in the spiritual context of the Qur'ān, see Toshihiko Isutzu, *Ethico-Religious Concepts in the Qur'ān* (Montreal, 1966).

5. The word used in this definition is *'adl*; other words used to denote justice, with slightly different connotations, but always containing the sense of equity and fairness, are *inṣāf* and *qisṭ*. See the article ''Adl' by E.Tyan in *EI2*, vol.1, pp.209–210; and for a comprehensive discussion of justice in theological context, see Murtaḍā Muṭahharī, *'Adl-i ilāhī* (Tehran, 2001).

6. *Nahj*, p.495, saying no.429; *Peak*, p.668, saying no.446.

7. *The Republic of Plato*, tr. F.M. Cornford (Oxford, 1951), p.124.

8. Ibid., p.256.

9. Fakhry, *Ethical Theories*, pp.61–147. This is not to deny the uniqueness, self-sufficiency and 'Islamicity' of the conception and practice of ethics in Islam, rooted as they are in the Qur'ān and Sunna. The 'influence' referred to here relates to formal articulation, not essential provenance.

10. See Bahrām Kāẓimī's 'Barresī-yi taṭbīqī-yi mafhūm-i 'adālat dar andīsha-yi Imām 'Alī wa Aflāṭūn' ('A comparative analysis of the concept of justice in the thought of Imam 'Alī and Plato'), in *Proceedings of the International Congress on Imām 'Alī* (Persian articles), ed. Mehdi Golshani (Tehran, 2001), especially p.170, for sayings of the Imam which closely parallel the Platonic view of justice.

11. This is a complex issue, and all we wish to suggest here is that, at the very highest level, 'remembrance'—however this be expressed linguistically—is of fundamental importance to spiritual realization. It might be argued that the differences between *dhikr* and *anamnesis* are so fundamental that any correspondence can only be superficial. But as we hope to show at the end of the essay and further in Chapter 3, this is a theme that warrants further exploration.

12. These processes have been masterfully analysed by S.H. Nasr in his works, *Knowledge and the Sacred*, especially Chapter 1, 'Knowledge and its Desacralization', pp.1–64; and *Man and Nature: The Spiritual Crisis of Modern Man* (London, 1968), Chapter 2, 'The Intellectual and Historical Causes', pp.51–80. See also Frithjof Schuon, *Light on the Ancient Worlds* (Bloomington, IN, 1984), especially Chapter 2, 'In the Wake of the Fall', pp.28–57, for a profound treatment of the metaphysical roots of the decline of the sacred in modern thought.

13. This is the first part of a tradition which is strongly attested in both Sunni and Shiʿi sources. See for the full text in English and Arabic, *ḥadīth* no.2 of *An-Nawawī's Forty Hadith*, tr. E. Ibrahim and D. Johnson-Davies (Damascus, 1976), pp.28–33 (our translation is slightly modified). See also the Shiʿi compendium of traditions compiled by Muḥammad Bāqir al-Majlisī, *Biḥār al-anwār* (Tehran, 1397/1977), vol.70, p.196.

14. As is stressed by Sachiko Murata and William Chittick in their excellent introduction to Islam, *The Vision of Islam* (New York, 1994), pp.xxxii, 267–273. In drawing attention to the aesthetic connotation of this key term, the authors cast into a different light the many verses in the Qur'ān that mention *iḥsān* and its derivatives. For example, 53: 31: '... [that He may] recompense those who do what is beautiful with the most beautiful.'

15. Though one should not forget Imam 'Alī's definition of the true *faqīh*, given in Chapter 1: he is one who does not make people despair of the mercy of God.

16. See S.H. Nasr, *Islamic Art and Spirituality* (Ipswich, UK, 1987).

17. On this subject, see the collection of essays by Western Muslim scholars edited by Joseph Lumbard, *Islam: Fundamentalism and the Betrayal of Tradition* (Bloomington, IN, 2004); especially the essay by Joseph Lumbard, 'The Decline of Knowledge and the Rise of Ideology in the Modern Islamic World', pp.39–77, which properly locates the *iḥsānī* tradition at the very heart of the Islamic faith.

18. This is not to say that there is no ethical tradition in Islamic thought outside of Sufism, but that Sufism plumbs the spiritual roots of ethical action within the soul. In its origins, Sufism is fundamentally about inner states, intentions and virtuous dispositions, in contrast to the formal legal disciplines which are more concerned with outward action.

19. Abū Naṣr al-Fārābī was one of the most versatile figures in the Islamic intellectual tradition, epitomizing the integration of diversity that characterizes traditional Islamic discourse. Not only was he a major Peripatetic philosopher and a polymath—the first to classify the various Islamic sciences

and disciplines—he also wrote important treatises in such diverse fields as physics and ethics, music and mathematics, political philosophy and Sufism. As regards the latter, S.H. Nasr writes in his *Science and Civilization in Islam* (Cambridge, 1987), p.47: 'He was a practising Sufi and the spirit of Sufism runs throughout his works. He was also one of the foremost medieval theoreticians of music and some of his musical works have survived in the rites of Sufi brotherhoods, especially those in Anatolia, until modern times.' His most important contribution to ethics is his *al-Madīnat al-fāḍila*, tr. Richard Walzer, in *al-Farabi on the Perfect State* (Oxford, 1985).

20. See, for example, Timothy J. Winter's comments in his Preface to his translation of Books 22 and 23 of the *Iḥyā'*, in *Al-Ghazālī on Disciplining the Soul, and Breaking the Two Desires* (Cambridge, 1995), p.v.

21. See, for example, the classic Sufi text of Abū Bakr al-Kalābādhī, *Kitāb al-ta'arruf li-madhhab ahl al-taṣawwuf*, tr. A.J. Arberry as *The Doctrine of the Sufis* (Cambridge, 1935), pp.32–106.

22. *Nahj*, p.330; *Peak*, p.487. I have translated the word *taba'* as 'dependent', but the word also connotes the ideas of 'consequence', 'following on from' and 'as a result of'. The import is clear: the quality of one's action is determined by the quality of one's prayer. This sentence comes in the Imam's letter appointing Muḥammad b. Abī Bakr, as governor of Egypt in 36/656, i.e., over a year before Mālik al-Ashtar was appointed to this position. See for details Madelung, *Succession*, p.192.

23. *Nahj*, p.382; *Peak*, p.546.

24. *Nahj*, p.288; *Peak*, p.384.

25. The epistle is also found in numerous texts long predating the compiler of the *Nahj al-balāgha*, al-Sharīf al-Raḍī (d. 404/1013). For a list of these sources, see 'Abd al-Zahrā', *Maṣādir*, pp.419–420; and for a list of the important commentaries on the letter, pp.415–419. See also Ni'ma, *Maṣādir*, pp.246–248. These and several other sources cite important early evidence for the authenticity of the attribution of this letter to Imam 'Alī. Many chains (*asānīd*, sing. *isnād*) of transmission are found linking the first transmitter of the letter, al-Aṣbagh b. Nubāta—considered highly 'trustworthy' in the discipline of *rijāl*, or appraisal of individuals mentioned in chains of narration—to al-Sharīf al-Raḍī. See, for example, Abū Ja'far al-Ṭūsī, *al-Fihrist* (Mashhad, 1351/1932), pp.62–63; Abu'l-'Abbās al-Najāshī, *Rijāl al-Najāshī* (Qom, 1407/1986), p.8; and Abu'l-Qāsim al-Khu'ī, *Mu'jam rijāl al-ḥadīth* (Qom, n.d), vol.3, pp.219–223. This 'internal evidence' upholding the authenticity of the attribution to Imam 'Alī is completely overlooked by Wadād al-Qāḍī in her article 'An Early Fāṭimid Political Document' (*Studia Islamica*, XLVIII, 1978, pp.71–108), which critically

investigates the question of the authorship of the letter. See our Prologue for the general position adopted in this book with regard to the sources of the Imam's intellectual legacy.

26. See S.H.M. Jafri, *Political and Moral Vision of Islam* (Lahore, 2000). In addition to discussing the Medina Constitution and the letter of the Imam to Mālik – of which he gives a full translation – this book is a welcome addition to the scanty works in Western scholarship that address the relevance of the intellectual legacy of the Imam to contemporary political and ethical discourse in Islam.

27. See Chapter 1 above for a discussion of the relationship between revelation and the intellect in what we have called the 'spiritual ethos' of the Imam.

28. This is a reference to ʿAmmār b. Yāsir who was killed at the battle of Ṣiffīn by Muʿāwiya's troops. The killing of ʿAmmār dealt a heavy blow to the morale of Muʿāwiya's army, given the well known prophecy of the Prophet that ʿAmmār would be killed by 'a rebellious people' (*qawm baghī*). See *Ṣaḥīḥ Muslim* (English translation), Chapter MCCV, pp 1508–1509, nos. 6966–6970.

29. Cited by Madelung, *Succession,* p.266. Mālik's assassination took place in the year 38/658.

30. *Nahj*, p.496, saying no.435; *Peak*, pp.668–669, saying no.452. In relation to the legacy of Mālik, it is of interest to note that a tomb associated with him in Baʿlabakk was described in the travelogue of ʿAlī b. Abī Bakr al-Harawī (d.611/1215), *Kitāb al-ishārāt ilā maʿrifat al-ziyārāt* (Damascus, 1953), p.9. See the translation by Josef Meri, *A Lonely Wayfarer's Guide to Pilgrimage* (Princeton, NJ., 2005).

31. *Nahj*, p.368; *Peak*, p.535.

32. This is the beginning of Sermon no.205 in *Nahj*, p.248. In *Peak*, it is Sermon no.213, p.431. Sayed Ali Reza renders the sentence 'I stand witness that He is just', which is a possible rendering of '*ashhadu annahu ʿadl*'. But the translation offered above brings out the strongly expressed theological principle of the Imam, namely, that the divine attributes are absolutely one with the divine Essence, not superadded to it as so many appendages. In the first sermon of the *Nahj al-balāgha*, God is described as 'He whose attribute has no binding limitation, no existing description, no time appointed, no term extended'. It is because His attribute is absolutely one with His Essence that it acquires these properties. *Nahj,* p.7; *Peak*, p.91. See our translation of the sermon in Appendix I.

33. *Nahj*, p.251; *Peak*, p.433.

34. See the volume of essays noted above, *Proceedings of the International*

Congress on Imām ʿAlī, which address diverse aspects of the theme of justice in relation to the Imam's life and thought; as well as the collection of legal judgements delivered by the Imam, *Qaḍāʾ Amīr al-muʿminīn ʿAlī ibn Abī Ṭālib*, compiled by ʿAllāma Shūshtarī (Tehran, 2001); the 27 essays devoted to the Imam in *Farhang: Quarterly Journal of Humanities and Cultural Studies*, vol.13, nos.33–36, Winter, 2001; and finally, a biography of the Imam, by George Jordac, *The Voice of Human Justice*, tr. M. Fazal Haqq (Qom, 1990), the title of which brings out the centrality of the theme of justice in his life.

35. Ṭabarī, *Taʾrīkh al-rusul waʾl-mulūk* (Leiden, 1964, vol.VI), p.3084.

36. The sole exception was Abū Mūsā al-Ashʿarī, whom ʿUthmān had been compelled to appoint as governor of Kūfa, in 34/654–5, when the rebels ejected the previous governor, Saʿīd b. al-ʿĀṣ. See for details Madelung, *Succession*, pp.84–85.

37. *Nahj*, p.424, saying no.103; *Peak*, p.592, no.106.

38. *Nahj*, p.438, saying no.152; *Peak*, p.605, no.160.

39. *Nahj*, p.366; *Peak*, p.534.

40. *Nahj*, p.367; *Peak*, p.534. The Qurʾān also refers to the 'upbraiding soul' (*al-nafs al-lawwāma*) (75: 2), the soul whose conscience is awakened and thus blames or upbraids itself for its own transgressions; and to the 'soul at peace' (*al-nafs al-muṭmaʾinna*) (89: 27), the sanctified soul, no longer subject either to vice or self-reproach. For an explanation of these terms in the context of a discussion of Sufi psychology, see the article 'Sufi Science of the Soul', by M. Ajmal, in S.H. Nasr, ed., *Islamic Spirituality*, vol.1, *Foundations* (London, 1987), pp.294–307.

41. This state of fallen nature, together with the means of remedying it, are succinctly expressed in the chapter of the Qurʾān called *al-ʿAṣr* (The Age), already cited: 'By the Age, truly man is in a state of loss, except those who believe and perform virtuous deeds, and exhort one another to truth and exhort one another to patience' (103: 1–3).

42. *Nahj*, p.367; *Peak*, p.534.

43. *Duʿāʾ Kumayl*, in *Supplications: Amīr al-Muʾminīn*, tr. W.C. Chittick (London, 1995), verses 4, 6, and 7.

44. This saying, sometimes attributed to the Prophet, though not in the major sources of prophetic sayings, is quoted by Ibn al-ʿArabī, who adds, 'That is Sufism'. Cited in William Chittick, *The Sufi Path of Knowledge: Ibn al-ʿArabī and the Metaphysics of the Imagination* (Albany, NY, 1989), p.283.

45. At the first attempted seduction, this grace is implicitly present through Joseph's 'vision' of the 'evidence' of his Lord. The verse is as follows: 'She desired him and he would have desired her, had he not seen the evidence of his Lord;

thus it was, so that We might turn away from him evil and lewdness' (12: 24). At the second attempt, when it was not just Zulaykhā but also her invited guests who were trying to seduce him, the indispensability of God's grace is more explicitly articulated by Joseph himself, when he makes the following utterance: 'O my Lord ... unless Thou turn away their snare from me, I would feel inclined towards them ...' (12: 33).

46. As noted above, this is *al-nafs al-muṭma'inna*. In the Qur'ān, God addresses this soul as follows: 'O thou soul at peace, return unto thy Lord, being content with Him and He with thee; enter among My slaves, enter My Paradise' (89: 27–30).

47. These rules, or rather counsels, are punctuated by penetrating insights into human nature. It is these insights, together with the transcendent openings alluded to in the letter, that make this document so much more than just a treatise on governance.

48. *Nahj*, p.367; *Peak*, p.534.

49. *Nahj*, p.288; *Peak*, p.384.

50. *Nahj*, p.290; *Peak*, p.385. The word 'watchtower' translates *maslaḥa*, which is based on Lane's definition '... a place of arms ... an elevated place of observation, wherein are parties that watch the enemy, lest they should make an invasion unawares, and, when they see them, inform their companions in order that they may prepare themselves for them.' Lane, *Lexicon*, vol.1, p.1403.

51. *Nahj*, p.414, saying no.43; *Peak*, p.581, saying no.46.

52. *Nahj*, p.382; *Peak*, p.546.

53. Cited by Sayyid Ḥaydar Āmulī in his commentary on Sūrat Yūsuf, 12: 106, 'And most of them believe not in God, except that they are polytheists (*illā wa hum mushrikūn*)'. See his *al-Muḥīṭ al-a'ẓam wa'l-baḥr al-khiḍamm fī ta'wīl kitāb Allāh al-'azīz al-muḥkam* (Qom, 2001), vol.1, p.284. The saying is also found, in slightly differing versions, in Ibn Ḥanbal's *Musnad* and Ḥākim's *Mustadrak* as noted by the editor of *al-Muḥīṭ*, vol.1, p.284, n.54.

54. *Nahj*, p.83; *Peak*, p.216.

55. *Nahj*, p.288; *Peak*, p.384.

56. *Nahj*, p.368; *Peak*, p.535.

57. *Nahj*, p.368; *Peak*, p.535.

58. Plato's description of the utter misery of the tyrant's soul is apposite here: '... the despot's condition, my dear Glaucon, is supremely wretched ... Whatever people may think, the actual tyrant is really the most abject slave, a parasite of the vilest scoundrels. Never able to satisfy his desires, he is always in need, and to an eye that sees a soul in its entirety, he will seem the poorest

of the poor. His condition is like that of the country he governs, haunted throughout life by terrors and convulsed with anguish ... power is bound to exaggerate every fault and make him ever more envious, treacherous, unjust, friendless, impure, harbouring every vice in his bosom, and hence only less of a calamity to all about him than he is to himself.' *The Republic*, p.299. Conversely, the happy man is the virtuous man, as it is only in a life of virtue that true happiness can be attained. In the tradition of ethics stemming from Plato and Aristotle, man can only be happy when that which distinguishes him as man, that is, his wisdom, is brought to fruition; and wisdom is only fully itself when it determines one's entire conduct, not when it is merely thought about. The Imam expresses this principle succinctly in his saying: 'Only he who acts according to what he knows, and whose knowledge harmonizes with his action, can be called a true knower.' Cited by Aḥmad Daylamī, in 'Mabānī wa niẓām-i akhlāq', in Rashād, ed., *Dānish-nāmah*, vol.4, p.136.

59. See the discussion of this theme in Chapter 1 above.

60. *Ghurar*, vol.1, p.781, no.1.

61. *Nahj*, p.329; *Peak*, p.487.

62. *'Awsaṭuhā fi'l-ḥaqq'*. One has here a good expression of the principle defined by the Aristotelian term 'the golden mean'.

63. *Nahj*, p.368; *Peak*, p.535.

64. *Nahj*, pp.243–244; *Peak*, pp.419–420.

65. This is a *ḥadīth qudsī*, a divine saying uttered through the Prophet. See Wensinck et al., *Concordance et indices*, vol.2, p.239, for references to this saying in the standard sources of *ḥadīth*, including those of Bukhārī, Muslim and Ibn Māja.

66. *Ghurar*, vol.1, p.580, no.1.

67. Ibid., p.581, no.9.

68. Ibid., p.581, no.4.

69. *Nahj*, p.374–5; *Peak*, p.540.

70. *Nahj*, p.322; *Peak*, p.481.

71. See Madelung, *Succession*, p.264, for the context of this request and the consequences of its refusal.

72. *Nahj*, p.264; *Peak*, p.444.

73. This letter, no.41 in most editions, is simply addressed to 'one of his [i.e. 'Alī's] administrators', and refers to the recipient of the letter only as his cousin. Some historians and commentators doubt whether the cousin in question is indeed Ibn al-'Abbās. See al-Khu'ī's *Minhāj al-barā'a fī sharḥ Nahj al-balāgha* (Tehran, n.d.), vol.20, pp.75–76, for a brief discussion of this letter,

and Madelung, *Succession*, pp.271–278, for details of the angry exchange of letters between the two, based on the historical sources.

74. *Nahj*, p.355; *Peak*, p.511.

75. See Madelung, *Succession*, pp.81–113 for a balanced appraisal of the injustices that came to characterize 'Uthmān's government, the grievances against him as caliph, and the rebellion that led to his being killed.

76. *Nahj*, p.367; *Peak*, p.534–5.

77. Cited by Shaykh Ḥusayn Nūrī Hamadānī in 'Uṣūl wa mabānī-yi ḥukūmat-i Islāmī az manẓar-i Imām 'Alī' ('Principles and foundations of Islamic government from the viewpoint of Imam 'Alī'), in *Proceedings of the International Congress on Imām 'Alī*, p.8.

78. *Nahj*, p.16; *Peak*, p.106.

79. Plato, *The Republic*, p.256. This attitude was exemplified to perfection in the wise and saintly Boethius (d. 525)—whose synthesis between the Hellenic philosophy and Christianity was to dominate medieval Christian thought—who entered the service of the Gothic emperor Theodoric, but was cruelly executed on false charges. As he wrote in his classic work, *The Consolation of Philosophy*, composed in his prison cell while awaiting his death sentence to be carried out, he entered political life motivated by 'Plato's opinion that commonwealths would be blessed if they should be ruled by philosophers'. He continues, in his address to 'Lady philosophy', that it was she who taught him that the reason why 'it was necessary for philosophers to take part in government was to prevent the reins of government falling into the hands of wicked and unprincipled men, to the ruin and destruction of the good. And it was upon this authority that I decided to transfer to public administration what I had learned from you in the course of our private leisure.' *The Consolation of Philosophy* (tr. V.E. Watts) (London, 1969), p.41.

80. *Nahj*, p.252; *Peak*, p.434.

81. *Nahj*, p.369; *Peak*, p.536.

82. This point of view is based on the principle, 'God made man in His image,' a *ḥadīth* found in both Shi'i and Sunni sources. See al-Majlisī, *Biḥār al-anwār* (Tehran, 1397/1977), vol.4, p.11; and for references in Bukhāri, Muslim and Ibn Ḥanbal, see Wensinck, *Concordance*, vol.2, p.71.

83. A famous saying of the Prophet. See the compendium of Rayshahrī, *Mīzān al-ḥikma*, vol.4, p.69, *ḥadīth* no.6963.

84. *Nahj*, p.371; *Peak*, p.537.

85. *Nahj*, p.370; *Peak*, p.537.

86. *Nahj*, p.372; *Peak*, p.538.

87. It is also, apparently, a good description of Mālik's own combination of

toughness and gentleness, as the commentator of the *Nahj*, Ibn Abi'l-Ḥadīd says, *Sharḥ*, vol.15, pp.101–102.

88. The answer is that the 'spirited' disposition, for which 'gymnastic' was necessary, must be tempered by 'music', that is all those arts over which the Muses presided: music, art, letters, culture and philosophy. See *The Republic*, Chapter 9, pp.65–99.

89. *Nahj*, p.374; *Peak*, p.539.

90. *Nahj*, p.375; *Peak*, pp.540–541.

91. *Nahj*, p.375–6; *Peak*, p.541.

92. *Nahj*, p.376; *Peak*, p.541.

93. *Nahj*, p.377; *Peak*, p.542–543.

94. See Chapter 1 for further discussion of the role played by notions of the Hereafter in the spiritual ethos of the Imam.

95. *Nahj*, p.449, saying no.229; *Peak*, p.619, saying no.238.

96. One is touching here upon that oft-debated theological question: is an injunction just because God enjoins it or does He enjoin it because it is just? While Ashʿarī theology tends towards the former, the adherents of the ʿAdliyya school, Shīʿa and Muʿtazila alike, affirm the latter of the two positions.

97. See for example al-Zamakhsharī, *al-Kashshāf*, vol.4, pp.567–658; Fakhr al-Dīn al-Rāzī, *al-Tafsīr al-kabīr*, vol.10, pp.746–747; al-Bayḍāwī, *Anwār al-tanzīl*, vol.5, p.428.

98. *Nahj*, p.302; *Peak*, p.394.

99. 'And who despaireth of the mercy of his Lord, except those who go astray?' (15: 56).

100. The contrast being made here is one of principles and not of practice, the respective ideals, and not the historical record pertaining to ostensibly 'Islamic' or 'religious' societies on one hand, and avowedly 'secular' societies on the other. For it is evident that justice in practice is not to be found exclusively within the one or the other type of society. The argument here, rather, is based on faith as an ideal, in contrast to atheism, and, therefore is of relevance to any individual, whether the context be a secular or religious society.

101. *Nahj*, p.422, saying no.91; *Peak*, p.590, saying no.95.

102. *Nahj*, p.222; *Peak*, p.367–368.

103. *Nahj*, pp.378–379; *Peak*, p.543.

104. *Nahj*, p.330; *Peak*, p.487.

105. As noted earlier, when someone mentioned in the presence of the Imam that a certain Khārijite was known for his long prayers at night, he said, 'A sleep with certainty is better than a prayer with doubt.' *Nahj*, p.422, saying no.93; *Peak*, p.591, saying no.97. See the discussion of this point in the previous chapter.

106. See the eloquent and moving description of the truly pious given by the Imam in response to the request by Hammām who, it is said, fell into a swoon and died after hearing it. *Nahj*, Sermon no.184; *Peak*, Sermon no.192.

107. See for the full text of this *ḥadīth* in English and Arabic, *An-Nawawī's Forty Hadith*, p.118, no.38. It is cited there from *Ṣaḥīḥ al-Bukhārī*, *Kitāb al-riqāq*, p.992, no.2117; see also Kulaynī, *Uṣūl*, vol.2, p.362, for a slightly different variant of this saying.

108. *Nahj*, p.475, saying no.330; *Peak*, p.65, saying no.347.

109. *Nahj*, p.260, *Peak*, p.440.

110. Cf. 'He who invokes God, glorified be He, God enlivens his heart and illuminates his inner substance (*lubb*).' *Ghurar* (Anṣārī), p.764, no.9545.

111. The Qur'ān informs us of the night vigils of the Prophet and a group (*ṭā'ifa*) with him: 'Truly thy Lord knoweth that thou standest in prayer for almost two-thirds of the night, and half of it, and a third of it—as doth a group from those with thee' (73: 20).

112. Plato, *The Republic*, p.210.

113. Ibid., p.256.

114. Plato, *The Republic*, p.211.

115. For an English translation of the rest of this dialogue, see Chittick, *A Shi'ite Anthology*, pp.38–39. See the following chapter for further discussion of this 'vision of the heart'.

116. For the most explicit exposition of this Platonic doctrine, see the dialogue entitled *Meno*, in *Protagoras and Meno*, tr. W.K.C. Guthrie (London, 1979).

117. According to al-Fārābī, Plato hid his *'ilm* behind devices and symbols lest it fall 'into the hands of those who do not deserve it'. See Joshua Parens, *Metaphysics as Rhetoric. Alfarabi's Summary of Plato's Laws* (Albany, 1995), p.xxiv.

118. *Phaedrus and Letters VII and VIII*, tr. W. Hamilton (London, 1978), p.136. This comment contradicts the judgement of Plato made by Peter Kingsley in an important recent book. He argues that Plato marks a shift in the Pythagorean/Orphic tradition, away from the intensely practical, mystical and magical concerns of his philosophical forebears, towards a more cerebral approach to philosophy. With Plato and Aristotle, he writes, 'the philosophical life as an integrated combination of practice and perception fell apart at the seams, and another ideal came to predominate instead: "a new type of man, the unworldly and withdrawn student and scholar"' [quoting Jaeger]. *Ancient Philosophy, Mystery and Magic: Empedocles and Pythagorean Tradition* (Oxford, 1995), p.158. While this 'new type of man' does appear to reflect Aristotle's kind of philosopher, it is wide of the mark in respect of Plato. It

certainly does not conform to the image of Plato in the Islamic tradition of mystical philosophy, and it ignores the sub-text or hidden references ('spiritual switches', as Rappe calls them) to attitudes, practices, and orientations that are presupposed by the text. See on this subject Sara Rappe, *Reading Neoplatonism: Non-discursive Thinking in the Texts of Plotinus, Proclus, and Damascius* (Cambridge, 2000). The outstanding work by Algis Uždavinys, *Philosophy as a Rite of Rebirth* (London, 2006, forthcoming), demonstrates beyond any doubt the mystical discipline, or spiritual praxis, underlying the Platonic approach to knowledge; philosophical 'discourse' is but the tip of an iceberg, an outward expression of that spiritual transformation which Uždavinys aptly refers to as a 'rebirth'.

CHAPTER THREE

Realization through Remembrance: Imam ʿAlī and the Mystical Tradition of Islam

This chapter addresses the meaning of *dhikru'Llāh*, 'the remembrance of God', one of the most fundamental principles in Islamic spirituality, doing so by focusing upon the Imam's sayings—viewed essentially as commentaries on the Qur'ānic notion of *dhikru'Llāh*—and engaging also with relevant doctrinal formulations which have emerged from within the mystical traditions of Islam. At the outset of this book we stated that to speak of Imam ʿAlī is to speak of the quintessential spirituality of the Islamic faith. His influence is to be felt wherever spirituality has flourished in Islam, whether this be in the more clearly defined spiritual disciplines of Sufism and Shiʿi 'Irfān, or in the realms of *futūwwa* (spiritual chivalry), the craft guilds, music, poetry and the arts.[1] His presence, as the 'gate' to the city of prophetic wisdom, leaves its mark on all the noblest manifestations of the spirit of Islam. As regards the tradition of Sufism, however, one discerns a particularly organic connection with the Imam. For whether they be Shiʿi or Sunni, Arab or Persian, Turk or Malay, Mauritanian or Bosnian, the Sufi orders are united in the figure of ʿAlī b. Abī Ṭālib, as it is he who stands at the summit of all of the chains of affiliation (*salāsila*, sing. *silsila*) by which the Sufi masters trace their spiritual descent from the Prophet.[2]

'Alī's unifying role is also apparent as regards the most important subdivision within Islam, that between Sunnism and Shiʿism. Apart from the vast ground that is shared between the two traditions in regard to essential beliefs and practices, these two branches of Islam are brought together in a particularly direct and existential manner by their common orientation towards sanctity (*walāya*) and gnosis (*ma'rifa*) as the goal of the religious life. In this connection, Seyyed Hossein Nasr writes: 'Islamic esotericism or gnosis crystallized into the form of Sufism in the Sunni world, while it poured into the whole structure of Shī'ism, especially during its early period.'[3] Thus, the esoteric core of Islam expresses itself in Sunni Sufism and in Shi'ite 'Irfān with different 'accents', taking on different forms and expressions, without this spiritual attunement to the essence of the Islamic message of *tawḥīd* being fundamentally altered. Indeed, according to one of the great figures in whom Shi'ism and Sufism are combined, Sayyid Ḥaydar Āmulī (d. 787/1385), the true Shi'i cannot but be a 'Sufi' if he plumbs the mystical depths of the teachings of the Imams; conversely, the Sufi is a Shi'i if he becomes aware that the most important roots of Sufism are the Imams of the Ahl al-Bayt, the first poles (*aqṭāb*, sing. *quṭb*) of the spiritual tradition through whom the mystical blessings of the Prophet were transmitted in an initiatic context. The differences of outward form as regards the two traditions are melted, for Āmulī, in the fire of *walāya*, sanctity, the true substance and goal of Sufism and Shi'ism alike.[4] And for both traditions, 'Alī is the *walī Allāh*, the 'friend/saint of God', *par excellence.*

The following reference to 'Alī by 'Alī Hujwīrī (d. 464/ 1071), author of the first manual of Sufism written in Persian, *Kashf al-maḥjūb*, can be taken as altogether representative of the way in which 'Alī is viewed within the Sufi tradition:

> Among them [i.e. the Sufis] is the son of Muḥammad's uncle, he who drowned in the ocean of trying affliction, and was consumed in the fire of loving passion, (*gharīq-i baḥr-i balā' wa ḥarīq-i nār-i walā*) the leader of the saints and the pure ones (*muqtadā-yi awliyā' wa'l-aṣfiyā'*). In this Path he holds a place of tremendous honour and elevated degree. He had complete mastery over the precise expression of the principles of the supernal realities, such that Junayd[5] said of him, "Alī is our master as regards principles and affliction (*shaykhunā fi'l-uṣūl wa'l-balā'*)'... That is, 'Alī is the Imam of this Path in respect of both theoretical knowledge and practical application (*andar 'ilm*

> *wa muʿāmalat imām-i īn ṭarīqat*), for the adepts of Sufism call the knowledge of this Path its 'principles', while its practice is summed up in the endurance of affliction.[6]

The mention here of the 'endurance of affliction' reminds us of the Imam's reference to the sages as those who 'befriend that by which the ignorant are estranged', noted in Chapter 1 above. A possible meaning of this elliptical sentence, as advanced earlier, is that one of the things which the sages befriend and the ignorant flee is prayer, and more specifically, the act of pure concentration on the Absolute, excluding all other thoughts; for this is a kind of death, the ego and all its preoccupations being as it were 'sacrificed' before the divine Reality on which concentration is exclusively focused. The remembrance of God, the focus of this essay, can be conceived both as the consummation of this concentration as well as constituting the path leading to the summit of spiritual realization: self-effacement before the sole reality of God.

The corpus of Imam ʿAlī's teachings elucidates in a remarkable manner the notion, the principle and the practice of the *dhikru'Llāh*, a theme of central importance both in the Qur'ān and in the *Sunna* of the Prophet. The sayings of the Imam constitute a valuable commentary on those verses of the Qur'ān referring to the *dhikr*; and, given the centrality of the *dhikr* within Sufi practice and doctrine, these sayings also help one to appreciate why it is that the Sufis refer to the Imam as the first spiritual 'Pole' (*quṭb*) of Sufism after the Prophet himself. The close relationship between remembrance and spiritual realization will also be explored in the light of both the sayings of the Imam and the expositions of representatives of the Sufi tradition, particularly those belonging to the school of Ibn al-ʿArabī, known in the tradition as *al-Shaykh al-akbar*, 'the greatest Master', on account of his preponderant influence upon the subsequent expressions of Sufi thought.[7] These expositions can be seen as doctrinal reverberations of the dense, often elliptical, pronouncements of the Imam. Key aspects of the spirituality of the Islamic tradition are brought into sharp focus by these sayings of the Imam, together with the elaborations of the Sufis, on the meaning and the implications of 'the remembrance of God'.

First, one must look at what is meant by this term *dhikr* and ask why it is given such prominence in the sphere of Islamic devotional practice. The term is extremely rich and no single word in English can do justice to its polyvalence. It comprises the following lexical meanings: remembrance, recollection, invocation, repetition, incantation, recitation; it can also mean memory, mention, telling, relating (as of a story), praise, glorification, celebration, fame, eminence, honour, exhortation, warning, as well as denoting the Qur'ān itself,[8] or any book of revelation or religion. But the definition that brings us close to the spiritual principle expressed by the term is that given by al-Rāghib al-Iṣfahānī in his Qur'ānic dictionary. He writes that *dhikr* is that by means of which 'man preserves that knowledge (*ma'rifa*) which he has attained, so it is akin to memory (*ḥifẓ*), except that memory is spoken of in respect of its function of acquisition (*iḥrāz*), whereas *dhikr* is spoken of in respect of its function of rendering present (*istiḥḍār*). *Dhikr* is also used to refer to the presence of a thing in one's consciousness (lit. 'heart') or in one's speech. Thus, it is said that there are two types of *dhikr*: *dhikr* of the heart and *dhikr* of the tongue, and each comprises two further kinds of *dhikr*: a *dhikr* which follows forgetfulness, and a *dhikr* which does not follow forgetfulness but which, on the contrary, expresses a continuous remembering.'[9]

As will be seen later, there is much in this definition of *dhikr* which resonates with the Imam's perspective. What is to be stressed for now is that when the thing remembered, or 'rendered present' to consciousness, is God, the importance of the principle of *dhikru'Llāh* becomes clear. *Dhikru'Llāh* should thus be seen, in the first instance and above all else, as a principle of awareness, an in-depth assimilation of the divine presence; but it must also be seen as an action, a practice or a series of practices,[10] and thus as a spiritual discipline. In other words, *dhikru'Llāh* can be understood both as the end and a means to that end, both spiritual awareness and methodic practice aiming at that awareness. It is in the Sufi tradition that this relationship between the practice of the *dhikr* and the principle of consciousness intended by the practice is most highly elaborated. That is, the *dhikr* is presented both as a contemplative discipline centring on the methodic invocation or repetition of a Name of God;[11] and as the cognitive consequence and mystical fruit of this methodic discipline.

The *dhikr* is thus the spiritual method *par excellence* of the Sufis, a discipline which contributes to the realization or assimilation in depth, within the heart, of that which is present to the mind, thus transforming an abstract, notional comprehension of certain ideas into a concrete perception of spiritual realities.[12] Insofar as *dhikru'Llāh* is conceived as the permanent awareness of the divine Reality, it can be presented as the quintessence of religion as such, being that which 'once again binds' (*re-ligare*) the human being to God; and thus as the *raison d'être* of all religious rites and practices. If prayer constitutes the core of religious practice, the *dhikru'Llāh* is, as the Qur'ān puts it very simply, *akbar,* that is, 'greater' or 'greatest':[13] 'Truly, prayer keepeth [one] away from lewdness and iniquity, and the remembrance of God is greater' (29: 45).

Numerous sayings of the Prophet attest to the pre-eminence of the remembrance of God. For example, it is related that the Prophet asked his companions: 'Shall I not tell you about the best and purest of your works for your Lord, and the most exalted of them in your ranks, and the work that is better for you than giving silver and gold, and better for you than encountering your enemy, with you striking their necks and them striking your necks?' Thereupon the people addressed by him said: 'What is that, O emissary of God?' He said, 'The perpetual invocation of God—exalted and glorious (*dhikru'Llāh ʿazza wa jalla dāʾiman*).'[14]

Likewise, Imam ʿAlī affirms, 'Perpetuate the *dhikr*, for truly it illumines the heart, and it is the most excellent form of worship (*huwa afḍal al-ʿibāda*).'[15] The performance of *dhikr* is given much importance in the Shiʿi tradition, which records many sayings of the early Imams on the virtues of invoking the Names of God and various sacred phrases.[16] Indeed Imam Jaʿfar al-Ṣādiq (d.148/765) described his followers in terms of *dhikr*: 'Our Shīʿa are those who, when alone (*idhā khalaū*, invoke/remember God much.'[17] The *khalwa*, the spiritual retreat where one seeks to be 'alone' with God, is referred to as follows by 'Allāma Ṭabāṭabāʾī, one of the most important masters of Shiʿi gnosis in the 20th century: 'As to the particular spiritual retreat (*khalwat-i khāṣṣ*) it is distancing oneself from people … it is especially required during certain types of verbal invocations (*adhkār-i kalāmiyya*)… and is considered essential by the masters of the path.'[18]

As regards the Sufi tradition, the following statement by Shaykh Aḥmad al-ʿAlawī (d.1934) on the *dhikr*, can be taken as altogether representative:

> Remembrance is the mightiest rule of the religion ... The law was not enjoined upon us, neither were the rites of worship ordained but for the sake of establishing the remembrance of God ... In a word, our performance of the rites of worship is considered strong or weak according to the degree of our remembrance while performing them.[19]

Al-Ghazālī poses the question as to why the *dhikr* should be the most meritorious practice, when it is so simple to perform, compared to all the other acts of worship which are so difficult. He replies that full verification of the reason for this superiority of the *dhikr* can only be arrived at through the 'science of unveiling' (*ʿilm al-mukāshafa*). But what can be said, from the viewpoint of the practical religious sciences (*ʿilm al-muʿāmala*) is that the most efficacious *dhikr* is that which is perpetually performed with the presence of the heart (*ḥuḍūr al-qalb*). This is the aim of the *dhikr*, and it is this which 'takes precedence over all acts of worship; nay, it is through this that the other acts of worship are dignified; this is the ultimate fruit of the practical acts of worship.'[20]

One is therefore justified in asserting that the principle of *dhikru'Llāh* relates to the highest levels of religious practice, contemplative discipline and spiritual realization—and thus to the very heart of Islamic spirituality. Despite all their variety in time and space, their divergent perspectives and accentuations, the Sufis are unanimous on the centrality of the *dhikru'Llāh* to their way. Likewise, as seen above, despite all their differences of name and orientation, schools of thought or modes of practice, the Sufi orders are united in the pivotal figure of Imam ʿAlī as the one who connects all the later masters of the spiritual path to the Prophet himself. Now this coincidence between the Imam and the *dhikru'Llāh* in the Sufi tradition is far from adventitious. For the Imam's elucidation of the meaning of the *dhikr*, in addition to his actual initiation of disciples into its methodic practice, constitutes a key aspect of his role as spiritual guide, the *walī Allāh*, or the Pole (*quṭb*) of his age; it is thus central to his esoteric function within the spiritual tradition of Islam, in both its Sunni and Shiʿi manifestations.

As regards the esoteric function of the Imam, it is true that we have little historically firm information about his initiatic role in this domain—that is, his actual initiation of disciples into the practice of invocation (known in the tradition as *talqīn*); just as we have precious little about his own initiation into the esoteric practice by the Prophet. This is hardly surprising, given that the practice is, precisely, esoteric; that is to say, it is not enjoined upon all (the exoteric majority) as an obligatory rite. Instead, within both Sufism and Shiʿi ʿIrfān, the invocation is bestowed upon those with a particular vocation, to those who have received a 'calling' to practise something in addition to the obligatory rites that are binding upon all.[21] Nonetheless, one should note that there are historical accounts which provide *prima facie* evidence of the role of the Imam in transmitting the *dhikr*. The individuals described in the earliest sources as being devoted to the *dhikr* as a particular practice were known as close associates, if not disciples, of the Imam.[22]

The role of the Imam in this initiatic domain is stressed in the orally transmitted sources of the Sufi way, and it is also expressed in several written sources.[23] These refer to reports of the transmission of the *dhikr* from the Prophet to the Imam and from him to several other disciples who went on to initiate others into what later became called the way of *taṣawwuf*.[24]

Despite the paucity of historically sound material on the period of the earliest usage and transmission of the *dhikru'Llāh*, we do have the extremely important literary data provided by the sayings recorded in the *Nahj al-balāgha* and the *Ghurar al-ḥikam*, as well as in the supplications attributed to the Imam. Taken together, these sayings certainly amount to a homogeneous corpus, a distinct body of doctrine, which furnishes the researcher with a rich source of philosophical reflection, spiritual meditation and metaphysical insight into the nature and meaning of this spiritual practice that occupies so central a place in the mystical tradition of Islam.

The sayings which we shall be examining shed light not only on the meaning of the practice of *dhikr*, but also upon the philosophy or epistemology underlying it; and they give precious allusions to the fruits of its practice, that is, its consummation in spiritual realization. Particular attention will be given to the way in which the Imam's sayings, on one hand, constitute an important source of commentary on the Qur'ānic verses that relate to this theme; and, on the other, present us with a clear foreshadowing of the more elaborate doctrines pertaining to the *dhikr* that one finds in the later Sufi and 'Irfānī traditions. The Imam's sayings in this domain are thus something of a bridge, connecting what came before him, by way of prophetic revelation, to what came after him, in the way of mystical elaboration. The texts and manuals of the mystical tradition seem to be making explicit what was more often than not implicit in the Imam's sayings. In other words, the mystics elaborated on the esoteric truths alluded to by the Imam in sayings that were concise, often paradoxical and elliptical, but always intellectually challenging and spiritually fruitful.[25] Reflection upon these sayings—in the context of the Qur'ān and the *Sunna*, which they illuminate, and in view of later Sufi doctrine, which they anticipate—can take one closer to a proper understanding of the role of *dhikru'Llāh* in the practical, operative and visionary aspects of Islamic spirituality.

DHIKRU'LLĀH AS A POLISH FOR HEARTS

The most appropriate place to begin this discussion is the comment on the *dhikr* given by the Imam in sermon 213 of the *Nahj al-balāgha*.[26] The Imam first quotes words from verse 37 of Sūra 24 of the Qur'ān, entitled *al-Nūr* ('The Light'), in which the invocation of God's Name is referred to, and then proceeds to comment on them. The words in question are: ' … men whom neither trade nor merchandise diverts from the remembrance of God'. Given the fact that this fragment of the verse is organically linked with the preceding 'verse of light'—the *āyat al-nūr*, so rich in mystical symbolism—the impact of the Imam's comment here is deepened considerably. The Imam clearly knew that his recitation of the words from verse 37 would evoke in the minds of his listeners the verses preceding them; the fact that he did not quote the verse of light in full only adds to the rhetorical impact of the ellipsis, such hints, implications, evocations and allusions being typical of Arabic *balāgha*.[27] To understand the context of the Imam's words, therefore, it would be as well as to cite in full the verse of light:

> God is the light of the heavens and the earth. A similitude of His light is a niche wherein is a lamp; the lamp is enclosed in a glass; the glass is as it were a shining star. [The lamp] is lit [by the oil of] a blessed olive tree, neither of the East nor of the West. The oil well-nigh shineth forth, though fire touch it not. Light upon light! God guideth to His light whom He will; and God striketh similitudes for mankind; and God knoweth all things (24: 35).

After this verse come the following two:

> In houses which God has allowed to be elevated, and that His Name be remembered therein, He is glorified in the mornings and in the evenings by men whom neither trade nor merchandise diverteth from the remembrance of God, and from establishing the prayer, and from the bestowing of alms … (24: 36–7).

After reciting the words 'men whom neither trade nor merchandise diverteth from the remembrance of God', the Imam begins his sermon:

> Truly, God has made the remembrance (*al-dhikr*) a polish for the hearts, by which they[28] hear after being deaf, and see after being blind and yield after being resistant ... There have always been slaves of God ... with whom He held intimate discourse through their thoughts and spoke with them through the essence of their intellects. They diffused illumination through the awakened light in their hearing and their seeing and their hearts, calling unto the remembrance of the days of God … Indeed, there is a special group (*ahl*) who belong to the *dhikr*; they have adopted it in place of the world, such that 'neither trade nor merchandise' distracts them from it. They spend the days of their life in it ... It is as though they had left this world for the Hereafter, and they are there, witnessing what is beyond this world ...[29]

In this passage it is important to note the Imam's description of the *dhikr* as a 'polish for hearts' (*jilā'an li'l-qulūb*), together with the reference to the 'awakened light' in the hearing, seeing and hearts of those who have applied this polish to their hearts. The relationship between the illumination of the heart to the verse of light is clear.[30] The latent light of the heart is disclosed by the remembrance of God;

the light within shines with the light from on high: 'light upon light'. Once the heart is illumined, all of the other faculties share in the luminosity generated by the invocation, so, again, there is further 'light upon light'. Also, the very word given for 'polish', *jilā'*, can be seen as an implicit commentary on the light verse, for it is derived from the verb *jalā*, the primary meaning of which is 'to become clear', exposed to view, disclosed, brought to light.[31] The Qur'ān refers to 'the night when it enshroudeth in darkness, and the day when it shineth forth in brightness (*idhā tajallā*)' (92: 1–2). Likewise: 'By the day, as it bringeth to light [the sun] (*idhā jallāhā*)' (91: 3). The consciousness which lies hidden within the heart is 'brought to light', through the effect of the polishing of the heart by the remembrance of God.

Here, it is a question of clarifying the organ of consciousness, the spiritual 'heart', both allowing it to function as a mirror reflecting truths from above, and also revealing its own hidden depths, thus disclosing truths from within, those concealed contents of consciousness referred to by the Imam as the 'buried treasures of the intellect' (*dafā'in al-'uqūl*).[32] The *dhikr* is presented here as a means of clarifying this spiritual mode of perception, the 'heart', which cannot be identified simply with the rational faculty, and still less with the organs of sensory perception, as discussed in Chapter 1.

The Qur'ān alludes to the deeper significance of the heart and its particular mode of 'vision': 'Have they not travelled in the land, that they might have hearts with which to comprehend, and ears with which to hear? Indeed, it is not the eyes that are blind, but blind are the hearts that are in the breasts' (22: 46). And again: 'They have hearts with which they understand not, eyes with which they see not, ears with which they hear not. They are like cattle—nay, even further astray. They are the heedless (*al-ghāfilūn*)' (7: 179).

Reference at the end of verse 179 to the 'heedless', the *ghāfilūn*, brings us back to the *dhikr*, for the *ghāfil* is the very opposite of the *dhākir*, the 'rememberer'; and in fact the verse that immediately follows it constitutes one of the most important 'methodic' foundations of the mystical practice of *dhikr*: 'Unto God belong the most beautiful Names, so call Him by them. And leave behind those who desecrate His Names; they will be requited for what they do' (7: 180). The relationship between remembrance and the heart is, in fact, clearly affirmed in these verses: '...Those who believe and whose hearts are at peace in the remembrance of God—is it not in the remembrance of God that hearts are at peace?' (13: 28); 'Truly, therein is a reminder (*dhikrā*) for him who hath a heart' (50: 37);[33] 'Those are true believers whose hearts quake with awe when God is invoked' (8: 2); 'Is he whose breast God hath opened up to submission (*islām*), such that he followeth a light from his Lord [like he who remains closed to submission and in darkness]? So woe be to those whose hearts are hardened against the remembrance of God, they are in plain error' (39: 22).

By contrast, the verse that follows this one refers to hearts that 'soften' to the *dhikru'Llāh*: 'God hath revealed the most beautiful saying, a Book [containing] similitudes and paired [threats and promises] at which the skins of those who fear their Lord quiver; then their skins and their hearts soften to the remembrance of God' (39: 23).

The Imam's comment on verse 37 of the 'Light' chapter, cited above, should thus be seen as shedding light also upon all of those verses of the Qur'ān in which there is a reference to the 'understanding' or spiritual vision to which the heart has access in principle; and which allude to the *dhikru'Llāh* as being the means of translating this potentiality into actuality. The heart needs to be 'polished' by the invocation of God. The Imam's comment here, in fact, echoes and reinforces a saying of the Prophet, oft-quoted in Sufi circles: 'For everything there is a polish (*ṣiqāla*), and the polish of the hearts is the *dhikru'Llāh*.'[34]

An actual discipline, a practice, an action, or regular series of actions is clearly being referred to here—without this in any way excluding the meaning of *dhikr* as awareness or as a state of recollectedness in the divine presence, a disposition of soul determined by the consciousness that 'if you cannot see Him, He sees you'. The 'polishing' in question can be understood both as purifying thought,[35] reflection and meditation, on one hand, and a regular methodic practice on the other, whether this take the form of glorification (*tasbīḥ*), magnification (*tamjīd*), praise (*taḥmīd*), sanctification (*taqdīs*), the declaration of divine unity (*tahlīl*) or the *dhikr* in the strict sense, that is, the invocation of God's Names, by means of which the 'rust' of forgetfulness is removed.

Imam 'Alī also refers in his comment to a particular group who 'belong' to the *dhikr*, referring to them as an *ahl*. It is to be noted that the Prophet also referred to the *ahl al-dhikr*: 'God has angels who rove the pathways, seeking out the *ahl al-dhikr*, and when they find a group of people (*qawm*) invoking God, they call out to one another, "Come to that which you desire!"'[36]

Likewise, moving forward in time to one of the greatest members of the *qawm*—one of the names by which the Sufis refer to themselves—Rūmī provides us with a poetic expression of the image of the heart being polished by the *dhikr*. It is the custom of kings, he tells us in the *Mathnawī*, to place the Sufis right in front of them:

> for they are a mirror for the soul, and better than a mirror:
> breasts polished by invocation and meditation,
> such that the mirror of the heart receives the pure, virginal image.[37]

Another aspect of this image of the polishing of the heart should be pondered, this time centring on the nature of the 'vision' experienced by the heart that is purified by the *dhikr* and vivified by faith. In the Imam's perspective, this vision is divinely inspired; it is nothing less than the spiritual vision of God to which we have already made reference earlier: 'Eyes see Him not through sight's observation, but hearts see Him through the verities of faith.'

In another saying the Imam refers to 'pure hearts' as the 'places' from where God can be seen, 'so whoever purifies his heart sees God'.[38] The relationship between the purification of the heart and the remembrance of God is affirmed in this saying: 'Where are they whose actions are accomplished purely for God, and who purify their hearts [so that they become] places for the remembrance of God?'[39]

Taken together, these sayings of the Imam on the impact of the *dhikr* on the heart can be seen as providing a commentary on the important *ḥadīth qudsī* cited in Chapter 2: 'My slave never ceases to draw near to Me through supererogatory acts (*nawāfil*) until I love him. And when I love him, I am his hearing by which he hears, his sight by which he sees, his hand by which he grasps, and his foot by which he walks.' The Sufis regard this 'divine utterance' as defining a basic principle of their metaphysical doctrine, and at the same time alluding to the goal of their mystical practice.

One observes here a mutual confirmation between the saying of the Imam and the *ḥadīth qudsī*. By means of the *dhikr*—the supererogatory act *par excellence*—the perceptions and actions of the individual are mysteriously assimilated to the divine Reality, and the result of this is that the heart attains spiritual vision. But then the heart, the centre of consciousness, can no longer be regarded in its exclusively relative, human dimension. Its inmost essence, or secret (*sirr*) pertains in truth to the divine, and it is this alone that can see as God sees and, ultimately, 'see' God Himself. As the Sufi master Abū Ṭālib al-Makkī wrote, 'None sees Him to whom nothing is similar but Him to whom nothing is similar'.[40] If it be true that God enters into the human acts of perception proper to the outward senses, then *a fortiori*, the supreme act of spiritual awareness—the vision of God—is in reality not a vision of God by man but a vision of God by God, effected *through* rather than *by* the individual's 'heart'. The Imam tells us, 'Know God through God (*i'rafū'Llāh bi'Llāh*)'.[41] In the final analysis, then, it is God who both 'sees' and is 'seen'. According to a typical Sufi interpretation of the Qur'ānic verse, 'by a witnesser and that which is witnessed' (85: 3), it is God Himself who is both the 'witnesser' (*shāhid*) and the 'witnessed' (*mashhūd*). For example al-Kāshānī writes in his esoteric exegesis (until quite recently, wrongly attributed to Ibn al-'Arabī) that the human witness is effaced in his witnessing, so that it is God who witnesses Himself through the individual whose separative consciousness is extinguished, such that 'He is the identity of the witness, there being no difference between the two except in terms of notional expression.'[42]

This discussion anticipates our final section, where the ultimate fruits of the invocation will be discussed in terms of spiritual realization through self-effacement. For now, the focus remains on a more relative aspect of the heart's vision of God, that whereby the reality of God is rendered clear and present to the heart by means of the 'verities of faith'. The agent here is the inner aspect of human consciousness, and the object 'perceived' is the divine Reality. To put this another way, profound faith reveals the objective presence of God, that presence which is ubiquitous and inalienable, constituting the ontological reality of all existing things. As the words in the Imam's famous *Du'ā' Kumayl* put it, noted earlier: 'By Thy tremendousness ('*aẓmatika*) which has filled all things ... *by Thy Names which have filled the foundations of all things*, by Thy knowledge which encompasses all things, by the light of Thy face, through which all things are illumined...' (emphasis added).

Nothing can exist without the 'foundation', the ontological infrastructure, as it were, that the Name, or combination of Names, of God furnishes for it. That which constitutes the true being and the positive qualities of each manifested thing is, thus, ultimately a divine Name or combination of Names. To see 'things' correctly means seeing the divine attributes manifested by and through them, and thus to see them as existential reflections of principial realities, as so many *tajalliyyāt* or theophanies, self-disclosures of the divine Reality. The 'heart' purified by the invocation comes to see God everywhere.

This vision of the divine in all things can be seen to derive from two principles affirmed in the Qur'ān: the first relating to the divine 'object', that is, the objective, metaphysical nature of reality, and the second relating to the human subject and the mystical assimilation of this reality. On the one hand, nothing that exists, even the most outward aspects of material existence, can be excluded from the divine Reality, for 'He is the First and the Last, and the Outward[43] and the Inward' (57: 3), and 'Wherever ye turn there is the Face of God' (2: 115); and on the other hand, 'We shall show them Our signs on the horizons and in their own souls, until it be clear to them that He is the Real' (41: 53).

The heart polished and purified by the *dhikr* can decipher these signs and thus 'see' God everywhere and in everything; but the possibility of such a vision in no way implies a reduction of the divine Reality to the level of sensible phenomena. As noted earlier, the first sermon of the *Nahj al-balāgha* proclaims that 'God is with every thing, but not through association; and other than every thing, but not through separation.'[44] This 'withness' (*ma'iyya*) of God does not imply any relativization of God, any association or con-joining (*muqārana*) of the divine Reality with created things, any diminution of the divine transcendence. The subtle combination of ideas here can be taken as a comment both upon the Qur'ānic verses which proclaim the divine immanence, the presence of God to and within all things, and upon those verses which stress the divine transcendence, surpassing and incomparable to all things. God may be 'absolutely' close to us, but we are infinitely far from Him. On the one hand, 'We are closer to man than the neck-artery' (50: 16), and on the other hand, '...there is none comparable unto Him' (112: 4).

Nothing that exists can be altogether separate from the all-encompassing reality of God, and yet this reality has no common measure with anything that exists. His oneness both includes and excludes all things; hence the affirmation of God's immanence within the world—His being 'with every thing'—does not imply any diminution of His transcendence; and conversely, the affirmation of God's transcendence above the world—His being 'other than every thing'—does not imply His absence from the world. The oneness of God implies all of this, just as it negates any numerical oneness, as was briefly discussed in the first chapter: God is One, in the Imam's perspective, not in the sense of a countable or merely numerical 'one', a unit or entity among other units, but insofar as His oneness brooks no 'other'. In his words, 'That which has no second does not enter into the category of numbers.'[45]

This can be taken as an esoteric commentary on the meaning of the Qur'ānic verse, 'Say: He, God is One' (112: 1). For the opposite of this oneness of God, that is, the multiplicity of gods implied in the error of *shirk*, is refined by this conception, and transformed into a statement of being, and not just theology. That is to say, the act of *shirk*, of associating 'partners' with God, is taken to a higher pitch, and implies not simply affirming false deities, but the attribution to God of a merely numerical oneness; for this is to reduce His oneness to the wholly relative category of number, a oneness which is confined to the level of determinate entities. Each of these entities is a unit, and from this point of view, God would be no more than one among other similar 'beings'. But, the Imam insists, God 'has no second', there is no other 'being' *in being* but Him. No other entity or unit that apparently exists can be compared, in reality, with His being, which is one in an infinitely all-encompassing sense, and unique in an absolutely exclusive sense: a oneness that is inclusive of all reality and exclusive of all alterity. This radical notion of a oneness that absolutely excludes the possibility of any 'otherness' in Being implies that created entities are so many false gods, in the very measure that their apparent 'oneness' in existence is compared with God's true oneness, or rather, with God's 'one-and-onliness'.

In another sermon, Imam ʿAlī refers to the aspect of divine immanence, this time centring on the nature of the awareness that the human intellect can have of the divine Reality. This relates back to the question of the kind of vision of God that is possible for the human being:

> Praise be to God who is present in the hidden inwardness of things,[46] and whose being is indicated by the signs of manifest things. The eye of the onlooker cannot behold Him, so the eye of one who does not see Him cannot deny His reality,[47] nor can the heart of one who affirms His reality see Him. He is utmost in elevation, so no thing is more elevated than He; but He is also close in His nearness, so no thing is closer than He ... God has not made the intellects capable of defining His qualities, but He has also not veiled the intellects from essential knowledge of Him.[48]

We are told in this passage, on the one hand, that human intellects cannot define and *a fortiori* know the divine attributes; and on the other, that 'essential knowledge' of Him is attainable. How can this apparent contradiction be resolved? By making an effort to understand this paradox one comes closer to another key aspect of *dhikr*, that of recollection, remembrance, recognition—in other words, one is reconstituting ('re-collecting') fragments of a knowledge that already exists, but which has been forgotten. One recognizes that which one has already known, and it is for this reason, precisely, that one is able to know it 'once again'. This does not mean that the knowledge in question is composed of parts that need to be put back together, for that would be knowledge of an empirical order; rather the remembrance in question is more like an awakening, an enlightenment, which dawns as the clouds of congenital forgetfulness[49] are dispelled.

This approach to knowledge through remembrance is frequently expressed in the Imam's sayings. For example, in Sermon 1 of the *Nahj* we find the following phrase: 'Foremost in religion is knowledge of Him (*awwal al-dīn maʿrifatuhu*).' The word *awwal* literally means 'the first' and can be understood as the starting-point, the foundation and hence the foremost element of religion. As for the word *maʿrifa*, this means not simply knowledge, but also connotes 'recognition'; the implication here is clearly that the basis of all religious orientation is man's pre-existing knowledge of the divine Reality. One 'recognizes,' that is, 're-cognizes' that which one has always known at the deepest level of consciousness; one 'ac-knowledges' that which one already 'knows' but which had been apparently forgotten.

Further on in the same sermon, as noted earlier, we are told that God sent to mankind 'His messengers, dispatching prophets in succession, in order to claim from them [His creatures] the fulfilment of the covenant of His creation; *to remind them of His forgotten graces*; to remonstrate with them through communication [of His revelation]; *to unearth for them the buried treasures of the intellects...*' (*dafā'in al-ʿuqūl*) (emphases added).[50]

The 'buried treasures' can be identified with the knowledge of divine realities ingrained in man's deepest nature, those realities to which mankind was made to testify at the dawn of creation: 'And when thy Lord brought forth from the children of Adam, from their loins, their seed, and made them testify of themselves, "Am I not your Lord?" They said, "Yea, we testify". [This was] lest ye say on the Day of Resurrection, "Truly, of this we were unaware"' (7: 172).[51]

These divine realities can also be understood in reference to the divine spirit breathed into man at the creation of the human soul: 'Then He fashioned [man] and breathed into him of His Spirit' (32: 9);[52] to the 'names' taught by God to Adam: 'And He taught Adam the names, all of them...' (2: 31); and to the *fiṭra*, the primordial nature of man, patterned upon that of the divine nature: '... the nature of God (*fiṭrat Allāh*), that according to which He created man' (30: 30).[53] The primordial nature of the human soul, then, can be seen to comprise the very element—knowledge of God—to which the whole of humanity is made to bear witness in the pact (*mīthāq*) mentioned in the Qur'ānic verse above. This identification between the *fiṭra* and the knowledge of God is made explicitly by Imam Muḥammad al-Bāqir, in a saying quoted by al-Khu'ī, by way of commentary upon this sentence of the first sermon. Al-Bāqir was asked about the meaning of the words in the Qur'ān, 'the nature of God, that according to which He created man'. He answered, 'He created them [such that their primordial nature was] in conformity with *tawḥīd*, at the covenant regarding knowledge of Him, [when they testified] that He is indeed their Lord.'[54]

Knowledge of God, then, essentially defines human nature; it is for this reason that the human intellect cannot be veiled, as the Imam said, from 'essential knowledge of God.' But even though this knowledge is ingrained in human nature, forgetfulness (*ghafla*) has become man's second nature. In Qur'ānic terms, the very flow of time smothers and thus 'hardens' the heart: 'Hath not the moment come for the believers, that their hearts be humbled to the remembrance of God, and to what hath been revealed of the truth; and that they not become as those who were given the Book aforetime. *Then the term was prolonged for them, so their hearts were hardened*; and many of them are evil-doers' (57: 16, emphasis added).

The verse refers both to this hardening of the heart over time, which can be identified with the *ghafla* of second nature, and to its opposite, the heart's being present, here and now, to the *dhikru'Llāh*. To remedy forgetfulness, more is needed than a simple factual reminder, in the sense of some item of information, some element of formal, conceptual, discursive knowledge. No amount of empirical data, coming exclusively from without, can bring man to knowledge of God; rather, it is integral remembrance, spiritual awareness, welling up from within and crystallizing upon contact with revelation from without, that renders present once again to the heart and mind the innate knowledge of God, that knowledge which is 'buried' deep in the intellect.

There is no common measure between this consciousness of God and ordinary empirical knowledge of phenomena. The incommensurability between the two kinds of knowledge is expressed by the Imam in such sayings as, 'Praise be to God who is well-known (*maʿrūf*) without being seen.'[55] The paradox in this statement is sharpened by the following formulation of the same principle: 'By things their Creator manifests Himself to the intellects; and by things He is guarded from the sight of the eyes.'[56]

This brings us to a complex theme in the Imam's perspective, the nature of the 'veil' constituted by created phenomena, and how this is to be understood in the light of the infinite and inalienable reality of God. On the one hand, all created phenomena are a veil, in that they prevent the divine Essence from being seen by outward vision; but on the other hand, all phenomena cannot but manifest the divine, bearing witness to its creativity, revealing something of its reality—this being clear to the intellect in its normative state, and dazzlingly evident to the heart illumined and purified by the remembrance of God.

The following aphorisms of one of the great masters of Sufi gnosis or *maʿrifa*, Ibn ʿAṭāʾillāh, are altogether pertinent in the present context. They can be seen as a series of comments on the paradox expressed so succinctly by the Imam. Ibn ʿAṭāʾillāh writes: 'That which shows you the existence of His omnipotence is that He veiled you from Himself by that which has no existence alongside of Him.' In one respect, God is 'guarded from the eyes', in the words of the Imam, and thus veiled by 'things'; but insofar as God alone 'is', these 'things' do not really exist, so God is veiled by 'nothing'. Through their very 'appearance'—both in the sense of their coming into existence and in their 'apparent' existence—it is 'by things' that 'their Creator manifests Himself'. The mystery of this self-manifestation of God by and through all things is rigorously impressed upon the reader by the following rhetorical questions of Ibn ʿAṭāʾillāh:

> How can it be conceived that something veils Him, since He is the one who manifests everything?
>
> How can it be conceived that something veils Him, since He is the one who is manifest through everything?
>
> How can it be conceived that something veils Him, since He is the one who is manifest in everything?
>
> How can it be conceived that something veils Him, since He is the Manifest to everything?
>
> How can it be conceived that something veils Him, since He was the Manifest before the existence of everything?
>
> How can it be conceived that something veils Him, since He is more manifest than anything?
>
> How can it be conceived that something veils Him, since He is the One alongside of whom there is nothing?
>
> How can it be conceived that something veils Him, since He is nearer to you than anything else?

> How can it be conceived that something veils Him, since were it not for Him the existence of everything would not be manifest?
>
> It is a marvel how Being has been manifested in non-being, and how the contingent has been established alongside of Him who possesses the attribute of Eternity![57]

The import of all of these sayings can be grasped within this paradox, tersely expressed by the Imam: 'The veils do not veil Him (*lā taḥjubuhu al-ḥujub*).'[58] The veils cannot help revealing what they are supposed to veil; they are not just transparent to the reality they cannot hide, but in and of themselves, they reveal rather than conceal that reality. This reminds us of the famous saying of the Imam, noted earlier, and which is so often quoted by the Sufis: 'Were the veil to be removed, I would not increase in certitude.' The veils of creation ultimately reveal what they initially conceal, but this revelation is perceived only by the eye of the heart that has been purified by the *dhikr*, and which now 'sees after being blind'. The Imam continues, deepening even further the initial paradox:

> The veil between Him and His creatures is His very creation of them. [This veil is] for the sake of His prevention of that which is possible in their essences, and for the sake of making possible that which is prevented in regard to Him; and to distinguish the Creator from the created, and the limit from the limited, and the Lord from the vassal.[59]

The whole of creation—all of the 'veils' constituted by creation—are thus grasped as nothing but the divine dimension of *al-Ẓāhir*, the Apparent, the Clear, the Evident, the Manifest. However, it is not on its own account that the creation is *al-Ẓāhir*, but by virtue of the divine reality of which the creation is a projection, a form of *tajallī*. God, as *al-Ẓāhir*, projects something of His 'hidden treasure'[60] within, and *as*, the creation. The world manifests the 'apparent' aspect of God—that which 'appears' from Him, that which can be manifested by Him or created by Him—even while concealing the mystery of God—that which remains 'hidden', *al-Bāṭin*, the supra-manifest source of being, the uncreated essence. Therefore, the veil of creation is nothing other than the self-revelation of God; but it is important to stress that it is so only by dint of that which pierces the veil of its own apparent otherness, that divine creativity which the creation cannot in fact veil, even though, in principle, it has the nature of a veil.

The veil constituted by creation prevents that which the essences of creatures make possible. What is it that the essences make possible? The realization of inmost identity with the divine Reality—*tawḥīd* at the very highest level—a possibility deriving from the fact that this same divine Reality is the ontological foundation of 'their essences'. As we saw above, it is the divine Names, qualities or attributes which 'fill the foundations of all things'. At the foundations—or in the 'essences'—there is but the one and only divine Reality. If the realization of this truth of identity is thus 'possible', what then does the veil 'prevent'? It can be seen to prevent the affirmation of this identity on the wrong level of being, that of empirical existence, instead of at the deepest level of being, there where the 'essences' of things are nothing other than the divine qualities and thus the divine Reality itself. To equate created phenomena with God is tantamount to pure *shirk*, the cardinal sin of 'association', and it is this which a vision of divine oneness must guard against. One must always 'distinguish the Creator from the created, and the limit from the limited, and the Lord from the vassal'.

The veil of the creation, in other words, acts as a barrier against pantheism, the reduction of the infinite transcendence of the Creator to the finite forms constituted by creatures. However, insofar as the veil has no existence apart from the self-manifestation of the Real, it paradoxically also makes possible 'that which is prevented in regard to Him': the veil, being thus rendered transparent to the divine Reality of which it is one expression, cannot prevent the immanent reality of God from shining through and within all things. On the one hand, there is essential identity, without this implying any diminution of divine transcendence; and on the other hand, there is existential distinction, without this attenuating in any way the divine immanence. We return to the foundational sentence of the first sermon of the *Nahj*: 'He is with every thing, but not through association; and other than every thing, but not through separation.' We are also reminded of a basic theme in Sufi metaphysics, the dynamic relationship between *tanzīh*, the declaration of divine incomparability and of transcendence, and *tashbīh*, the affirmation of similarity, and at the deepest level, of immanence. In the words of Ibn al-ʿArabī:

> He is not declared incomparable in any manner that will remove Him from similarity, nor is He declared similar in any manner that would remove Him from incomparability. So do not declare Him nondelimited and thus delimited by being distinguished from delimitation! For if He is distinguished then He is delimited by His nondelimitation. And if He is delimited by His nondelimitation, then He is not He.[61]

To return to the powerfully evocative statement of the Imam: 'The veils do not veil Him'. Both *tanzīh* and *tashbīh* can be veils unless each be seen in the light of the other; both transcendence and immanence can be veils unless the two viewpoints be combined in spiritual vision; both the creation—as divine manifestation—and the uncreated Essence—above and beyond all manifestation—can be veils unless they be integrated in the spiritual vision proper to *tawḥīd*, and thus rendered transparent, each 'revealing' the other. Likewise, a unilateral stress on God as 'the Apparent' will become a veil, as it blinds us to God as 'the Hidden', and conversely: for even the hidden aspect of God, if considered alone, will, despite its non-manifest nature, constitute a conceptual veil preventing us from seeing God's 'evidence', His 'evident-ness', in the very bosom of the created world. In other words, the 'veils' are not only created phenomena, but also the limitations inherent in all human conceptions of God, including the divine qualities, and attributes—whence the need, as we shall see shortly, for a radical negation, on the plane of human conception, of the divine attributes. Only on the basis of such an apophasis can consciousness begin to fathom the true nature of divine transcendence, and see through the veils that 'do not veil Him'.

It is clear that these perspectives on the nature of the 'veil' must be taken more as the evocation of a spiritual vision than the logical expression of some empirical observation; they are the fruits of contemplative synthesis, not the conclusions of rational analysis. It is a vision which resolves apparent contradiction by intuitive awareness of the unitive simplicity[62] of reality; it is not the result of some tortuous mental effort to reconcile the complexities of existence. It is at once a vision reflected by the heart burnished by the remembrance of God and also itself a form of this very remembrance. What the rational faculty will only ever perceive as irreducible contradiction, the spirit of the intellect can apprehend as a fruitful paradox. This aspect of the Imam's teaching can be seen to be well expressed by the famous Sufi, Abū Saʿīd al-Kharrāz, who said, when asked how he came to know God: 'through the fact that He brings opposites together (*jamʿuhu al-ḍiddayn*)'. He then recited the Qur'ānic verse, 'He is the First and the Last, and the Outward and the Inward'.[63]

It is spiritual intuition which imparts the capacity to see as one (in the unifying vision of *tawḥīd*) that which appears on the surface as many. In sharpening the paradox on the conceptual plane, Imam ʿAlī is, to use modern parlance, 'deconstructing' the artifices of mental conception, and in so doing paves the way for receptivity to intuitive apprehension and spiritual contemplation. It is only at these deeper levels of consciousness that the complementary process of 'reconstruction' can take place, a 're-cognition' of the Real, *al-Ḥaqq*, deriving from the heart's vision of God through 'the verities of faith' (*ḥaqā'iq al-īmān*). It is only these *ḥaqā'iq* that are truly commensurate with *al-Ḥaqq*, only these realities hidden within the depths of faith, and brought to light in a heart polished by the remembrance of God, that can do justice to the reality of God.

REMEMBRANCE AS THE QUINTESSENCE OF WORSHIP

To focus now on the actual performance of the *dhikru'Llāh*, we ought to turn in the first instance to certain Qur'ānic verses which allude to the *dhikr* as a practice:[64]

> And invoke the Name of thy Lord morning and evening (76: 25).
>
> And invoke the Name of thy Lord, devoting thyself to Him [or: it] with utter devotion (73: 8).
>
> O ye who believe! Invoke God with much invocation (33: 41).
>
> Call upon thy Lord in humility and in secret (7: 55).
>
> And invoke thy Lord within thyself, in humility and awe, and beneath thy breath, in the morning and in the night (7: 205).

All of these verses appear to point to an actual practice, one which is to be maintained according to different modes ('within thyself, 'in humility', 'in awe', 'in secret', 'beneath thy breath', etc.). But perhaps most important of all, the invocation is to be done much, in abundance—*dhikran kathīran*. As noted before, the intensity and duration of the devotions of the Prophet and the first Muslims is referred to in the Qur'ānic chapter *al-Muzzammil* ('The Enwrapped'), where the long night vigils maintained by these early Muslims are mentioned: 'Truly, thy Lord knoweth that thou standest in prayer for almost two-thirds of the night, and a half of it, and a third of it—as doth a group from those with thee' (73: 20). It is important to note that the first part of the Sūra contains the verse quoted above, instructing the Prophet to 'remember/invoke the Name of thy Lord, and devote thyself to Him with utter devotion' (73: 8).[65] The pronoun in the word *ilayhi*, 'to Him', can refer either to Him as 'thy Lord' or to 'it' as the 'Name of thy Lord', so that the hidden, operative meaning of the verse comes to be, 'Invoke the Name of God and devote yourself to this Name with utter devotion'. This recalls the explicit injunction contained in the verse, 'Glorify the Name of thy Lord, the Exalted' (87: 1).[66] Thus, devotion to the *Name* of the Absolute is—on the plane of devotional praxis—tantamount to devotion to the Absolute itself. The Absolute in itself is above and beyond all forms, and thus all verbal forms; but It is nonetheless rendered accessible through the divine Name—a Name not defined by some human linguistic inventiveness but bestowed through divine self-disclosure: God reveals the sacrament of His own Name.[67] Distraction from the remembrance or invocation of the Name is, likewise, distraction from God Himself, as alluded to in the verses, 'The devil hath overcome them, causing them to forget the remembrance of God' (58: 19), and 'O ye who believe, let not your wealth nor your children distract you from the remembrance of God' (63: 9).

This identification between devoting oneself to God and devoting oneself to His Name can be seen to flow naturally from the principle enunciated by Imam 'Alī in the following simple affirmation, 'He who loves a thing dedicates himself fervently to its invocation (*man aḥabba shay'an lahija bi-dhikrihi*).'[68] It is thus that the lover of God should devote himself utterly to the invocation of the Name of God, to give himself to it in abundance (*kathīran*). The combination between the words *lahija*—meaning 'to be devoted to', as well as 'to mention repeatedly'[69]—and *dhikr*, clearly indicating the constant, verbal repetition of the invocation, figures also in the Imam's *Duʿāʾ Kumayl*, here with an additional, explicit reference to the tongue: '... my tongue has devoted itself to thy invocation (*lahija bihi lisānī min dhikrika*).' He implores God, 'Make my times in the night and the day inhabited by Thy remembrance', and 'make my tongue invoke Thee with utter dedication *(ijʿal lisānī bi-dhikrika lahijan*)'. Finally, the invocation as a practice is clearly confirmed by him in these words: 'O He whose Name is a remedy and whose invocation is the cure (*yā man ismuhu dawāʾ wa dhikruhu shafāʾ*).'[70]

Here, the Name of God is more than just a name among other names, a word or a sound among other such symbols: it is the remedy for man's congenital forgetfulness, the spiritual amnesia or *ghafla* that has become his 'second nature', as noted above. But to be effective, the Name must be actively invoked and not merely thought about, just as a medicine must be taken and not merely contemplated if it is to exercise its healing power. As the Imam puts it in one of his sermons, describing the greatness of the Qurʾān: 'It has made the *dhikr* incumbent upon your tongues.'[71] And, as we have seen, the invocation is to be done *kathīran*, 'much' or in abundance. The following *ḥadīth* of the Prophet should also be noted in this context. It makes absolutely clear that *dhikr* has an operative, practical dimension, and is not to be restricted by a purely theoretical interpretation of its meanings and implications:

> ʿAbd Allāh b. Busr reported that a man said, 'O Messenger of Allāh, the laws of Islam are too many for me, so tell me something that I may cling to.' He replied, may God bless him and give him peace, 'Let your tongue never cease to be moist from invoking Allāh.'[72]

It is also worth quoting here the verses which follow the Qurʾānic exhortation to invoke much: 'O ye who believe, invoke God with much invocation, and glorify Him early and late. He it is who blesseth you, as do His angels, so that He may bring you forth from darkness into light; and He is ever merciful to the believers' (33: 41–43).

Here, the reciprocity between the *dhikr* of the believers and the *ṣalāt*, the prayer or blessing of God, over the believers should be noted. However, the relationship between the human act of invocation and the divine act of blessing is more complex than at first appears. Indeed, exploring this relationship and delving deeper into the ontological dimensions of the invocation takes us close to the mystery expressed by the verse, 'Remember Me, I will remember you' (2: 152).

We shall turn to the possible meanings of this reciprocity below. For now, remaining with the Qur'ānic verses cited above (33: 41–3), the relationship to be noted is that between the invocation and illumination, being brought from darkness into light. The Imam refers to the manner in which human invocation results in divine illumination, and can be taken as a comment on this aspect of the meaning of the verses: 'Whoever invokes God, glorified be He, God enlivens his heart and illuminates his inner substance (*lubb*).'[73] Mention of the word *lubb* (pl. *albāb*) here evokes the Qur'ānic verse which describes the *ūlu'l-albāb*, the 'possessors of substance', in which the *dhikr* once again figures prominently: 'Truly in the creation of the heavens and the earth, and in the alternation between night and day, there are signs for those of substance, those who invoke God standing, sitting and reclining on their sides, and reflect upon the creation of the heavens and the earth...' (3: 190–191).

In addition to underlining further the practical or methodic aspect of the remembrance, we have here also a clear indication of the relationship between *dhikr* and *fikr*, between invocation and reflection or meditation. Going back to the observations above, the practice of the invocation is held to polish the inmost organ of awareness, resulting in an enhanced capacity for meditation upon the 'signs of God' in the creation and within oneself. When one interposes the element of love between the invocation and meditation—for 'he who *loves* a thing dedicates himself fervently to its invocation'—one comes to understand the possibility of entering into a 'virtuous circle' within which each element strengthens and deepens the other two. As one begins to ponder more seriously the 'signs' of God—and appreciate more fully their beauty—the more one comes to love God; the more one loves God, the more one invokes His Name; the more one invokes, the more sharply one perceives the sacred message of the 'signs' in the universe. Thus, *fikr* intensifies *dhikr* and *dhikr* deepens *fikr*.

These verses, 3: 190–1, are also important in that they highlight the supra-formal aspect of the invocation. The *dhikr* is presented here as the quintessence of all religious activity, or as the spiritual act *par excellence*. For the universality of its modes—standing, sitting, reclining, as this verse says, and 'within thyself, 'in humility', 'in awe', 'in secret', 'beneath thy breath', according to the verses cited above—transcend the formal rules pertaining to the fixed canonical prayers, which involve prescribed words, movements and conditions. The *dhikr*, by contrast, is described as something to be performed at all times, in all places, in all postures, and is thus to be woven into the texture of everyday life, rather than super-imposed upon life as an extraneous, formalistic practice.

It would not be out of place to mention here that, according to Imam Ja'far al-Ṣādiq, the invocation is the sole practice that should be performed in all circumstances and at all times, there being no limit placed on its practice: 'Everything has a limit, at which it terminates, except the *dhikr Allāh*. God has made obligatory the religious duties (*al-farā'iḍ*), so whoever fulfils them, that fulfilment constitutes their limit. For the month of Ramaḍān, whoever fasts therein, that constitutes its limit...' He proceeds to mention other rites, and then cites the Qur'ānic verse: 'O ye who believe, invoke God with much invocation', and adds that his father, Imam Muḥammad al-Bāqir, never ceased invoking, even while eating and walking.[74]

In this light it is easier to understand those referred to in the Qur'ān as 'men whom neither trade nor merchandise diverts from the remembrance of God'. The verse also helps to explain the description of the believers as those who are 'perpetually at prayer (*'alā ṣalātihim dā'imūn*)' (70: 23). They are not only regular in the performance of the canonical prayer at the appropriate times; there is no time when the men of substance are not 'at prayer', if one understands by 'prayer' the remembrance of God. The Qur'ān instructs mankind to 'establish the prayer for the sake of My remembrance' (20: 14). The very purpose and goal of the prayer, its spiritual value and substance, is thus the remembrance of God.

The following saying of Imam 'Alī is relevant here: 'Continuous invocation is the food of the spirit and the key to prayer (*miftāḥ al-*

ṣalāt).'[75] One understands better in this light why the Qur'ān tells us, as was noted at the outset of this essay, that 'prayer keepeth [one] away from lewdness and iniquity, and the remembrance of God is greater' (29: 45). The formal, canonical prayer is described here in negative or constraining terms; it is a *preventative*. Its very formality is defined as a ritual necessity, but it is also, unavoidably, an existential limitation; it is performed and operative at one time and not another, expressed in certain forms and movements and not others. The remembrance of God is *greater* in that it is the positive, enlivening substance of prayer; it is that which liberates consciousness from the limits—verbal, mental, existential—by which all formal prayer is defined. Since all formal prayer is thus inescapably defined, objectively, within certain limits, its *baraka* or blessedness, can all too easily become confined, subjectively, within those same limits. One feels close to God only in formal prayer, and not in one's everyday life outside the prayer-times. It is *dhikr*, in the sense of recollectedness, constant awareness of God, that allows prayer (or the consciousness conditioned by prayer) to open out into its intended essence, into an awareness of the unconditional presence of God. It thus transforms a preventative measure vis-à-vis moral transgression into a positive apprehension of spiritual reality. One might say here that the *dhikru'Llāh* is 'greater' than the ritual or canonical prayer in the measure that spiritual awareness transcends moral conscience, or in the measure that essence transcends form. The 'lesser' is not negated by the 'greater', but rather, comprised within it, enriched by it, attaining a greater plenitude and scope within it than it is capable of attaining on its account. In this light one can understand better at least some of the reasons why the Imam, following the Prophet and the Qur'ān, presents *dhikru'Llāh* as the quintessence of worship and devotion.

THE REALITY OF REMEMBRANCE

In this final section, our discussion turns to the spiritual fruits of the remembrance of God, and in particular to 'realization', *taḥqīq*, the process by which *al-Ḥāqq*, the Real, is 'made real' within oneself. This is closely related to the process referred to earlier, which the Imam described as *tawaḥḥud*, self-integration, the spiritual assimilation of oneness within oneself, as opposed to the simple theological affirmation of oneness, *tawḥīd*, in its conventional sense. In conformity with the Imam's own use of paradox, the fruit of remembrance can be addressed in the first instance by taking stock of its very opposite, which is *ghafla*, heedlessness, or *sahw*, forgetfulness, distraction. In following this line of inquiry, we will observe another interesting example of the way in which the Imam's sayings function implicitly as a commentary on verses of the Qurʾān, while opening out onto a rich terrain of mystical speculation and spiritual contemplation pertaining to the ultimate consequences of the invocation/remembrance of God.

The Qurʾān is severe in its condemnation of those who pray in an ostentatious and hypocritical manner; these are the ones who 'give the lie to religion': 'Woe to those who pray, those who are heedless of their prayer, those who make a show ...' (107: 4–6). The Imam likewise warns against remembering God heedlessly or with distraction, and in describing its opposite, perfect or complete *dhikr*, expresses a paradoxical return to a kind of 'forgetting' which goes to the very heart of the Sufi principle of 'extinction in remembrance' (*al-fanāʾ fīʾl-dhikr*):

> Do not remember God absent-mindedly (*sāhiyan*), nor forget Him in distraction; rather, remember Him with perfect remembrance (*dhikran kāmilan*), a remembrance in which your heart and tongue are in harmony, and what you conceal conforms with what you reveal. But you will not remember Him according to the true reality of the remembrance (*ḥaqīqat al-dhikr*) until you forget your own soul in your remembrance.[76]

In this very important saying, one is given a summary of the entire mystical path. What is implied here is the whole series of spiritual 'stations' (*maqāmāt* sing. *maqām*) by which total sincerity is attained—Sufism is itself often referred to simply as 'sincerity', that is, *ṣidq* or *ikhlāṣ*.[77] On the one hand, the *dhikr* itself helps to realize sincerity by 'polishing' the heart, on the other hand, it is the virtue of sincerity that bestows 'perfection' or 'completion' upon the spiritual efficacy of the *dhikr*. What matters in this stage of 'perfect' *dhikr* is that the outward verbal form of the invocation must harmonize with heart-felt intention. There must be no contradiction between that which is articulated by the tongue and that which motivates the heart. Bringing the heart and the tongue into harmony means that the divine Reality invoked by the tongue reverberates in the heart, whence arise the fundamental dispositions of the soul, the virtues.

The divine qualities comprised within the Name of the Absolute must, to some degree at least, be reflected in the heart and soul of the invoker, in the form of the virtues, which are summed up in the sincerity or 'purity' of soul to which *ikhlāṣ* refers. When the soul is completely pure, sincerely and utterly at one with the highest ideals proclaimed by the tongue and the intellect, then it becomes transparent to the spiritual qualities embedded within its own substance, the *fiṭra*, or primordial nature. These are the qualities 'brought to light' and also brought to life, by the *dhikr*; these are the qualities that shine forth from the heart once it is polished by the *dhikr*. In the absence of these moral and spiritual qualities, however, the purely technical act of invocation is 'heedless' and lacking in all efficacy: one who does not make any effort to attain sincerity—who does not engage with the 'greater' *jihād* referred to in Chaper 1—is heedless of God, neglecting the moral concomitants of authentic remembrance, and ignoring the moral pre-requisites for the efficacy of the remembrance.

But what is most remarkable in this saying of the Imam is the presentation of the ultimate stage of *dhikr* in terms of its apparent opposite. The 'reality' of *dhikr*, its *ḥaqīqa*, opens out into the supreme *ḥaqīqa*, the divine Reality as such. This degree of *dhikr* demands the 'forgetting' of the individual: the veil of the self must be cast aside if the spiritual vision of divine Reality is to be attained. There can be no *maʿrifa* without self-effacement, initially, and 'extinction' (*fanāʾ*) ultimately.[78] The reality of 'remembering' calls for the most radical 'forgetting'.

In other words, there is a clear distinction between 'perfect' *dhikr* and the 'reality' of *dhikr*. Indeed there is a radical disjuncture between the one and the other, such that the move from 'perfection' to 'reality'—from human perfection to divine Reality, one might say—requires an ontological 'leap' of consciousness. In the first degree—where the aim is the elimination of hypocrisy, the attainment of sincerity, integrity, totality, hence perfection on the plane of the human soul—the individual as agent of the act of *dhikr* retains his identity. The harmonious reverberation between hidden intent and outward act is here given the name of 'perfect' *dhikr*. But it is still a *dhikr* which pertains to the individual as agent. In the higher degree, by contrast, the *dhikr* can no longer be defined in relation to the individual, since the individual has been 'forgotten'—by himself.[79] This can only mean that the centre of consciousness has shifted from the invoker, *al-dhākir*, to the Invoked, *al-Madhkūr*. The *ḥaqīqa* of the *dhikr* is thus one with the object of invocation, the Real itself, *al-Ḥaqq*. Esoterically, then, it can be said that the true agent of the invocation is God Himself, the apparent invocation by man being but an outward appearance, an illusion which is extinguished by the very act of the invocation itself.

This takes the discussion back to the question broached earlier, that of agency. The *ḥadīth qudsī* quoted earlier, 'My slave never ceases to draw near to Me through supererogatory acts (*nawāfil*) until I love him…' should be recalled here. The Imam's commentary on the words of the Qur'ān referring to those who are not distracted by the world from the remembrance of God made it clear that the *nawāfil* in question are centred on the practice of the invocation. At this point what is to be stressed is that the invocation can be seen as disclosing the reality of God's ontological agency within all acts: God is the hearing and the seeing of the individual who is loved by God as a result of his devotions. But it must be stressed that this report of the penetration of the Divine into the faculties of the soul and body of the individual describes a universal reality, the true state of affairs, and not any change of state, either for God or for the individual: for God does not 'change' in order to enter into the acts and perceptions of one person as opposed to another. His 'becoming' one with the acts of perception is to be understood in terms of a reality 'becoming clear' to the soul that is unveiled, so that it sees through the illusory appearance of its own agency. By virtue of the invocation, the soul is enabled to see the deeper meaning of the Qur'ānic verses, 'God hath created you and what ye do' (37: 96), and 'thou didst not throw when thou threwest [the stones], but God threw' (8: 17).[80]

To return to the kind of 'vision' that is made possible by the *dhikr*, the very title of one of Ibn al-'Arabī's treatises, *Kitāb al-fanā' fi'l-mushāhada* (The Book of Extinction in Contemplation), appears to point to the Imam's paradox of forgetting in the very bosom of remembrance, for being extinguished in contemplation can be seen as akin to the state of being forgotten in invocation. At the outset of this extremely important treatise, Ibn al-ʿArabī writes that the divine Reality is too elevated to be witnessed by the creaturely eye. The vision of God is impossible for as long as there subsists a 'trace of the condition of the creature in the eye of the witness'.[81] It is only towards the end of the treatise that this apparently insuperable barrier before the vision of God is removed. The problem is resolved by Ibn al-ʿArabī by means of the Prophet's definition of *iḥsān*, discussed in Chapter 1 above: 'It is to worship God as though you see Him, and if you see Him not, yet truly He sees you.' The Arabic wording is such that, by effecting a stop in the middle of the phrase 'if you see Him not (*in lam takun: tarāhu*)', the meaning is completely transformed into, 'if you are not, you see Him'.[82]

This vision of God cannot, then, pertain to the individual, who is 'forgotten' in the Imam's words, or non-existent according to Ibn al-ʿArabī. The vision of God can only be by God, not man. We will return to this possibility of 'ontological transference' and its metaphysical underpinnings in relation to the divine Names shortly. But here it is useful to reinforce the message of 'extinction in contemplation' by referring to the discourse as narrated by Ibn al-ʿArabī, which took place between him and Moses in the sixth heaven. This is presented by Ibn al-ʿArabī in his account of his own visionary ascent, his own spiritual *miʿrāj* through the heavens to the divine presence within his own soul.

> He addresses Moses: 'You requested the vision (of God), while the Messenger of God (Muḥammad) said that "not one of you will see his Lord until he dies."?'
>
> Moses replies: 'And it was just like that: when I asked Him for the vision, He answered me, so that I "fell down stunned" (7: 143).[83] Then I saw Him in my (state of) being stunned.'
>
> Ibn al-ʿArabī asks: 'While (you were) dead?'
>
> Moses: 'While (I was) dead ... I did not see God until I had died.'[84]

We have here a 'supra-personal vision', which is entirely congruent with Imam 'Alī's 'un-selfconscious remembrance'. What appears to be implicit in both types of spiritual assimilation is what was called above an 'ontological transference' of agency. The true vision of God cannot take place for as long as anything creaturely subsists in the 'eye' of the beholder. It is interesting to see how the spiritual principle (and even some of the language) of this dialogue is expressed in condensed fashion in a supplication attributed to the Imam. He pleads with God to make him 'one of those whom You have called and he has replied to You, upon whom You have glanced and who falls unconscious before Your majesty.'[85] It should be noted that the word, *ṣaʿiqa* ('to fall unconscious', 'be stunned'), which is used in this supplication is the same as that used in the verse of the Qur'ān (7: 143) in relation to Moses' state when God revealed Himself to the mountain. The one 'glance' of the Real is enough to precipitate this denouement of self-awareness, which is the shadow cast, on the plane of individual consciousness, by the fulgurating light of the self-disclosure, the *tajallī*, of God.

Also, to speak of this divine 'glance' (*lāḥiẓa*) takes us back to Ibn al-ʿArabī's evocative phrase 'extinction in contemplation'. In his *Tarjumān al-ashwāq*, he refers to the divine wisdom as a peacock which 'kills with her glances', and then adds, in his own commentary, that this refers to 'the station' of *al-fanā' fi'l-mushāhada* (extinction in contemplation).[86] Earlier in the same commentary on this poem, he refers to the 'murderous glances' of this divine wisdom 'which accrues to a man in his hours of solitude, and which assaults him with such violence that he is unable to behold his personality, and which exercises dominion over him.'[87] The commentary given on the following lines is also instructive in underlining the relationship between *dhikr* and *fanā'*: 'Wild is she, none can make her his friend; she has gotten in her solitary chamber (*bayt khalwatihā*), a mausoleum for remembrance (*dhikr*).' The commentary adds: ' … because contemplation of the Essence is a passing away (*fanā'*) … Her solitude is her looking on herself, for God says, "Neither My earth nor My heaven contains Me, but I am contained by the heart of My believing servant,"[88] and since the heart which contains this essential wisdom of the race of Jesus is bare and empty of all attributes, it is like a desert and she is like a wild animal.'[89]

Realization through remembrance, then, strictly implies the extinction of individual consciousness. This principle is far from being purely speculative or theoretical. Quite apart from the wealth of Sufi literature on the states of consciousness (*aḥwāl*, sing. *ḥāl*) into which the mystic passes, we have the following evidence of the Imam's own immersion within such states. Abu'l-Dardā', an eminent companion of the Prophet, reported that he once saw 'Alī lying down in one of the palm orchards of Medina. His body seemed completely lifeless, as stiff as wood. He went to condole with 'Alī's family, but was told by his wife, Fāṭima, 'My cousin [that is, 'Alī, her 'cousin' by virtue of being the cousin of the Prophet] has not died. Rather, in fear of God he has fainted. This condition overcomes him often.'[90] The 'fear' in question here is evidently to be understood in the sense of 'awe', and is to be related to the heavenly aspect of *khawf*—heavenly because Paradise is said to be the consequence of realizing to perfection the kind of fear in question—indicated by the Qur'ān: 'But whoso feareth (*khāfa*) the station of his Lord and restraineth his soul from caprice, verily, the Garden will be his abode' (79: 40–41). 'Fear of God', in the spiritual and not moralistic sense of the term, does not so much terrify as beatify, it produces not simply quaking awe in the face of the transcendent Absolute, but also intimate absorption within the immanent divine presence. As is oft quoted in Sufism, when one fears creatures one flees from them, but when one fears God one flees *to* Him. 'There is no refuge from God except [fleeing] to Him' (9: 118), as the Qur'ān puts it.

This report also shows that the following saying of the Imam is not just extravagant rhetoric; rather, it appears to allude to an authentic state of spiritual intoxication, and a total re-absorption of consciousness within its divine source: that is, a description of the conditions leading up to the experience of the state which 'overcomes him often', as Fāṭima put it:

> Truly, God has a drink for His friends (*awliyā'ihi*). When they drink it, they are intoxicated (*sakarū*); and when they are intoxicated, they are enraptured (*ṭarabū*); and when they are enraptured, they are blessed (*ṭābū*); and when they are blessed they dissolve (*dhābū*); and when they dissolve, they are free (*khalaṣū*); and when they are free, they

> devote themselves purely (*akhlaṣū*); and when they devote themselves purely, they seek (*ṭalabū*); and when they seek, they find (*wajadū*); and when they find, they arrive (*waṣalū*); and when they arrive, they are at one (*ittaṣalū*); there is no difference between them and their Beloved.[91]

This saying of the Imam evokes that of the Prophet who claimed that he had states or 'moments' (*waqt*), which no 'angel brought close' nor 'prophet sent forth' could encompass[92]—the implication being that neither angel nor prophet can subsist as such in the ineffable 'moments' of absolute *tawḥīd*, which is not 'union', it must be stressed: it is, rather, the realization of oneness. For union implies two entities becoming one, whereas God is, as the Imam put it, 'that which has no second'. This ultimate realization of *tawḥīd* can be seen as the fruit of the invocation—the most potent of all intoxicating 'drinks', if prayer be described as drink—and leads one to take careful note of the true agent of the invocation, the true 'drinker'. For what appears to be man's invocation of God is transformed into the divine invocation of man; whereas at the outset it appears that man 'drinks' God through His Name, the ultimate result of the invocation—unitive realization—reveals that, in fact, it is God who 'drinks into Himself' the essence of the consciousness of man, an essence from which the impurity of self-consciousness has been extracted. The true nature of the *dhikr*, masked by the outward form of man's invocation of God, is alluded to in another saying of the Imam: 'The invocation is not a formality of speech nor a way of thinking; rather, it comes forth firstly from the Invoked, and secondly from the invoker (*awwal min al-madhkūr wa thānin min al-dhākir*).'[93]

It is thus God Himself who performs the invocation, first and foremost; man's invocation is but a shadow, a reflection or a consequence of this divine invocation. The polyvalence of the Imam's short sentence can give rise to a number of fruitful meditations on the meaning, the origin, the end and the very substance of the *dhikr*. Among other things, one recalls here the Qur'ānic verse cited above, 'Remember Me, I will remember you.'

Before addressing one of the metaphysical implications of the fact that God is Himself the Invoker, it is important to take cognisance of how this perception of the reality of the invocation reveals more clearly its spiritual efficacy. For the reality denoted by the term *dhikr* is no longer confined within the boundaries of the individual, still less is it definable in terms of his verbal or mental activity. Instead, what is meant by *dhikr* in its primary, metaphysical significance, opens out into the realm of engendering, implying the function of existentiation, the effusion of Being. The creative Word uttered by God, 'Be! (*kun*)', which brings into existence the possibilities of being, can be seen in this light as a form of *dhikr*: God utters the 'name' of the possible thing, 'calling' it from non-existence into existence. This passage from nothingness to being is what renders the possible thing 'remembered', *madhkūr*. Here, again, the Imam's sentence can be read as a commentary on a Qur'ānic verse, as well as an anticipation of the highly elaborate cosmogony associated with Ibn al-ʿArabī.

The Qur'ān poses the following question: 'Hath there come upon man any moment in time when he was not a thing remembered?' (76: 1). Man's being a 'thing remembered' is here tantamount to his coming into being, and his nothingness is equivalent to his being 'not remembered'—that is, not yet called forth from the abysm of pre-existential hiddenness into the light of manifest existence. In this pre-existential state, the human being is, according to Ibn al-ʿArabi, 'known', *maʿlūm*, but only by God. He refers to the above verse in the following lines of *al-Futūḥāt al-makkiyya* (*The Meccan Illuminations*):

> God said of Himself that He is *al-Badīʿ*, the Originator, that is, He created that which had no like/exemplar in all the degrees of being, for He knows, by His all-encompassing nature, every single thing that enters into the degrees of being. Therefore He says, as regards the creation of man, that he 'was not a thing remembered', for His is the remembrance ... so a thing has being in the remembrance of the one who remembers it.[94]

God's 'remembrance' of man thus precedes, ontologically and not just temporally, man's remembrance of God, this constituting another interpretation of the verse cited earlier, '...and the remembrance of God is greater', infinitely greater, that is, than man's remembrance of Him. The true being of man resides in the 'remembrance' that

God has of him. While man's devotion to God is articulated by the utterance of the divine Name, God's creation of man is articulated by His utterance of the creative Word. In Ibn al-ʿArabī's cosmogony, the utterance of this Word is not simply an event in time; rather, that Word never ceases to reverberate, furnishing each human soul with its divine substrate, support or foundation, its *mustanad ilāhī*. This Word 'breathes' existence upon the immutable entity, *al-ʿayn al-thābita* which, though inexistent in itself, determines the contours, the form, the configuration of being that will be manifested through it—just as a prism refracts the light that passes through it, or just as water takes on the colour of the cup, an image used by Junayd and often quoted by Ibn al-ʿArabī.[95]

It is also of interest to note that the *ḥadīth al-ḥaqīqa*, attributed to Imam ʿAlī, contains the essence of the Akbarī doctrine of the *tajallī* of the unique Light of God upon the differentiated 'receptacles', the loci of manifestation for that Light. The Imam is questioned by his disciple, Kumayl, on the meaning of *al-ḥaqīqa*. The response includes the following affirmations:

> *Al-ḥaqīqa* is the unveiling of the splendours of Majesty, without any allusion ... the effacement of that which is erroneously imagined (*al-mawhūm*), together with the clarity of that which is truly known (*al-maʿlūm*) ... the attraction of absolute unicity to the quality of *tawḥīd* ... a light dawning from the morn of eternity, its traces shimmering on the temples of *tawḥīd* ...

Al-Kāshānī comments on this last image: 'That is, the manifestation of the Light of the one Essence ... upon the loci of manifestation of the qualities of the Real, the Essence, these being the loci of the entities of existents (*aʿyān al-mawjūdāt*), which the Imam calls "temples of *tawḥīd*", that is, the forms of the divine Names in the station of *tawḥīd*.'[96] This *mustanad ilāhī* or divine support of each individual soul, then, is its particular Lord, the divine Name that engenders and sustains it. The soul is but the locus of manifestation, the *maẓhar*, where God discloses Himself in a particular, unique mode.

The following are the very first words of the *khuṭba* with which Ibn al-ʿArabī begins the *Futūḥāt al-makkiyya*: 'Praise be to Him who engendered things from nothing, then negated it; and established their being through the orientation towards them of His Words.'[97] This orientation (*tawajjuh*) of the divine Word towards the possible thing results in the manifestation of the properties of the Word in accordance with the receptivity of the possible thing; the possibility is then 'breathed' into existence, and becomes akin to a 'body', the 'heart' of which is the divine Name existentiating it: '... every slave has a Name which is its Lord; so it becomes the "body" of that Name, which is its "heart".'[98]

This analogy recalls the Imam's image of the *dhikr* as a 'polish' for hearts. The Name revealed from 'above' is mirrored by a Name that resounds from 'within'. The reciprocal reflection appears when the rust that obscures the surface of the heart is removed by the polish of the *dhikr*. A mode of union between two divine realities is evoked here, which again reminds one of the phrase 'light upon light'.

Earlier we saw that the Imam referred to the Names of God 'which have filled the foundations of all things'; this clearly foreshadows Ibn al-ʿArabī's conception of the divine Names as the supports or substrata of all things. But there arises a question here, the answers to which might help to take us another step closer to comprehending the powerful and mysterious efficacy of the *dhikr*. What is the difference between the divine Names, conceived as the metaphysical roots of all things, and the particular Names of God as revealed in the Qurʾān? For, on one hand, the whole of creation is the 'Book of God', all phenomena being so many 'words' of God; and on the other, the revealed text contains specific words and Names, and it is these that are to be recited and invoked. Why? One clear answer to this question is given in the following verse: 'Call upon Allāh or call upon *al-Raḥmān*. By whatever Name you call upon Him, His are the most beautiful Names' (17: 110). The Qurʾān itself enjoins the believers to invoke these specific, revealed Names, and not others. These Names, therefore, are totally unlike the names of the idolators' gods: 'They are but names that ye have named, ye and your fathers, for which God hath revealed no authority' (53: 23).

Names of idols are similar to conventional names of phenomena in that they are only arbitrary labels or signs with no intrinsic relationship with the phenomena themselves, let alone the principles of those phenomena. By contrast, the Names of God, revealed by God, are penetrated by the very substance of that reality which they denote; therefore, these Names do have 'authority' (*sulṭān*), by virtue of which they have the power to transform and not just inform. They are, in other words, impregnated with a theurgic power, the capacity to render present to one's mind and heart the immanent reality of God. Though God's presence is inalienable—for nothing existent can possibly be situated 'outside' of His all-encompassing presence—nonetheless, this presence can become veiled, at least subjectively. The heart can be veiled from God by the 'rust' of forgetfulness covering it, such that the divine Reality comes to be 'veiled' by the very phenomena which manifest it. As was noted earlier, the Imam challenges us to think of how it is 'by things' that the Creator manifests Himself, and yet it is also 'by things' that He is hidden from sight.

This being the case, what is needed to open oneself up to the divine presence within and beyond all things is both a polishing, by the *dhikr*, of one's own 'within' and an unveiling or revelation from that 'beyond'. This latter form of disclosure can be viewed as a direct revelation of God within that indirect revelation of Him that consists in the entirety of the created cosmos, which both reveals and veils the divine Reality.[99] Even if, from a certain point of view, the two 'revelations', cosmic and scriptural, are both defined as manifestations of God, from another point of view, the scriptural revelation is charged with a spiritual power that renders it incomparably more 'revealing' than the created cosmos. There is no common measure, in respect of spiritual method, between the cosmos as the manifested divine 'Word', and Allāh as a revealed Name of God. On one hand there is differentiated manifestation, and on the other, a unique revelation. One might also say that the divine Name is the quintessential manifestation, at once summing up the whole realm of manifestation *and* transcending it. The difference between cosmic manifestation and scriptural revelation might be seen in one respect[100] as analogous to that between shadow and light. Revelation is like a projection of the pure Light of God, and, therefore, it is of one substance with the source whence it emanates, whereas manifestation is like the shadow cast by that light. Both are projections of one and the same reality, but this does not diminish the incommensurability between light and darkness.[101] In the words of Ibn al-ʿArabi, 'The very Being of the Real is a verified Light, the very existence of creation is a shadow following after.'[102]

There is a remarkable supplication attributed to Imam 'Alī, the *Du'ā' al-Mashlūl*, 'supplication of the lame man'.[103] It consists of 122 verses containing a multitude of divine Names, attributes and titles. Towards the end of the supplication one reads a verse which can be taken as the key to the entire text: 'I ask Thee by every Name with which Thou hast named Thyself'.[104] It is the fact that God 'names Himself' that imparts to His Names their theurgic power, their sacramental substance, their mystical efficacy. It is the revealed substance of the Names that accounts for these distinctive properties, and which renders them incomparable to other names. It is for this reason that, as is so commonly asserted in Sufi texts, the Name is the Named (*al-ism huwa'l-musammā*).[105]

These observations on the ontological relationship between the Names of God and the nature of being, while helping to explain certain aspects of the *dhikr* as a mystical practice, nonetheless fall short of accounting for that ontological leap of consciousness, that extinction of self-awareness, to which the Imam refers in the words, 'you will not remember Him according to the true reality of the remembrance until you forget your own soul in your remembrance'. Why and how, it may be asked, does the *dhikr* produce this extinction of consciousness, or this effacement of individual being, especially since the function of *dhikr* appears to be the very opposite, that is, to actualize or precipitate a heightened mode of consciousness, and to enhance or deepen one's quality of being?

The first point to be made by way of response is this: the individual is unable on his own to make this leap from remembrance to forgetfulness. It is impossible for a conscious person, concentrating on the invocatory act, to make himself unconscious of himself *during* his invocation. It is to be noted carefully that the Imam says that the soul is to be forgotten '*in*' the remembrance. Any effort to will oneself into a state of unconsciousness emanates from a conscious will, and thus entrenches, rather than effaces, self-consciousness.[106] So it cannot be a question here of forcing oneself to forget oneself whilst invoking God; it is, rather, an effort of total concentration on the Name, an attempt to be so focused on the Name that there is no 'space', mentally or existentially, for anything but the Named, the reality being invoked. A certain initial degree of self-effacement can thus be seen as a concomitant of total concentration. But the ultimate consummation of self-effacement in *fanā'* comes about as a divine grace, as something that surpasses all individual effort, even if the act of invocation is deemed to attract this grace—or to remove from the heart the 'rust' that obscures the vision of one's nothingness in the face of the sole reality of God, 'that which has no second'.

This part of the response to the question posed above can be summed up by an esoteric reading of the words of the Qur'ān, ' ... thou wilst not forget, unless God willeth it so' (87: 6–7).[107] It is also noteworthy that al-Kalābādhī, author of one of the most important early manuals of Sufism, begins his chapter on *dhikr* with these words, which echo those of the Imam: 'The *ḥaqīqa* of the *dhikr* is this: that you forget everything other than the *madhkūr* (the Invoked) in the *dhikr*. For He says: "So remember thy Lord when thou hast forgotten" (18: 24). That is, when you have forgotten what is not God, then you have remembered God.'[108]

The second response to the question above can be framed in terms of the principle of inverse analogy. That is, the human invocation is analogous to the divine invocation, being, as was said earlier, a kind of reflection thereof; and, like any reflected image, the human act of invocation positively participates in what it reflects but also inverts it.[109] In the first respect, the human act of invocation leads to a greater plenitude of consciousness and a fuller participation in being for the invoker; while in the second respect, the human invocation finds its consummation in the apparent opposite: the effacement of the individual in the object invoked. But this is only apparently opposed to the enhancement of consciousness and being: in reality it is the fulfilment of that process, but the last stage of the process involves a quantum leap, the negation of the limits constituted by individuality as such. Insofar as the individual is limited, and insofar is limitation is a negation, the negation of this negation is tantamount to pure affirmation, or the affirmation of unconditional, supra-individual being. This negation of negation, on the plane of the self, can be seen as the reflection of that negation of nothingness referred to by Ibn al-'Arabī in the line quoted above: 'Praise be to Him who engendered things from nothing, then negated it.' In this connection it is worth recalling this enigmatic saying of the Imam, cited earlier: 'I am the death of the dead'.[110] This recalls the words which Rūmī has the Imam utter, in the following renowned lines of his *Mathnawī*:

> He said, 'I am wielding the sword for God's sake, I am the servant of God, I am not under the command of the body.
>
> I am the Lion of God, I am not the lion of my passion: my deed bears witness to my religion.
>
> In war I am (manifesting the truth of) *thou didst not throw when thou threwest*: I am (but) as the sword, and the wielder is the (divine) Sun.
>
> I have removed the baggage of self out of the way, I have deemed (what is) other than God to be non-existence.
>
> I am a shadow, the Sun is my lord; I am the chamberlain, I am not the curtain (which prevents approach) to Him.
>
> I am filled with the pearls of union, like a (jewelled) sword: in battle I make (men) living, not slain.[111]

In other words, whereas the cosmic unfolding of creation—the movement from God to man—requires the negation of that relative nothingness[112] which is pregnant with the possibilities of being, the realization of God by man requires the negation of that same 'nothingness' that was breathed into being by God. Returning to Ibn al-ʿArabī's treatise *Extinction in Contemplation*, what is in question here is 'the extinction of that which never was ... and the subsistence of that which never ceased to be'.[113] The following verses of the Qurʾān are clearly implied: 'Everything thereon perisheth (*fān*), and there subsisteth (*yabqā*) only the Face of thy Lord, possessor of glory and bounty' (55: 26–27).

But all things, insofar as they exist, have two aspects, or 'faces', as noted above: the divine aspect, which is the true being of the thing, and the created aspect, which is 'nothing'. Thus, the 'Face' of the Lord which alone subsists is not simply the divine Reality above and beyond all things, but also the same reality within all things. This is the import of al-Ghazālī's esoteric commentary on the Qurʾānic verse, 'Everything perisheth except His Face' (28: 88).[114] Al-Ghazālī comments:

> [It is] not that it perisheth at some particular moment, but rather it is forever perishing, since it cannot be conceived except as perishing. For each thing other than God is, when considered in and by itself, pure nothingness; and if considered from the *face* (*wajh*) to which existence flows to it from the Prime Reality, it is viewed as existing, but not in itself, solely from the *face* which accompanies Him Who gives it existence. Therefore, the divine *face* is the sole thing in reality.[115]

He then relates the mystical realization of this oneness to the invocation of God, and to the forgetting of the self in the invocation. In doing so, he provides a valuable commentary on the meaning of this total denouement of self-consciousness. The Sufis who verify this oneness through mystical 'taste' (*dhawq*), he writes, are 'drowned in oneness', such that they become 'dumbfounded':

> No capacity remained within them save to recall Allāh; yea, not so much as the capacity to recall their own selves ... when this state prevails, it is called in relation to him who experiences it Extinction, nay Extinction of Extinction, for the soul has become extinct to itself, extinct to its own extinction; for it becomes unconscious of itself and unconscious of its own unconsciousness, since were it conscious of its own unconsciousness, it would be conscious of itself.[116]

The following statement attributed by al-Qushayrī to Abū 'Uthmān, should also be noted in this context, as it helps to shed light on another aspect of the 'unconsciousness' realized through the invocation: 'Whoever has not tasted the loneliness of unconsciousness will not find the food of the intimacy of remembrance.'[117] Here, losing consciousness of oneself is equated with 'loneliness', while becoming fully conscious of God through invocation results in 'intimacy'. In other words, one cannot find true intimacy with the divine Reality except through depriving the self of its false 'intimacy', that is, its intimate self-satisfaction, that habitual self-centredness which is the shadow cast by self-awareness: it is this awareness of self—to return to the Imam's statement—that must be forgotten. This higher forgetfulness cannot arise except on the basis of the remembrance of God, for it is the source of Being, unconditional Consciousness and eternal Life that, alone, is capable of extinguishing, eclipsing or effacing the relative existence, partial consciousness and apparent life of the individual. This, the *ḥaqīqa* of the *dhikr*, is expressed succinctly in the simple expression of the Imam, '... forget your own soul in your remembrance'.

The state of *fanā'*, the ultimate degree of 'forgetting' of oneself, is therefore a grace; it cannot be attained by the individual, however much effort the individual may exert, as was seen earlier. But this does not imply any abandonment of effort on the part of the invoker. On the contrary, as is abundantly attested in the Sufi tradition, *fanā'* is closely linked with the practice of *dhikr*, being its climax. Subsequent to this state or *ḥāl*, of extinction, there is the station, or *maqām*, of subsistence, *baqā'*, that is, a return of consciousness to the self, a self now transfigured by the knowledge of reality impressed on the soul in the state of *fanā'*.[118] For it is only in the state of *fanā'* that the ultimate 'vision' is attained of absolute oneness, wherein there is no room for the ontological duality that is the inescapable concomitant of the condition of individuality. To posit the 'individual' is to posit its correlate, the Lord, and thus to affirm duality.

This is expressed by al-Kāshānī in his commentary on the Qur'ānic verse, 'Remember Him as He hath guided you' (2: 198). He refers to the guided ascent through the degrees of the *dhikr*. The first is the *dhikr* of the tongue, which corresponds to the soul (*al-nafs*); then that of the heart (*al-qalb*) which corresponds to the divine acts, those which manifest His graces; then that of the 'secret' (*al-sirr*), corresponding to the vision of the divine acts, together with the 'unveiling of the sciences of the manifestation of the divine qualities'; then that of the spirit (*al-rūḥ*), corresponding to 'the contemplation of the lights of the manifestations of the divine qualities, with an apprehension of the light of the Essence'; then comes the *dhikr* of 'the hidden' (*al-khafī*), which is 'the contemplation of the beauty of the Essence along with the subsistence of duality'; finally, comes the *dhikr* of the Essence, 'which is essential vision, attained through the removal of duality.'[119]

The same point is made in the following counsel of Ibn 'Aṭā'illāh, which brings to light the manner in which the *dhikr* generates receptivity to the divine presence and to the grace by which, alone, the individual can truly 'forget' himself, in the sense of becoming 'unconscious of his own unconsciousness' as Ghazālī put it:

> Do not abandon the invocation because you do not feel the Presence of God therein. For your forgetfulness *of* the invocation of Him is worse than your forgetfulness *in* the invocation of Him. Perhaps He will take you from an invocation with forgetfulness (*ghafla*) to one with vigilance (*yaqaẓa*), and from one with vigilance to one with the Presence of God (*ḥuḍūr*), and from one with the Presence of God to one wherein everything but the Invoked (*al-Madhkūr*) is absent. 'And that is not difficult for God' [emphasis added].[120]

In his commentary on the *Ḥikam*, Ibn ʿAjība adds: 'So, in the measure that one is extinguished in the Name, one is extinguished in the Essence.'[121] This is because, as mentioned above, the Name is the Named. In another treatise, a commentary on a poem by Shūshtarī on the divine Name Allāh, he states more explicitly this cardinal tenet of the invocatory discipline in Sufism. The first line of the poem reads, in reference to the letters of which Allāh is composed: 'The *alif* before two *lām*s, then a *hā*': coolness of the eyes.' Ibn ʿAjība comments: 'The "coolness of the eyes", this is joy, for tears of joy, as one knows by experience, are cool. The author means this: this Name is the joy of my heart, its happiness, its beatitude.' He then cites some lines from al-Ḥallāj on the letters of the Name Allāh, adding one verse of his own, and then this comment: 'The Name is not other than the Named, for joy cannot come from anything but the essence [of a thing], not from the name [as such].'[122]

This summarizes the doctrine of the identity between the Name and the Named, the rationale for the Sufi practice of *dhikru'Llāh*. But here, we encounter a certain problem. However congruent the Imam's pronouncements on the *dhikr* may be with these later Sufi expressions of the principles underlying the practice of *dhikr*, this particular stress on the identity between the Name and the Named appears, on the surface, contrary to the numerous sayings of the Shiʿi Imams which deny that the Name is the Named. For example, Imam Jaʿfar al-Ṣādiq is reported as saying:

> The Name of Allāh is other than Him. For everything to which the name of a thing is applicable is a creation, hence other than God. For whatever the tongue expresses, or is worked on by the hand, is a creation ... everything described is created, and the Creator of things cannot be described within the limits of a named object.[123]
>
> Allāh has ninety-nine Names. If the Name were the Named, then every one of the Names would be a god. But Allāh is the one meaning (or: spiritual reality, *maʿnā*) indicated by the Names, and all of them are other than Him.[124]

This apparent contradiction can be resolved in two ways. First, we should take careful note of exactly what is meant by the word 'Name' in the two contexts: that of doctrinal distinction, in terms of which the Absolute is to be rigorously distinguished from the relative, the Essence from all forms; and that of methodic concentration in which the Absolute is deemed to be the reality of the form by which it, the Absolute, reveals itself. Then we can turn to one of the most esoteric aspects of the Shiʿi Imams' conception of themselves, that is, their reference to their own selves as the 'most beautiful Names' (*al-asmāʾ al-husnā*).

First, as regards what is meant by 'Name', one can turn to Ibn al-ʿArabī for a precise definition: '[T]he Names have two connotations; the first connotation is God Himself who is what is named, the second that by which one Name is distinguished from another ... As being essentially the other, the Name is the Reality, while as being not the other, it is the imagined Reality.'[125] In other words, each Name is, on the one hand, identified with every other Name, by virtue of its essential identity with the Named, the one Essence, the source of all the Names; on the other hand, it has its own specific meaning and quality, the relationship by virtue of which the one Reality engages with the created cosmos. In this latter respect, each Name is distinguished from the other Names, and distinction implies limitation, hence relativity and, ultimately, a kind of illusion before the one and only Reality; it is in this manner that the Name assumes the nature of 'imagined Reality'. The Names, in Ibn al-ʿArabī's perspective, have no specific ontological entities; they all revert to the self-same, one and only Reality, that of the divine Essence. This resolves the problem of the different Names implying different 'gods', as raised earlier in the saying of Imam Ja'far.

In the lexicon of Sufi terms, *Laṭā'if al-i'lām fī ishārāt ahl al-ilhām* (*Subtle Disclosures in the Allusions of the Folk of Inspiration*), attributed to al-Kāshānī, one finds a definition of the divine Names which also helps to distinguish between these two connotations. Under the term 'Names of the Divinity', we read as follows:

> These are, in the terminology of the Sufis, expressive of the manifest aspect of being, in respect of its determination within a specific meaning. For every divine Name is the manifest aspect of being, which, in turn, is identical to the Essence, but not such as it is in itself, rather, in respect of its specification and determination within a particular meaning—or one might say 'quality'. For example, the Name *al-Ḥayy* ('The Living') is a Name of manifest, determined being, but in respect of its specification and determination as a particular meaning, it is Life. So in regard to being itself, *al-Ḥayy* is identical to the Essence, whilst in regard to its determination as a particular meaning, it is other than the Essence. If you have understood what we have said, you will know the meaning of their [i.e., the Sufis'] saying: the Name is not identical to the Essence, the Named, neither is it other than It.[126]

There is a nominal and cognitive distinction between the Name and the Named, in terms of which the Name is not the Named; but at the same time, there is a spiritual assimilation between the Name and the Named, such that the Name *is* the Named.[127] Following on from this, there is a further distinction to be taken into account: the verbal form of the Name is to be distinguished from the Name *qua* attribute of the Essence. On the one hand, the Name in this latter sense is nothing but the divine attribute it designates, and this in turn is identical to the Essence; on the other hand, there is the 'name' of this Name, which is but a verbal form. This distinction is brought to light by Qayṣarī, another key commentator of Ibn al-'Arabī. In the introduction to his commentary on the *Fuṣūṣ al-ḥikam* (which is a major work in its own right, a masterly and succinct exposition of the essential elements of the Akbarī perspective as a whole) he writes:

> The Essence, considered along with a determined quality, and in relation to one of Its theophanies, is named by a Name; so 'The Compassionate' has an essence, which is compassion; 'The All-Conquering' has an essence, which is all-conquering power. These spoken Names are Names of Names; from this it can be understood what is meant by the saying: The Name is identical to the Named.[128]

In his own, monumental, commentary on Qayṣarī's introduction, Jalāl al-Dīn Āshtiyānī, a contemporary authority on Shi'i 'Irfān, makes the following important observation after citing the above passage, an observation which brings the discussion back to the principle of extinction through the invocation of the Name, and also to the second point referred to above, that is, the Imams themselves constituting the 'most beautiful Names'. Āshtiyānī writes that the saints frequently refer to the Names as being one with the Named because they are implicitly referring to the referent (*miṣdāq*), which is the *ṣifa*, the divine attribute or quality: 'The *ṣifāt* are in one respect the specifications of the Essence, while in the station of unicity they are annihilated in the Essence, and are [thus] identical to the Essence.'[129]

This metaphysical conception of the relationship between the Name, the *ṣifa* and the Essence can be seen as mirroring, objectively and universally, the path traced subjectively and mystically, by the soul extinguished in and by the invocation of the Name. Just as the *ṣifāt* are 'annihilated' in the Essence—with which they are thus absolutely and unconditionally one—so the soul extinguished by the Name attains at one and the same time its total nullification *and* its ultimate realization, but then no longer *qua* individual soul. It is only by virtue of the divine theophany or the particular divine Name—the 'heart' that constitutes the true being of the soul, its *mustanad ilāhī*—that this 'extinction' on the plane of the individual soul is tantamount to 'realization' on the plane of transcendence. The deepest reality of *tawḥīd* is revealed: the individual no longer affirms the notion that 'there is no god but God', for the individual has been extinguished by the reality that 'there is no reality but the one and only Reality'. God is 'that which has no second'. Just as 'No one has truly said Allāh but Allāh',[130] likewise, no one realizes God but God. It is God alone who comes to 'know' or 'be' Himself, this constituting one aspect of the purpose of creation, as indicated in the *ḥadīth qudsī* cited earlier: 'I was a hidden treasure and I loved to be known.'

In this light the saints (*al-awliyā'*) can be seen as perfectly self-realized theophanies,[131] thus, as totally effaced in That of which they are theophanic manifestations, their very effacement in the divine Reality being the ultimate source of their knowledge of that Reality. Needless to say, this applies, *a fortiori*, to the Prophet himself, the prototype of all the saints, being the 'perfect man', *al-insān al-kāmil*. In this connection, Sabziwārī cites the saying of Imam 'Alī, 'We are the most beautiful Names', in his commentary on the divine Names: 'There is no doubt that they [the Imams] are His most exalted indicators and His greatest signs (*'alā'imihi'l-'uẓmā wa āyātihi'l-kubrā*), as the Prophet said, God bless him and his family, "Whoso sees me has seen the Truth (*al-Ḥaqq*)."'[132] He proceeds to equate the spiritual station or inner reality of the Imams with those of the divine Names and attributes, stressing that the divine Essence transcends all Names and attributes, and is forever ineffable, known only to itself. The Prophet, the Imam, the saint, the 'perfect man', thus manifest those aspects of the divine nature that can be perceived on the human plane. The more the divine Essence is exalted in transcendence above all Names and attributes, the more fulgurating is the reflection of those Names and attributes in the mirror constituted by the 'perfect man'. The unknowable transcendence of the hidden 'treasure' is, to some degree, compensated by the faithful reflection of the communicable aspects of that treasure in the 'friend of God'.

It is worth dwelling, in conclusion, on the implications of identifying the Imam with the divine Name or attribute; for in one respect this identification would appear to be *shirk*, the 'association' of a creature, however exalted his status, with the transcendent Reality. The same applies with regard to the ecstatic utterances (*shaṭḥiyyāt*) of many of the most famous Sufis, such as the *anā'l-Ḥaqq* ('I am the Real') of al-Ḥallāj, and the *subḥānī* ('Glory to me') of Bāyazīd.[133] However, when one adopts a viewpoint that is formed by the conception of the divine attributes offered by the Imam, a very different picture emerges, one which, far from being tainted by *shirk*, in fact rejoins the most profound application of *tawḥīd*. The first sermon of the *Nahj al-balāgha* contains, as we have seen, the following remarkable and highly important statements in regard to the attributes of God:

> The perfection of purification (*ikhlāṣ*) is to divest Him of all attributes (*ṣifāt*) because of the testimony of every attribute that it is other than the object of attribution, and because of the testimony of every such object that it is other than the attribute. So whoever ascribes an attribute to God—glorified be He!—has conjoined Him [with something else] and whoever so conjoins Him has made Him twofold, and whoever makes Him twofold has fragmented Him, and whoever thus fragments Him is ignorant of Him.[134]

When the Imam says that pure devotion to God requires divesting God of all attributes, the negation here is not of the divine attributes as such; rather, it is a negation of them as separate, autonomous or super-added realities, conceived of as being substantially 'other than' or ontologically distinct from, the Essence of God. For the reality of God's attributes is clearly affirmed in an earlier phrase in the same sermon, '*He whose attribute* has no binding limitation (*alladhī laysa li-ṣifatihi ḥadd maḥdūd*).' What is denied is the possibility of confining the reality of any attribute of God within the boundaries of human conception and language. Since no divine attribute can be distinct from the divine nature, and since this nature is infinite, it follows that every attribute is likewise of infinite scope and thus beyond all the limitations that are presupposed by formal conception and linguistic definition.

In one respect, then, the attribute or Name is to be affirmed, and in another respect, it is to be negated; affirmed as being not other than the Essence, negated insofar as it is conceived in itself, on its own account. Now this metaphysical perception of the relationship between the attribute/Name and the Essence can also be applied, mystically, to the relationship between the individual soul and the divine Reality. On its own account the individual is nothing, while in respect of the divine substrate, the divine Name, the *mustanad ilāhī* that constitutes its essential reality, it is not other than the unique Real. According to Ibn al-ʿArabī, 'The final end and ultimate return of the gnostics ... is that the Real is identical with them, while they do not exist.'[135] This is a perfect expression of the dual aspect of the soul of the realized sage: insofar as he is aware that 'he does not exist', he knows that the Real is his true identity. Thus, however paradoxical it may appear, the mystic's realization of absolute Reality goes hand in hand with his realization of his own non-existence. These two aspects of the self-same realization are elliptically expressed by Ibn al-ʿArabī. He describes the climax of his spiritual ascent, his *miʿrāj*, when he claims that God removed from him his 'contingent dimension (*imkān*)', resulting in the attainment of 'the inner realities of all the Names'. He continues:

> Thus I attained in this nocturnal journey the inner realities (*maʿānī*) of all the Names, and I saw them returning to One Subject (*musammā*) and One Entity (*ʿayn*): that Subject was what I witnessed and that Entity was my Being. For my voyage was only in myself and pointed to myself, and through this I came to know that I was a pure 'servant' without a trace of lordship in me at all.[136]

This passage helps explain what is meant by so many of the ecstatic utterances of the Sufis and the apparently self-deifying statements of the Imams. Their personal servitude to God, far from being denied, is indeed fully realized by the knowledge of their true identity: for this identity as the Named is attained only upon effacement of their individuality. Like the divine attributes, they are *mustahlak*, annihilated, in the divine Essence, so that there can be no question of any individualistic appropriation of the glory of God. When, therefore, the Imam appears to be speaking of his own greatness, it is to be understood that this is nothing but the greatness of God that is being expressed through him, as a *maẓhar*, a locus for the theophanic manifestation of the divine, and this, precisely in the measure of his own effacement in that greatness.

The same point is reinforced by what ʿAṭṭār recounts in his *Tadhkiratu'l-awliyā'* about Imam Jaʿfar al-Ṣādiq. A person accused him of being proud and Imam Jaʿfar replied: 'I am not proud, for pride pertains to the divine greatness. Since I have gone beyond the pride of self, His pride has come and taken the place of my own pride. With pride of self present, there can be no divine greatness, but through the divine greatness, pride will be present.'[137] The divine qualities shine with greater, not lesser, brilliance through the prism of the soul that has been rendered transparent to the divine Reality, such transparency being the result of the dissolution of all the clouds of egoism and passion.

Let us recall the holy utterance cited earlier: 'My slave draws near to Me through nothing I love more than that which I have made obligatory for him. My slave never ceases to draw near to Me through supererogatory acts (*nawāfil*) until I love him. And when I love him, I am his hearing by which he hears, his sight by which he sees, his hand by which he grasps, and his foot by which he walks.'

In the light of the above considerations, one can now resolve the paradox contained in this divine utterance. On the one hand, the most beloved thing to God appears to be the obligatory rites; on the other, it is the supererogatory rites that lead to the slave drawing near to God until He loves him, this love being apparently greater insofar as it results in the divine penetration of the human faculties, the unitive realization proper to *tawḥīd*. The paradox can be resolved, however, if one understands that God's 'love' for the obligatory rites is a love directed toward something apart from Himself, whereas when His love is for the 'slave'—the pure slave effaced in his Lord—this love is infinitely greater, insofar as it partakes of the love of God for His own Self-manifestation, thus for Himself. In the beginning, God 'loved to be known', hence He created the world. In 'knowing' Himself *through* the effaced slave, the apparent 'other', His love to be known is realized through the saint whose greatest glory is, precisely, his own effacement, poverty or emptiness of self.

It is in this sense that the following statement of the Imam is to be understood: 'Down from me torrents do pour; up to me no bird can soar.'[138] Torrents flow down from him because—and in the measure that—he is extinguished in the source of the torrent. This image recalls that given in the Qur'ān in its description of the 'slaves of God' who, unlike the 'righteous', drink directly from the celestial spring of Kāfūr identified ultimately with the divine Essence: 'Truly, the righteous shall drink from a cup flavoured with Kāfūr, a spring wherefrom the slaves of God drink, making it gush forth abundantly' (76: 5–6). These slaves cause the flow of the spring to increase because, according to al-Kāshānī, 'they are [themselves] the sources of this spring; there is no duality or otherness ... were it otherwise, it would not be the fountain of Kāfūr, because of the darkness of the veil of egoity (*anā'iyya*) and duality.'[139]

Thus, we return to the final degree of the *dhikr*, such as al-Kāshānī defined it above: the *dhikr* of the Essence, 'which is essential vision, attained through the removal of duality'. The *dhikr* 'polishes' away not just the impurities of the heart and mind, but ultimately, through the grace of the *madhkūr*, all taint of duality, including pre-eminently that postulate of duality, the individual as such. It removes all subtle or hidden *shirk*—the 'partners' in being that are non-existent before the One 'that has no second'—and establishes the spiritual principle of *tawḥīd*, such that the heart transfigured by the knowledge of the sole Reality comes to perceive the light of that Reality reflected in all the mirrors of the created realm. To realize—to 'make real' in the fullest sense—this one and only Reality is, by the same token, to realize the unreality, or the merely apparent reality, of everything else.

There is, at this level of realization, an inescapable degree of perplexity which accompanies the revelation of the divine Reality all around one. The elevation of the divine Essence beyond all comprehension makes all the more inescapable the utter annihilation of creaturely consciousness if that Essence is to be 'realized', if gnosis of it is to be attained. On the one hand, one 'knows' God by knowing that His Essence is unknowable, utterly other, utterly transcendent, the essence of the Creator being beyond the veil constituted by the creation itself; on the other hand, the very distinction between creature and Creator is effaced when the creature has 'forgotten' itself—not just notionally but existentially, in a state of authentic contemplative extinction. Then, it is no longer a question of one type of self-consciousness replacing another, but of the 'self' being taken out of the equation altogether, leaving only pure consciousness *per se*, which cannot 'belong' or pertain to any entity, on pain of being reduced to the relativity proper to that entity. Thus, consciousness of the Absolute, that is, 'being conscious *of* the Absolute', is transmuted into absolute consciousness, the Real being 'realized' not *by* another, but *through* another, whence the designation *al-ʿārif bi'Llāh*, literally, 'the knower *through* God' rather than simply the 'knower *of* God.' As we noted earlier, the Imam tells us, 'Know God through God'. Knowledge of God at this deepest level is the Real knowing itself through the creature, and to say 'through' implies an unimpeded passage, the creature being qualified by perfect *faqr*, poverty, self-effacement and, ultimately, extinction.

Realization through remembrance, however, implies not only 'forgetting' everything in existence except God, but also finding that, in reality, there is nothing but God in being. To return to the Imam's image of the 'polish' effected by the remembrance, the heart is rendered capable of 'seeing' and 'hearing', after being blind and deaf. The heart sees the Face of God wherever it looks, and hears the cosmic hymn of remembrance and praise chanted by the whole of creation. For: 'Wherever ye turn, there is the Face of God' (2: 115), and '...whosoever is in the Heavens and the earth praises God; and the birds in flight with outstretched wings—each knoweth its prayer and glorification' (24: 41).

We conclude this chapter with the following reflection on a passage from the Imam's famous and much disputed[140] *Khuṭbat al-bayān*, 'The Sermon of Clarifying Expression':

> I am the Sign of the All-Powerful. I am the gnosis of the mysteries. I am the Threshold of Thresholds. I am the companion of the radiance of the divine Majesty. I am the First and the Last, the Manifest and the Hidden. I am the Face of God. I am the mirror of God, the supreme Pen, the *Tabula secreta*. I am he who in the Gospel is called Elijah. I am he who is in possession of the secret of God's Messenger.[141]

This extraordinary affirmation of the Imam's inmost reality may appear shocking to the exoteric mentality, and is all too easily misunderstood as a blasphemous self-deification, *à la* Ḥallāj. One of the keys to unlocking the correct comprehension of these expressions of 'his' true nature is: 'I am the gnosis of the mysteries'. If this be understood, all the other statements fall into place naturally. For here, the Imam is identifying himself not with God, but with the *knowledge* of God—not with his own knowledge of God, for this would still be a relative knowledge, belonging to or attributed to himself as a relative being. It is only the knowledge itself—the knowledge that God has of Himself, and not the knowledge that man has of God—that can be fully identified with the object known. The distinctions between knowledge, knower and known are dissolved only at this transcendent level, just as the distinction between knowledge and being is no longer operative at this level of consciousness. Thus, the knower *is* the known when the knowledge in question is that consciousness which the divine Reality has of itself; and the consciousness within the individual has access to this knowledge solely on condition of the extinction of all trace of individual, creaturely consciousness. To 'remember' God, one must have 'forgotten' oneself. To 'be' the knowledge of God is, by way of metaphysical reverberation, to 'be' everything that God is, for the consciousness that is absolutely at one with the Absolute is nothing but 'the radiance of the divine Majesty'. Insofar as this consciousness is one with the 'gnosis of the mysteries', and these mysteries (*asrār*) are all rooted in the ultimate mystery (*al-sirr*), the one and only Essence of God, it is perforce one with all the divine attributes. It is thus that the Imam can proclaim 'I am the First and the Last, the Manifest and the Hidden'.

Analogous remarks can be made about the claim to be 'the Face of God' (*wajh Allāh*). This is only comprehensible on the basis of first understanding that the Imam refers to himself as the 'mirror' of God. The mirror loses its identity as mirror when one's attention is focused exclusively on the object reflected in it, that is, to the total exclusion of the mirror itself: the object alone is seen, the surface of the mirror becomes, as it were, invisible. Conversely, when the mirror is focused upon, the face in it can no longer be seen. Thus the mirror is identified with the object/Face that is projected upon it—and which, in a certain sense, is 'in' the mirror—without the mirror itself ceasing to be a mirror, and without the Face ceasing to be absolutely independent of the mirror.[142] The 'veil' is here the mirror itself: if one's attention is directed to it as such, this very orientation prevents one from seeing the object reflected in it, but once one's attention is riveted to the object whose image the mirror 'contains', the mirror ceases to be a veil and instead reveals the object itself. In terms of this symbolism, the forgetting of the mirror is tantamount to the effacement of the self, and focusing on the image within the mirror, to the remembrance of God.

But this leads to another paradox: the deepest effacement of individuality goes hand in hand with the most perfect expression of humanity. The 'friends of God', who know they are nothing in the face of the Absolute, are the ones who most faithfully reflect the divine Names and qualities, which belong not to them but to God. It is for this reason that the great saints and sages are also exemplars of the virtues, whose true foundations are the 'most beautiful Names' and attributes of God. The reflections of these divine attributes shine through them most clearly precisely because the mirrors of their hearts have been polished by the remembrance of God; and the most persistent stains—those imprinted by egotism—have been removed. The creativity of the saint is raised to the highest possible pitch precisely because the divine qualities reflected by the heart are no longer impeded, subjectively, by the individualistic coagulations that are generated by egotism; nor are they constrained, objectively, by the cosmic coagulations of this lower world. For such saints are the ones whose 'hearts are in the Gardens [of Paradise] while their bodies are at work'.[143]

Such souls have not only understood, but have also been seized existentially by the principle expressed in the Qur'ānic verse, 'And the life of this world is naught but sport and play; and truly, the abode of the Hereafter—that is true life' (29: 64). Thus, their instincts are always attuned to that higher reality. When Imam 'Alī was struck by the poisoned sword of Ibn Muljam, he instinctively uttered the cry, 'I have triumphed, by the Lord of the Ka'ba!'[144] At the very moment of death, there was nothing but the remembrance of God, and the Imam passed away, it is said, with his tongue repeating the words *lā ilāha illa'Llāh*. His death was thus consummated, just as his life had been lived, according to the wisdom of the Prophet, who, upon being asked what was the most meritorious of all acts, replied: '[That] you die while your tongue is moistened with the invocation of God.'[145]

NOTES

1. All the rites and practices associated with the chivalric orders in Islam 'were traced, without exception, back to the Prophet's son-in-law, 'Alī ibn Abī Ṭālib, establishing him as the supreme source of the virtues of *futūwwa*.' Muhammad Ja'far Mahjub, 'Chivalry and Early Persian Sufism', in Lewisohn, ed., *Heritage*, vol.1, p.552. S.H. Nasr writes in similar vein that 'Alī, having received the 'truth and power' of *futūwwa* from the Prophet, 'became the

supreme source of *futūwwa* in Islam for both Sunnis and Shi'ites … The personality of 'Alī, at once sage and knight, contemplative and protector of laborers and craftsmen, has continued to dominate through the centuries over the horizon of *futūwwa* as it has over much of Sufism.' See his 'Spiritual Chivalry', in Nasr, ed., *Islamic Spirituality*, vol.2, pp.305–306. Nasr also draws attention in this article to the organic relationship between *futūwwa* and the guilds (*aṣnāf*, sing. *ṣinf*) of craftsmen and artists which were established throughout the length and breadth of the Muslim world.

2. It is often said that the Naqshabandī *ṭarīqa* is the exception to this rule, tracing its descent from the Prophet through the first caliph, Abū Bakr, rather than through 'Alī. But it should be noted that this affiliation with Abū Bakr pertains only to one of its three principal *silsilas*. In his work, *al-Ḥadā'iq al-wardiyya fī ḥaqā'iq ajilla al-Naqshabandiyya*, (Damascus, 1306/1889), p.6, 'Abd al-Majīd b. Muḥammad al-Khānī, himself a Naqshabandī-Khālidī shaykh, refers to the first *silsila* (*al-silsilat al-ūlā*) as the 'golden chain', and this begins with 'Alī, proceeding through the Shi'i Imams until 'Alī b. Mūsā, then to Ma'rūf al-Karkhī and the other masters. The second *silsila* (*al-silsilatu'l-thāniya*) likewise begins with 'Alī and proceeds through Ḥasan al-Baṣrī. It is only the third *silsila*, which is called *al-silsilat al-ṣiddīqiyya* which proceeds from the Prophet to Abū-Bakr (*al-ṣiddīq*). (I am grateful to Professor Mahmut Kiliç for providing me with this reference.)

For an overview of the *ṭuruq*, see J. Spencer Trimingham, *The Sufi Orders in Islam* (Oxford, 1971); for deeper insights into the spiritual principles and contemplative disciplines of eight of the most important orders, see *Islamic Spirituality* (New York, 1991), ed. S.H. Nasr, vol.2, 'Manifestations', pp.3–193; and for a concise account of the orders, see John O. Voll's article 'Sufi Orders' in *The Oxford Encyclopedia of the Modern Islamic World* (New York–Oxford, 1994), ed. John L. Esposito, vol.4, pp.109–117.

3. This statement comes in his important essay, 'Shi'ism and Sufism: their Relationship in Essence and in History', in *Sufi Essays* (London, 1972), p.105. Corbin states succinctly the case for the influence of Shi'ism upon Sufism: The 'great themes' of Sufism, he writes, are those of Shi'ism: 'the polarity of *sharī'ah* and *ḥaqīqah*, *ẓāhir* and *bāṭin*, the idea of the cycle of *walāyah* in hierohistory following on the cycle of prophecy. The idea of the *quṭb* or mystical pole, in Sunnī Sufism is simply the translation of the Shiite idea of the Imām …' Corbin, *History of Islamic Philosophy*, p.191. One must not, however, pretend that the two traditions can be conflated; they may have identical roots and overlap in certain key areas, but they also have very different manifestations. Within the tradition of Shi'i 'Irfān, one should note in particular the distinctiveness

of the manifold functions attributed to the Imams, and the informal, highly secret initiatic relationships between master and disciple, shorn of the public organizational features (titles, hierarchies, distinctive dress, etc.) which characterize the principal Sunni Sufi orders.

4. See Corbin's *En Islam iranien*, vol.2, pp.154–155, 178–190, for this aspect of Āmulī's thought. For a contemporary account of 'Irfān from a Shi'i perspective, see the overview by Murtaḍā Muṭahharī, "Irfān: Islamic Mysticism", in his *Understanding Islamic Sciences* (London, 2002), pp.89–141. It is noteworthy that Muṭahharī's historical account of the origins of 'Irfān, and his biographical overview of the first *'urafā'*, or sages/gnostics within this tradition, differs very little from any standard Sufi history of the origins of Sufism.

5. Abu'l-Qāsim al-Junayd (d. 298/910) was himself regarded as 'the leader of this group [the Sufis] and their Imam (*sayyid hādhihi'l-ṭā'ifa wa imāmuhum*)', in the words of al-Qushayrī, *al-Risāla al-qushayriyya* (Cairo, 1995), p.78.

6. *Kashf al-maḥjūb* (Tehran, 1376 Sh./1997), a reprint of the critical edition by Zhukovskii (St. Petersburg, 1899; repr. Leningrad, 1926), p.84. This edition was referred to by Nicholson as being a 'much fuller text' than that translated by himself (Preface to the 2nd edition, London, 1936). The first sentence of the quotation from Hujwīrī is not found in Nicholson's edition (p.74). In connection with this important reference to 'Alī, Leonard Lewisohn makes the following pertinent remark: 'The definition of the practice of Sufism as consisting "entirely in the endurance of affliction," which Hujwīrī describes during his retelling of the life of 'Alī, was the probable inspiration behind Rūmī's later, quite similar opinion that "Sufism is finding delight at the descent of affliction". In his commentary on this Arabic verse of Rūmī, Nicholson admitted not knowing "to whom this definition of *taṣawwuf* is due"'. See Leonard Lewisohn, "Alī b. Abī Ṭālib's Ethics of Mercy in the Mirror of the Persian Sufi Tradition,' in Ali Lakhani, ed., *The Sacred Foundations of Justice in Islam* (Vancouver, forthcoming).

7. For a comprehensive and spiritually engaging biography of Ibn al-'Arabī, see Claude Addas, *Quest for the Red Sulphur*, tr. Peter Kingsley (Cambridge, 1993). For a wide-ranging evaluation of the influence of Ibn al-'Arabī see the series of articles by James Morris on 'Ibn Arabî and his Interpreters', in *Journal of the American Oriental Society*, vol.106 (1986), pp.539–551, pp.733–756; vol.107 (1987), pp.101–119; and Alexander Knysh, *Ibn 'Arabi in the Later Islamic Tradition: The Making of a Polemical Image in Medieval Islam* (Albany, NY, 1999).

8. As is clear from several verses in the Qur'ān itself. The word is also used in the Qur'ān as a description of the Prophet, as in the following: '... And God

hath revealed a reminder (*dhikrā*), a prophet reciting unto you the verses of God ...' (65: 10–11).

9. Al-Rāghib al-Iṣfahānī, *Mu'jam mufradāt alfāẓ al-Qur'ān* (Beirut, n.d.), p.181. See also the article '*Dhikr*' by L. Gardet in *EI2*, vol.2, pp.223–227.

10. All religious practices that, in one way or another, are connected with the function of making the divine Reality present to the mind—including prayer, supplication, recitation of the Qur'ān, incantation of formulae from the Qur'ān or the tradition, and as will be stressed in this essay, the repetitive invocation of a Name of God—can be assimilated to *dhikr* in this active, practical or operative sense.

11. The invocation can also involve a series of divine Names or formulae, such as *Lā ilāha illa'Llāh*, and the invocation can be uttered aloud (*dhikr jalī*) or else silently (*dhikr khafī*).

12. The practice of the invocation or jaculatory prayer is found in the most diverse religious traditions, and thus might be said to constitute, on the plane of religious practice, evidence of the inner unity of the religious traditions. See the remarkable citations on the practice of invocation drawn from traditions as diverse as ancient Greco-Roman religion and Judaism, Native American religion and Orthodox Christianity, Japanese Buddhism, Hinduism, Taoism and Islam, given by Whitall Perry in his *Treasury of Traditional Wisdom* (London, 1971), section entitled 'Colophon: Invocation', pp.1001–1042. For an insightful treatment of the invocation within the context of Islamic contemplative disciplines, See J.-L. Michon, 'The Spiritual Practices of Sufism', in S.H. Nasr, *Islamic Spirituality*, vol.1, *Foundations*, pp.265–293; and M.I. Waley, 'Contemplative Disciplines in Early Persian Sufism,' in Leonard Lewisohn, ed., *The Heritage of Sufism* (Oxford, 1999), vol.1, pp.497–548.

13. The Arabic comparative is at the same time the superlative, so the word *akbar* can be translated either way.

14. Cited in Al-Ghazālī: *Invocations and Supplications* (Book IX of *Iḥya 'ulūm al-dīn*), tr. K. Nakamura (Cambridge, 1990), p.8 (we have slightly modified the translation of the last sentence of the *ḥadīth*.) See the Arabic text of this and several other *ḥadīth*s of similar import in al-Ghazālī's *Iḥyā' 'ulūm al-dīn* (Beirut, 1992), vol.1, pp.391–392. The same *ḥadīth* is found in al-Kulaynī, *Uṣul*, vol.2, p.489.

15. *Ghurar* (Anṣārī), p.177, no.2537.

16. See, for numerous sayings referring to different forms of *dhikr*, the section entitled *Kitāb al-du'ā'* ('Book of Supplications') in al-Kulaynī, *Uṣūl*, vol.2, pp.457–567.

17. Ibid., vol.2, p.489. See also the dialogue between Imam Ja'far and one of his disciples, Abū Baṣīr, on the qualities distinguishing the Shi'is, as reported in al-Qāḍī al-Nu'mān, *Sharḥ al-akhbār fī faḍā'il al-a'immat al-aṭhār*, ed. Muḥammad al-Ḥusaynī al-Jalālī (Qom, 1409–12/1988–92), vol.3, pp.435–510, section entitled 'Ṣifāt shī'at Amīr al-mu'minīn'.

18. 'Allāma Ṭabāṭabā'ī, *Kernel of the Kernel Concerning the Wayfaring and Spiritual Journey of the People of Intellect* (Risāla-yi lubb al-lubāb dar sayr wa sulūk-i ulu'l-albāb): *A Shi'i approach to Sufism*, ed. Sayyid Muḥammad Ḥusayn Ḥusaynī-Tihrānī, tr. Mohammed H. Faghfoory (Albany, NY, 2003), p.105.

19. Cited in M. Lings, *A Sufi Saint of the Twentieth Century: Shaikh Aḥmad al-'Alawī* (London, 1971), pp.96–97.

20. Al-Ghazālī, *Iḥyā'*, pp.399–400. See Nakamura's translation, pp.21–22, in Al-Ghazālī, *Invocations*, which we have not followed.

21. The second oath of allegiance—that is, an oath additional to that by which the first believers pledged themselves to Islam—given by a small group of Muslims to the Prophet at Ḥudaybiyya, is taken by the Sufis as the prototype of their initiation into the spiritual path. For details on this incident, see Martin Lings, *Muhammad*, pp.252–256.

22. This point was well brought out by David Dakake in his paper, 'The Practice of *dhikr* in the Early Islamic Community,' especially pp.186–193, in Zailan Moris, ed., *Knowledge is Light: Essays in Honor of Seyyed Hossein Nasr* (Chicago, 1999).

23. See for example, Ibn 'Ajība in his *Īqāẓ al-himam fī sharḥ kitāb al-ḥikam* (Cairo, 1893), p.136. In the tradition of Shi'i 'Irfān, all such initiatic practices and esoteric doctrines are deemed to have been imparted by the Prophet to the Imam when the latter was a youth, living with the Prophet and, as cited earlier, following him everywhere 'as a baby camel follows its mother'. Within this tradition one cannot find any public disclosure of such chains of transmission, apart from that constituted by the Imams. But the existence of such transmission is to be inferred from the fact that in our time, the invocation of different formulae and divine Names is still being practised, permission for its use being given from master to disciple, under strict conditions of confidentiality and privacy. See Roy Mottahedeh's *The Mantle of the Prophet* (Middlesex, 1987), pp.134–141, for a fascinating account of how a young religious student in Mashhad in the 1960s was initiated into an invocatory practice. Although the names in this story are fictitious, the characters and events are real, the story being based on the first-hand account given to Mottahedeh by the student, who wished to remain anonymous.

24. One should note here a well known definition of *taṣawwuf* quoted by Hujwīrī: 'Today Sufism is a name without a reality; formerly it was a reality without a name.' *Kashf al-maḥjūb*, tr. R.A. Nicholson (Lahore, 1992), p.44. This implies that the Sufis saw themselves as attempting to revive the spiritual heart of the Islamic tradition, that heart which was realized in all its fullness in the time of the Prophet—though in the absence of any formal reference to it as *taṣawwuf*—only to become gradually obscured by worldliness in the succeeding generations. So when the name *taṣawwuf* was given to this spiritual heart, its 'reality' was already much diminished.

25. Regarding the communication of esoteric truths, Ibn al-ʿArabī says that the gnostics cannot explain their spiritual states to others, rather, 'they can only indicate them symbolically to those who have begun to experience the like'. The *Tarjumān al-ashwāq*, tr. R.A. Nicholson (London, 1978), p.68.

26. See the previous chapter for a discussion of this comment in relation to the principle of justice.

27. On the use of such devices as *kināya* (metonymy: the mention of an attribute or part of a thing in order to refer symbolically to the thing itself) and *taʿrīḍ* (allusion) in Arabic *balāgha*, see Abū ʿUthmān ʿAmr b. Baḥr al-Jāḥiẓ (d. 254/868), *al-Bayān wa'l-tabyīn* (Beirut, 1968), vol.1, pt.1, p.64; and Jalāl al-Dīn al-Suyūṭī, *al-Itqān fī ʿulūm al-Qur'ān* (Beirut, 1987), vol.2, pp.101–105. Also, see Estelle Whelan, 'Forgotten Witness: Evidence for the Early Codification of the Qur'ān', in *Journal of the American Oriental Society*, 118, (1998), pp.1–14, who draws attention to the words of the Qur'ānic verses inscribed by order of the Umayyad ruler ʿAbd al-Malik upon the inner and outer faces of the Dome of the Rock in Jerusalem (built ca.72/691–692); she argues convincingly that these inscriptions, hitherto ignored because they were deemed to be departures from the 'canonical' text, are in fact evidence of an already prevalent received text. She maintains that the inscriptions express a rhetorical style engaging scriptural associations, a style which was 'dependent upon recognition of the text by the listeners or readers—a strong indication that the Qur'ān was already the common property of the community in the last decade of the seventh century' (p.8). Thus, she continues, the inscriptions are to be read as 'little sermons or parts of a single sermon addressed to an audience that could be expected to understand the allusions and abbreviated references by which ʿAbd al-Malik's particular message was conveyed.' The same can be said for the Imam's 'abbreviated reference' to the *āyat al-nūr*: there is an allusion to the relationship between the light mentioned in that verse, and the *dhikr* which illumines the hearts of the 'men' who devote themselves to it.

28. The pronoun 'they' refers to the hearts. As will be seen below, the fact that it is the heart that 'hears' and 'sees', and not the organs or the rational faculty, is significant.

29. *Nahj*, p.260; *Peak*, p.441.

30. Many commentators, exoteric and esoteric alike, refer to the verse of light as a simile for the illumination of the heart. See for example, Abū Jaʿfar Muḥammad b. Jarīr al-Ṭabarī, *Jāmiʿ al-bayān* (Beirut, 2001), vol.18, p.163; Nāṣir al-Dīn ʿAbd Allāh al-Bayḍāwī, *Anwār al-tanzīl wa asrār al-ta'wīl* (Beirut, 1996), vol.4, p.190; Abu'l-Qāsim al-Qushayrī, *Laṭā'if al-ishārāt* (Cairo, n.d.), vol.4, p.285. It is also of interest to note that in his commentary, al-Zamakhsharī explicitly cites Imam ʿAlī's interpretation, which refers to God's 'diffusion of the Truth in the heavens and the earth', by means of which 'they shine with His light'; the Imam also refers to the divine 'illumination of the hearts' of those in the heavens and the earth. See Abu'l-Qāsim Maḥmūd al-Zamakhsharī, *Tafsīr al-kashshāf* (Beirut, 1995), vol.3, p.235.

31. Whence the word *tajallī*, referring, in the Sufi tradition, to the theophany or self-disclosure of God. As will be seen shortly, there is an important connection between the polishing of the heart and the witnessing of the divine theophanies, both in the Imam's perspective and in later Sufi discourse. The theme of *tajallī* was so central to Ibn al-ʿArabī's teachings that 'before he was known as the great spokesman for *waḥdat al-wujūd* [the oneness of being], he had been called one of the Companions of Self-disclosure (*aṣḥāb al-tajallī*).' W.C. Chittick, *The Self-Disclosure of God: Principles of Ibn al-ʿArabī's Cosmology* (Albany, NY, 1998), p.52.

32. Al-Ghazālī refers to the heart as a well, the depths of which can only be fathomed when one stops, for a time, the flow of the 'streams' of the five senses that enter into the heart from without. See his *The Alchemy of Happiness*, tr. Claud Field (Lahore, 1987), pp.27–28.

33. Ibn al-ʿArabī's comment on this verse is helpful here: '"Surely in that", that is, in the constant change in the cosmos, "there is a reminder" of the constant change of the Root, "for him who has a heart", since the heart possesses fluctuation (*taqlīb*) from one state to another. That is why it is called "heart" (*qalb*). He who explains "heart" as meaning "reason" has no knowledge of the realities, for reason is a "delimitation" (*taqyīd*), the word *ʿaql* being derived from "fetter" [i.e., *ʿiqāl*].' W.C. Chittick, *The Sufi Path of Knowledge*, p.107.

34. Cited, for example, in ʿAbd al-Wahhāb al-Shaʿrānī, *al-Anwār al-qudsiyya fī maʿrifa qawāʿid al-ṣūfiyya* (Cairo, 1987), p.29.

35. 'We purified them with a pure quality: remembrance (*dhikr*) of the Abode [of the Hereafter]' (38: 46).

36. The *ḥadīth* is a long one, containing a dialogue between God and the angels, at the end of which God declares that 'they are such a group (*julasā'*, lit. 'those who sit together') that nobody who keeps their company will be wretched'. A Sufi 'session' of *dhikr* is thus quite appropriately referred to as a *majlis*. See for the full text, *Ṣaḥīḥ al-Bukhārī* (Summarized) (Riyad, 1996/1417), p.979, no.2090 (translation modified). It is to be noted that the term *ahl al-dhikr* is also mentioned in the Qur'ān at 16: 43 and 21: 7; and that the Shi'i Imams referred to themselves as the *ahl al-dhikr* (see, for example, Kulaynī, *Uṣūl*, vol.1, p.235).

37. *Mathnawī-i ma'nawī* (Tehran, 1371 Sh./1992), I, 3159–3160. Cf. Nicholson's translation, *Mathnawi*, I, lines 3153–3154.

38. *Qulūb al-'ibād al-ṭāhira mawāḍi'u naẓari'Llāh, fa-man ṭahhara qalbahu naẓara ilayhi*, cited in *Ghurar*, vol.2, p.1197, no.18. Cf. the sixth beatitude in Christ's Sermon on the Mount: 'Blessed are the pure in heart, for they shall see God.' Matthew, 5: 8. See also the fascinating discussion of the 'vision of the heart' in Amir-Moezzi's *Divine Guide* (section entitled 'Excursus: "Vision of the Heart"') pp.44–55. Here, and indeed throughout this remarkable work, Amir-Moezzi links the vision of God to the vision of what he calls 'the ontological Imam', that archetypal principle of which the historical Imams are the outward manifestations. We shall briefly discuss the complex relationship between the Imams and the divine qualities at the end of this chapter.

39. *Ghurar*, vol.2, p.1038, no.32.

40. Ibn al-'Arabī quotes this saying in his treatise *Kitāb al-jalāla wa huwa kalimatu'Llāh*, in *Rasā'il Ibn al-'Arabī* (Damascus, 1998), p.65. See the French translation by Michel Valsan, 'Le Livre du Nom de Majesté', in *Études Traditionelles*, no.268, July–Aug 1948, p.214.

41. Al-Kulaynī, *Uṣūl*, vol.1, p.107.

42. Al-Kāshānī, *Tafsīr Ibn al-'Arabī* (Cairo, n.d.), vol.2, p.384.

43. As will be seen shortly, it is God as 'the Outward' (*al-Ẓāhir*), which is, in a sense, the most challenging dimension of the divine Reality to grasp.

44. *Ma'a kulli shay', lā bi-muqārana; ghayr kulli shay' lā bi-muzāyala* (*Nahj*, pp.7–8). This remarkable sentence, combining spiritual profundity with literary elegance, is one of those pearls of the *Nahj al-balāgha* that help explain why al-Sharīf al-Raḍī, and countless scholars of the Arabic language before and after him, refer to the Imam as their teacher in *balāgha*, the art of eloquence. See our translation of Sermon 1 in the Appendix for the context of this statement.

45. See our discussion of this in Chapter 1 above. One might go so far as to say that we are given the quintessence of the complex doctrine of *waḥdat al-wujūd* (oneness of Being) associated with Ibn al-'Arabī, in these two short

sentences: 'God is with every thing, but not through association; and other than every thing, but not through separation,' and 'That which has no second does not enter into the category of numbers.' For the most comprehensive exposition of this theme in the writings of Ibn al-'Arabī himself, see Chittick, *The Sufi Path of Knowledge*, and for the most eloquent and succinct expression of the doctrine, see the chapter on 'Oneness of Being' by Martin Lings in *A Sufi Saint*, pp.121–131.

46. The Arabic here is this: '*Al-ḥamdu li'Llāhi'lladhī baṭana khafiyyāt al-umūr*'.

47. One has here a sharp and unanswerable refutation of atheism. The one who denies the existence of God cannot, in good logic, prove that what he does *not* perceive has no existence. It is only one who perceives an object that can know for certain that that object exists. The objective reality of God, such as this is perceived by the heart in spiritual vision—that is, in supra-phenomenal mode—cannot therefore be denied by one whose perception is limited to the realm of sensible phenomena.

48. *Nahj*, p.53; *Peak*, p.181.

49. The word for man, *insān*, is derived from the root *anisa*, 'to be intimate, social', but in Sufism it is said to be connected also to the root *nasiya*, 'to forget'. The spiritual path is thus seen as consisting in the return from an accidental state of natural forgetfulness of God to an original state of supernatural intimacy with the divine Reality.

50. Cf. the *ḥadīth* of the Prophet: 'The word of wisdom is the stray camel of the believer; wherever he finds it, he has the greatest right to it.' See Wensinck et al., *Concordance*, vol.1, p.491, for references to this saying in the collections of Tirmidhī and Ibn Māja.

51. It should be noted that the phrase in the Qur'ān which is translated here as 'we were unaware' could also be translated as 'we were forgetful', the Arabic being *innā kunnā 'an hādhā ghāfilīn*; as has been noted above, the *ghāfil* is the opposite of the *dhākir*, the 'rememberer/invoker'.

52. See the discussion in Chaper 1 above.

53. In his commentary on these words of Imam 'Alī, Ibn Abi'l-Ḥadīd refers to the prophetic saying, 'Every child is born in accordance with the primordial nature (*fiṭra*),' and says that the covenant mentioned by the Imam here (*mīthāq fiṭratihi*) should be understood in the light of this primordial nature, which entails the implanting of 'knowledge of God and the evidences of *tawḥīd* and of justice (*'adl*)' within the intellects. The function of the prophets is to confirm these intellectual evidences. Ibn Abi'l-Ḥadīd, *Sharḥ*, vol.1, p.115.

54. Mīrzā Ḥabību'Llāh al-Khu'ī, *Minhāj al-barāʿa fī sharḥ Nahj al-balāgha*, vol.2, p.150.

55. *Nahj*, p.220; *Peak*, p.366.

56. *Nahj*, p.277; *Peak*, p.373.

57. Ibn ʿAṭā'illāh al-Iskandarī, *Kitāb al-ḥikam*, tr. Victor Danner as *Sufi Aphorisms* (Leiden, 1973), pp.25–26.

58. *Mawsūʿa*, vol.10, p.85 (referring to *al-Uṣūl min al-kāfī*, 1/139).

59. Ibid. The Arabic reads as follows: *Al-ḥijāb baynahu wa bayna khalqihi khalquhu iyyāhum, li-imtināʿihi mimmā yumkin fī dhawātihim, wa li-imkānin mimmā yamtaniʿ minhu, wa li-iftirāq al-ṣāniʿ min al-maṣnūʿ, wa'l-ḥadd min al-maḥdūd, wa'l-rabb min al-marbūb*.'

60. According to an extremely important *ḥadīth qudsī* (a divine utterance expressed through the Prophet), which plays a major role in Sufi thought: 'I was a hidden treasure and I loved to be known, so I created the world.' Although this *ḥadīth* does not figure in the canonical collections, its meaning is accepted as valid, even by the exoteric scholars, as it conforms with the interpretation given by Ibn al-ʿAbbās, accepted as valid, of the Qur'ānic verse, 'I created not the *jinn* and mankind except that they might worship Me' (51: 56). The word 'worship' here means 'knowledge' (*maʿrifa*), according to Ibn al-ʿAbbās, so that the phrase '*illā li-yaʿbudūni*', 'except that they might worship Me', becomes '*illā li-yaʿrifūni*', 'except that they might know Me'. This interpretation is widely cited in Sufi texts. See, for example, Hujwīrī's *Kashf al-maḥjūb*, p.267. As an example of an exoteric scholar accepting the same interpretation also, see Fakhr al-Dīn al-Rāzī, who cites the *ḥadīth* of the 'hidden treasure', as well as the interpretation *illā li-yaʿrifūni*, at the end of his commentary on 51: 56, in his *al-Tafsīr al-kabīr*, vol.10, p.194.

61. Chittick, *The Sufi Path of Knowledge*, p.112.

62. It should be noted that the root of the word 'simplicity' is the Proto-Indo-European 'sem', meaning 'one', 'together', whence also the English word 'same'.

63. Cited in Chittick, *The Sufi Path of Knowledge*, p.67.

64. In what follows, we shall translate the word *dhikr* as 'invocation' wherever the context makes it clear that a practice is being indicated; this, despite the fact that the word 'remembrance' can also be employed in such a way as to connote a practice in addition to its primary, cognitive meaning of recalling, recollecting, 'making present to the mind'.

65. Immediately preceding these words is a verse acknowledging the weighty duties of the Prophet during the day. This combination of momentous responsibilities by day and long vigils by night reminds one of

the way in which the Imam enjoined exertion in prayer upon Mālik al-Ashtar, as seen in the previous chapter, even though Mālik's days would be filled with a multitude of administrative tasks. It is worth repeating the words of the Imam to Mālik: 'Give unto God of your body [i.e. your vital energy] in your nights and your days, and perform fully that by which you draw near to God, doing so perfectly, without becoming dull or deficient, exerting your bodily energy to its utmost (*bālighan min badanika mā balagha*).' *Nahj*, p.378–379; *Peak*, p.543.

66. This accords with the Sufi maxim, 'the Name is the Named (*al-ism huwa'l-musammā*),' to which we shall return later in this chapter.

67. Cf. Tz'u-min, eighth century CE Chinese master in the Buddhist Pure Land tradition, describing the universal vow of compassion made by Amida: 'The Buddha, in the causal stage, made the universal vow: "When beings hear my Name, and think on me, I will come to welcome each of them ...Solely making beings turn about and abundantly say the *nembutsu* [invocation of the Name of Amida] I can make bits of rubble change into gold".' Cited by Taitetsu Unno, 'The Practice of *Jodo-shinshu*', in Alfred Bloom (ed.), *Living in Amida's Universal Vow: Essays in Shin Buddhism* (Bloomington IN, 2004), p.65.

68. *Ghurar* (Anṣārī), no.8528, p.690. Cf. the following statement by al-Ghazālī: 'Truly, when a man loves a thing, he invokes/remembers it much (*akthara min dhikrihi*), and he who invokes/remembers a thing much loves it.' *Iḥyā' 'ulūm al-dīn*, p.400. See the translation (which we have not followed) by K. Nakamura, *Al-Ghazālī: Invocations and Supplications*, p.23.

69. The derivative *lahja* means 'tip of the tongue', and, by extension, 'dialect', 'vernacular'—that language or dialect which one speaks effortlessly, through absorption of all its subtleties, such language being 'on the tip of one's tongue'. See Lane, *Lexicon*, vol.2, p.2672.

70. Chittick, *Du'ā' Kumayl*, p.28, verse 63; p.36, verse 132; p.38, verse 148; p.40, verse 156 (we have slightly modified Chittick's translation). Cf. the description of the 'man of substance' (*dhū lubb*): 'renunciation has curbed his desires and invocation quickens his tongue (*awjafa al-dhikr bi-lisānihi*).' *Nahj*, p.77; *Peak*, p.210. In connection with the healing power of the invocation, the following image of the Prophet is also to be noted: '[He was like] a physician roving with his medicine, having fortified his remedies and heated up his implements, ready to place them at the disposal of those who need them: hearts which are blind, ears that are deaf, tongues that are dumb. With his medicines he sought out the domains of heedlessness (*ghafla*) and the homelands of perplexity.' *Nahj*, p.120; *Peak*, p.251–252.

71. *Nahj*, p.221; *Peak*, p.367.

72. Quoted in Waley, 'Contemplative Disciplines', p.509. This *ḥadīth* is found in such canonical sources as Tirmidhī and Ibn Māja, as noted by Waley.

73. *Ghurar* (Anṣārī), p.764, no.9545. The word *lubb* lterally means 'kernel', 'core', 'marrow', etc.; in mystical literature it is often contrasted with *qishr*, meaning 'husk'.

74. Al-Kulaynī, *Uṣūl*, vol.2, p.489.

75. *Ghurar* (Anṣārī), p.836, no.10456.

76. Ibid., p.621, no.7524.

77. Witness the title of one of the earliest Sufi manuals, that by Abū Sa'īd al-Kharrāz (d.286/899), *Kitāb al-ṣidq*, tr. A.J. Arberry, *The Book of Truthfulness* (Oxford, 1937).

78. Needless to say, extinction is a finality only from one point of view—that of the soul still susceptible to egocentricity; for the realized souls—the prophets and the saints—this *fanā'*, implying the effacement of the ego, is the end of one mode of life and the beginning of another, a life lived in complete conformity with the Real, this manner of living being referred to in Sufism as *al-baqā' ba'd al-fanā'*, 'subsistence after extinction'.

79. Note this remarkable *ḥadīth*, found in the collection of Ibn Ḥanbal: 'Increase the *dhikru'Llāh* until they say, "madman (*majnūn*)!"' For this and several other traditions of similar import, together with relevant Qur'ānic verses relating to the *dhikr*, see the Shaykh al-'Alawī's powerful rebuttal of accusations made against the Sufis by 'reformers' in Algeria in the 1920s and 1930s, in Lings, *A Sufi Saint*, pp.93–95.

80. As will be seen below, Rūmī cites this verse in connection with the utter selflessness and absence of passion that characterized the inner spirit motivating 'Alī in his battles; they were truly fought *fī sabīli'Llāh*, 'in the path of God', not for the sake of self-glorification nor out of rage or bitterness.

81. 'Kitāb al-fanā' fi'l-mushāhada' in *Rasā'il Ibn al-'Arabī* (Damascus, 2001), p.11. Cf. French tr. M. Valsan, *Le Livre de l'Extinction dans la Contemplation* (Paris, 1984), p.27.

82. Ibid., p.18; cf. the French tr. Valsan, *Livre de l'Extinction*, pp.48–49.

83. The Qur'ānic context of these words is as follows: 'And when Moses came to Our appointed tryst and his Lord had spoken to him, he said, "My Lord, show me [Thyself] that I may look at Thee". He said, "Thou wilt not see Me, but look at the mountain, if it remain in its place then thou wilt see Me". And when his Lord manifested (*tajallā*) Himself to the mountain He sent it crashing down. And Moses fell down, stunned (7: 143).'

84. Cited by James Morris, 'Ibn 'Arabī's Spiritual Ascension,' in M. Chodkiewicz et al., eds., *Les Illuminations de La Mecque: The Meccan Illuminations. Textes Choisis/Selected Texts* (Paris, 1988), p.375.

85. *Kulliyyāt mafātīḥ al-janān*, compiled by Shaykh 'Abbās al-Qummī (Qom, n.d.), p.293.

86. Ibn al-'Arabī, *Tarjumān*, p.51.

87. Ibid., p.50.

88. We have slightly modified Nicholson's translation of this *ḥadīth qudsī*.

89. Ibid., p.52.

90. Cited in 'Allāmah Ṭabāṭabā'ī, *Shi'ite Islam*, ed. and tr. S.H. Nasr (Albany NY, 1975), p.194.

91. Cited by Āmulī, *Muḥīṭ*, vol.1, p.266. The commentator cites this saying and then quotes certain verses of the Qur'ān describing the drink which is given to the believers of different ranks in Paradise. See 76: 5–6; 76: 21; 83: 25–28; *et passim*.

92. See Ṭabāṭabā'ī, *Kernel*, pp.24–28, for a discussion of this saying.

93. *Ghurar* (Anṣārī), p.135, no.2098.

94. Ibn al-'Arabī, *al-Futūḥāt al-makkiyya*, vol.4, p.315, lines 21–24. (Cairo, 1911). See the important points made in this regard by M. Chodkiewicz in his essay 'Une Introduction à la Lecture des *Futūḥāt Makkiyya*', in *Les Illuminations de La Mecque,* especially p.37, where he comments on Ibn al-'Arabī's interpretation of 76: 1 in the context of his metaphysics: the 'moment' in time when man was not is an ontological 'degree', that of *aḥadiyya*, absolutely unconditioned oneness.

95. For a detailed and illuminating exposition of Ibn al-'Arabī's ontology and the role played in it by the 'immutable entities' (*al-a'yān al-thābita*), see Chittick, *Sufi Path,* Chapter 3, 'Ontology', pp.77–143; and his *Self-Disclosure of God*, Chapter 1, '*Wujūd* and the Entities', pp.3–47.

96. For both the text of the *ḥadīth* itself and al-Kāshānī's commentary, see his 'Commentary on the *Ḥadīth al-ḥaqīqa*' in the collection of his treatises entitled *Majmū'-i rasā'il wa muṣannafāt*, ed. M. Hādīzādah (Tehran, 2000), pp.640–645. See also the forthcoming publication, *A Tradition of Esoteric Commentary: Imam 'Alī's Ḥadīth al-ḥaqīqa*, by Bruce Wannell and Hermann Landolt, which analyses and translates twelve commentaries on this *ḥadīth* by a range of luminaries in the tradition of Shi'i 'Irfān. The question of the authenticity of its attribution to the Imam is also addressed.

97. *Futūḥāt*, vol.1, 2.1. See Chodkiewicz, 'Une Introduction', *Les Illuminations,* pp.35–38 where this part of the *khuṭba* is analysed.

98. *Futūḥāt*, vol.1, 2.7. Cf. the response by the Ismā'īlī guide to his disciple,

when the latter asked whether the initiatic name he was to be given would be 'his': 'The Name is your owner'. Jaʿfar b. Manṣūr al-Yaman, *Kitāb al-ʿālim wa'l-ghulām*, ed. and tr. James Morris as *The Master and the Disciple: An Early Islamic Spiritual Dialogue* (London, 2001), p.119.

99. From a higher metaphysical point of view, even the revealed scriptures can be seen as a veil obscuring, as well as a revelation unveiling, the divine Reality. This point of view is well expressed by Ibn al-ʿArabī in the lines of a poem addressed to the lady Niẓām, together with his important commentary upon them: 'She has baffled everyone who is learned in our religion, every student of the Psalms of David, every Jewish doctor and every Christian priest.' His commentary: 'All the sciences comprised in the four Books (Qur'ān, Psalms, Torah and Gospel) point only to the divine Names and are incapable of solving a question that concerns the divine Essence' (*Tarjumān*, pp.49, 52). No manifestation or revelation can be placed on the same level as the absolutely transcendent Essence. Insofar as any revelation is 'other than' that which it reveals, it is, in this respect, a 'veil' over it.

100. In one respect only, and not in all respects, since in principle the phenomena of nature are so many 'signs' or 'verses' (*āyāt*) of God, and are thus complementary to the verses of the revealed Book: 'We shall show them Our signs on the horizons and in their own souls that it be clear to them that He is the Truth' (41: 53). Concerning *al-Qur'ān al-takwīnī*, the Book of creation, as opposed to *al-Qur'ān al-tadwīnī*, the written Qur'ān, the 14th century Sufi ʿAzīz al-Dīn Nasafī writes: 'Each day, destiny and the passage of time set this book before you, *sūrah* for *sūrah*, verse for verse, letter for letter and read it to you…' Quoted by S.H. Nasr in 'The Cosmos and the Natural Order,' in *Islamic Spirituality*, vol.1, p.355, n.1.

101. As the Gospel of St John (1: 5) says, 'The Light shone in the darkness and the darkness comprehended it not'.

102. Quoted in Chittick, *Sufi Path*, p.380.

103. It is said that this was recited to a youth who had been stricken on account of sins he had committed against his father. Thereafter, he saw the Prophet in a dream. The Prophet passed his hands over the youth's body and said, 'Safeguard God's greatest Name, and your affair will turn out well.' The youth woke up and was healed. See the Imam's *Supplications—Amīr al-Muʾminīn*, p.43.

104. Ibid., verse 109, p.60.

105. See, for example, Chittick, *Sufi Path*, p.37.

106. 'Allāma Ṭabāṭabā'ī alludes to this important principle in his reference to the impossibility of the individual attaining detachment on his own, using

his own resources, his will, intelligence and so on, 'because the very same struggle to attain detachment and catharsis (*tajrīd*) implies the presence of attachment and is an indication of the wayfarer's struggle for a special personal purpose.' He continues by citing the words of his mentor, Āqā Ḥājj Mīrzā Qāḍī: 'When he finds himself helpless and unable to free himself of greed, he will have to entrust his affair to God and set aside any thought of eradicating greed from his soul by himself. The admission of helplessness and weakness burns down the very root of greed and purifies him.' *Kernel*, p.101. Applied to the invocation, the need 'to entrust his affair to God' translates into a more resolute effort to concentrate on the Name of God, which, alone, can 'burn' the root of egocentricity, allowing one to forget oneself utterly.

107. The context of these words indicates a quite different literal meaning: 'We shall make thee recite, and thou wilst not forget, unless God willeth.'

108. Kalābādhī, *Ta'arruf*, pp.103–104. Cf. Arberry's translation in *The Doctrine of the Sufis* (Cambridge, 1953), p.95, which we have not followed.

109. For a profound exposition of this principle in relation to the metaphysics underlying the practice of the invocation, see Frithjof Schuon, *Stations of Wisdom* (Bloomington, IN, 1995), pp.125–135.

110. Cited by Todd Lawson, 'The Dawning Places', in Lewisohn, *Heritage of Persian Sufism*, vol.2, p.272. As noted earlier, the Imam also said, 'People are asleep; when they die, they wake up.'

111. *Mathnawī*, tr. Nicholson, Book 1, 3787–3792. These words are spoken when 'Alī had sheathed his sword, refusing to kill his defeated opponent who had spat at him in a last gesture of defiance. Had he killed him at that moment, he would not have acted out of the dispassionate spirit which motivated him to fight *fī sabīli'Llāh*, 'in the path of God'. Rather, it would have been out of personal anger, and thus for the sake of the slighted ego.

112. This is *'adam iḍāfī* as opposed to *'adam muṭlaq*, absolute nothingness, an important distinction in Ibn al-'Arabī's metaphysics. The first is a pre-existential nothingness, ready to be brought into existence by the attention (*tawajjuh*) directed to it by the divine Names; the second is simply nothingness as such, that which has no existence, and is not susceptible to existentiation.

113. See the Arabic text in *Rasā'il Ibn al-'Arabī*, pp.11–12; tr. Valson, *Livre de l'Extinction*, pp.27–28.

114. *Al-Ghazzālī's Mishkāt al-Anwār (The Niche for Lights)*, tr. W.H.T. Gairdner (New Delhi, 1988), p.59.

115. Ibid., p.59 (translation modified).

116. Ibid., pp.60–61. It is interesting to note that one version of the poem of Manṣūr al-Ḥallāj referring to the 'extinction of extinction' is attributed by Ibn

'Ajība to Imam 'Alī. This is the poem that begins, 'I saw my Lord with the eye of my heart.' The line in question is, 'So in my extinction, my extinction was extinguished, so in my extinction, I found You (*fa-fī fanā'ī fanā fanā'ī fa-fī fanā'ī wajadtu anta*)'. See Ibn 'Ajība, *Īqāẓ al-himam*, p.84; for the original version of the poem, see *Dīwān al-Ḥallāj*, ed. S. Ḍannāwī (Beirut, 1988), p.31.

117. Abu'l Qāsim al-Qushayrī, *al-Risāla al-Qushayriyya*, tr. R. Harris as *Sufi Book of Spiritual Ascent* (Chicago, 1997), p.198.

118. Al-Ghazālī writes that the ultimate spiritual sciences are only revealed in the state of *fanā'* because the individual faculties act as obstacles to inspired disclosure, being bound up with the sensible world, 'a world of error and illusion'. Quoted in F. Jabre, *La Notion de la Ma'rifa chez Ghazālī* (Paris, 1958), p.124. It is also to be noted that al-Ghazālī refers to the invocation as one of the principal means of 'polishing the heart', rendering it capable of reflecting the verities of *ma'rifa*. Ibid., pp.18 and 124. The importance of *dhikr* as the method *par excellence* of the Sufis is further attested by al-Ghazālī when he refers to the advice given him by a Sufi master in response to his request to follow the path of direct experience. He was told to break all his ties with the world and to enter a retreat in which he was to perform only the obligatory prayers and the invocation: '... being seated, concentrate your thoughts on God, without other interior preoccupation. You will do this, first by saying the Name of God with your tongue, repeating without ceasing Allāh, Allāh, without relaxing your attention.' This comes from Ghazālī's *Mīzān al-'amal*, cited by J.-L. Michon in 'The Spiritual Practices of Sufism', *Islamic Spirituality*, vol.1, p.288.

119. Al-Kashanī, *Tafsīr Ibn al-'Arabī*, vol.1, p.80.

120. Ibn 'Aṭā'illāh, *Sufi Aphorisms*, p.32, no.47. The final quotation is from the Qur'ān, 14: 20. See also Ibn 'Aṭā'illāh's volume devoted entirely to the invocation, *Miftāḥ al-falāḥ wa miṣbāḥ al-arwāḥ*, tr. Mary A.K. Danner as *The Key to Salvation: A Sufi Manual of Invocation* (Cambridge, 1996).

121. Ibn 'Ajība, *Īqāẓ al-himam*, p.136.

122. See J. L. Michon, *Le Soufi Marocain, Aḥmad Ibn 'Ajība (1746–1809) et son Mi'rāj* (Paris, 1973), p.124.

123. Kulaynī, *Uṣūl*, vol.1, p.135.

124. Ibid., vol.1, p.136.

125. Ibn al-'Arabī, *Fuṣus al-ḥikam*, tr. R. Austin, *The Bezels of Wisdom* (New York, 1980), p.125.

126. 'Abd al-Razzāq al-Kāshānī, *Laṭā'if al-i'lām fī ishārāt ahl al-ilhām*, ed. M. Hādīzādah (Tehran, 2000), p.91. See also the shorter lexicon of al-Kāshānī, *al-Iṣṭilāḥāt al-ṣūfiyya* (Cairo, 1992), p.54, for the meaning of *al-ism*, 'the Name':

'In their [the Sufis'] terminology, this is not the verbal expression, rather, it is the essence of the Named (*dhāt al-musammā*).'

127. It is interesting to note what the great spokesman of Hindu Advaita Vedanta, Shankaracharya (Śaṃkara), says on this subject. The 'Name' he refers to here is *Om*: 'The purpose of knowing the identity of the Name and the Named is to enable oneself to dismiss Name and Named altogether and realize the Absolute, which is quite different from either.' *A Śaṃkara Source-Book*, vol.2, *Śaṃkara on the Creation*, tr. A.J. Alston, (London, 1983), p.144. He affirms the essential identity between the Name and the Named, and at the same time stresses the transcendence of the Absolute beyond the formal polarity assumed by these two elements on the conceptual plane. Thus, as regards the relationship between the Name and the Named, he affirms both mystical realization through invocation *and* metaphysical distinction through discernment. See, for further discussion, our forthcoming *Paths to Transcendence*.

128. Jalāl al-Dīn Āshtiyānī, *Sharḥ-i muqaddam-i Qayṣarī bar Fuṣūṣ al-ḥikam* (Qom, 1372/1953), p.243.

129. Ibid., pp.243–244.

130. This is a saying of Shiblī, quoted by Ibn 'Aṭā'illāh in *Key to Salvation*, p.170.

131. It is important to note that, as regards the highest spiritual realization—pertaining to the ultimate meaning and reality of the oneness of God—the *awliyā'* or 'saints', despite being distinguished from the Imams as regards outward function, are deemed by Shi'i spiritual authorities to have access to this ultimate degree of *walāya*. This is because this dimension of *walāya* is regarded as *muktasab*, that is, capable of being 'acquired' by those who exert themselves spiritually and receive the grace which leads to the realization of this mystical degree of *walāya*, which is identified with the summit of *tawḥīd*. As 'Allāma Ṭabāṭabā'ī explains: 'One may argue that these stations are exclusive, and attainment of this level of divine knowledge is solely confined to exalted Prophets and infallible Imams—may God's greeting and peace be upon them all—and that others have absolutely no access to it. In response we say that the positions of prophethood and imamate are exclusive, but reaching the station of absolute *tawḥīd* and annihilation in the divine Essence, which is considered the same as *wilāyat* [sic], is not exclusive at all. In fact, it is to this plane of perfection that the Prophets and Imams...have called the community of believers.' Ṭabāṭabā'ī, *Kernel*, p.25.

132. Quoted by Ḥasanzādah Āmulī, *Insān-i kāmil az dīdgāh-i Nahj al-balāgha* (Qom, 1379 Sh./2000), p.95.

133. For a fine translation of the poem in which this famous line comes, see Martin Lings, *Sufi Poems* (Cambridge, 2004), p.28. See also the valuable discussion of such *shaṭḥiyyāt* by Carl W. Ernst, in his *Words of Ecstasy in Sufism* (Albany, NY, 1985).

134. See Appendix I for a translation of the whole of the first sermon.

135. Quoted in Chittick, *Sufi Path*, p.375.

136. Quoted in Morris, 'Ibn 'Arabī's Spiritual Ascension', in *Les Illuminations de La Mecque*, p.380.

137. Farīd al-Dīn 'Aṭṭār, *Tadhkiratu'l-awliyā'*, ed. R.A. Nicholson (London, 1905), p.12.

138. *Nahj*, p.15; *Peak*, p.105.

139. Kāshānī, *Tafsīr*, vol.2, pp.360–361. See also Martin Lings (Abū Bakr Sirāj ad-Dīn), *The Book of Certainty* (Cambridge, 1992) for an illuminating exposition of the spiritual themes connected with the different 'fountains' of Paradise, based on al-Kāshānī's exegesis. The image of the 'flood' in connection with the experience of union should be noted in this description by the Shaykh al-'Alawī of the state of 'submersion' of the mystic: 'Extinction and submersion and annihilation come suddenly upon the gnostic, so that he goeth out from the sphere of sense and loseth all consciousness of himself, leaving behind all his perceptions, nay his very existence. Now this annihilation is in the Essence of the Truth, for there floweth down over him from the Holiness of the Divinity a flood which compelleth him to see himself as the Truth's Very Self in virtue of his effacement and annihilation therein. In this state he giveth utterance to such sayings as "Glory Be to Me" (Abū Yazīd al-Basṭāmī) and "There is no god but I Alone", speaking with the Tongue of the Truth, not with his own tongue, and telling of the Essence of the Truth, not of himself.' Quoted in Lings, *Sufi Saint*, p.163.

140. The authenticity of its attribution to Imam 'Alī is disputed, but we see no reason to doubt that it is indeed one of his sermons, delivered in all likelihood to very few disciples, precisely on account of its esoteric character. From the following saying of the Imam—indicating the gulf separating the knowledge of Salmān al-Fārisī from that of Abū Dharr al-Ghifārī—one can gauge the extent to which esoteric truths were deemed to be so dangerous as to be divulged only to those who could truly understand and benefit from them: 'If Abū Dharr knew what there is in the heart of Salmān, he would kill him.' See Corbin's comments on Salmān al-Fārisī as the embodiment of receptivity to the *bāṭin* of the Islamic revelation in his *Cyclical Time*, pp.123–130, 143–148. The *Khuṭbat al-bayān*, together with another highly 'gnostic' one, entitled *al-Taṭanjiyya*, is found in Rajab Bursī's, *Mashāriq anwār*. For editions of this

important work, the controversy surrounding these sermons, and the status of Bursī himself—the degree to which the traditional authorities in Shiʿism regard him as a *ghālī* or 'exaggerator'—see the article entitled '*Mashāriq anwār al-yaqīn*', by Abu'l-Faḍl Ḥāfiẓiyān Bābulī, in Rashād, ed. *Dānish-nāmah*, vol.12, pp.483–495.

141. This translation is taken from Corbin, *History of Islamic Philosophy*, p.49.

142. This expresses the difference between particular incarnation (*ḥulūl*)—one thing entering into another—and universal theophany (*tajallī*)—there being no thing that is not the locus (*maẓhar*) for the manifestation of God. According to the latter viewpoint, the vision of divine immanence in no way implies compromising the principle of divine transcendence: the Essence is always infinitely beyond all those self-manifestations by virtue of which its immanence is inescapable. To repeat the words of the Imam: 'God is with every thing, but not through association; and other than every thing, but not through separation.'

143. *Nahj*, p.302; *Peak*, p.394.

144. Cited in al-Ghazālī, *Remembrance of Death*, p.84. Cf. the poem by al-Ḥallāj: 'Slay me, my trusted friends; truly, my life lies in being slain. And my dying is in my living, and my living is in my dying.' *Dīwān*, p.31.

145. Al-Ghazālī: *Invocations*, p.7. The *ḥadīth* is given in al-Ṭabarānī's *al-Muʿjam al-kabīr*, 20.107, as noted by the editor and translator of this work, K. Nakamura.

The First Sermon of *Nahj al-balāgha*[1]

Praise be to God, whose laudation those who speak cannot deliver, whose graces those who count cannot number, whose rightful due those who strive cannot render; He who cannot be grasped by far-reaching aspirations, nor fathomed by profound intuitions;[2] He whose attribute has no binding limitation, no existing description, no time appointed, no term extended. Through His power He originated all created things, and through His mercy He diffused the comforting winds;[3] and He entrenched with rocky pillars His swaying earth.

Foremost in religion is knowledge of Him,[4] and the perfection of this knowledge is believing in Him,[5] and the perfection of this belief is affirming His oneness,[6] and the perfection of this affirmation is to purify one's devotion to Him,[7] and the perfection of this purification is to divest Him of all attributes—because of the testimony of every attribute that it is other than the object of attribution, and because of the testimony of every such object that it is other than the attribute.[8] So whoever ascribes an attribute to God—glorified be He!—has conjoined Him [with something else], and whoever so conjoins Him has made Him twofold, and whoever makes Him twofold has fragmented Him, and whoever thus fragments Him is ignorant of Him. And whoever points to Him confines Him, and whoever confines Him counts Him;[9] and whoever asks 'in what?' encloses Him, and whoever asks 'upon what?' isolates Him.[10]

Being, but not by way of any becoming; existing, but not from having been non-existent;[11] with every thing, but not through association; and other than every thing, but not through separation;[12]

acting, but not through movements and instruments; seeing, even when nothing of His creation was to be seen; solitary, even when there was none whose intimacy might be sought or whose absence might be missed.

He brought forth creation, originating it from the very beginning, without pondering over any deliberation or benefiting from any [previous] experience; without initiating any movement or engaging in any unsettling exertion. He assigned to all things their span of time and harmonized their differences; He instilled within them their natural dispositions, impressing upon them their respective forms; knowing them before their genesis, encompassing their boundaries and their finalities; aware of their configurations and their contours.

Then[13] He—glorified be He!—created a fissure in the atmospheres, cleaving up directions and the uppermost levels of air;[14] then He caused water to flow therein, a current of surging waves, swelling and swirling in overflowing abundance. Then He mounted it upon a tempestuous wind, a thunderous gale; then He made the wind prevent the return of the water, enabling it to dominate the violence of its flow, and aligning it with the boundaries of the water; the air beneath the wind was spread wide open, while the water above it flowed copiously.

Then He raised up a wind, making it sterile,[15] fixing its course, intensifying its current, distancing it from its source. Then he ordered it to agitate the swelling waters and to stir up oceanic waves. The wind churned up the waters—as one churns up milk in a milk-bag—imparting to the water its own violence in the atmosphere, turning its foremost back upon its hindmost, and its stillness to its motion, so that its torrents surged and its swelling waves threw up foam. Then He elevated [the foam] within a cleft air and a vast open atmosphere and formed from it the seven heavens,[16] making the lowest of them a suspended wave and the highest a protected shelter and an elevated ceiling, without any pillars to support them or any clinch to transfix them. Then He adorned the heavens with the ornaments of the stars and the effulgence of the firmament; and made a radiant lamp [the sun] and an illuminating moon to follow an orbit, in a revolving sphere, [beneath] a roof in motion and a firmament in flux.[17]

Then He split up the highest heavens and filled them with angels of different dispositions: some prostrating and not bowing; others bowing and not standing upright; some arrayed in ranks, not separating from each other; others glorifying, never wearying—not overcome by sleepiness in the eyes, distraction in the mind, fatigue of the body or the negligence of forgetfulness. And among them are custodians of His Revelation, and conveyors [of His Words] to His Messengers, and those who come and go with His Decree and His Command. And among them are the guardians of His slaves, and the wardens of the gates of His Gardens. And among them are those whose feet stand firmly on the lowest worlds,[18] and whose necks surpass the highest heaven, and whose sides exceed all bounds, and whose shoulders are proportioned to the pillars of the Throne, their eyes cast down before it, enwrapping themselves in their wings beneath it. Between them and all others there is a barrier: veils of Glory and screens of Might. They do not imagine their Lord through formal representation, nor ascribe to Him created attributes; they do not confine Him within places, nor do they allude to Him through similitudes.

Then He—glorified be He!—gathered up a quantity of dust, from some hard earth and some soft, some sweet earth and some salty, and poured water onto it until it was pure,[19] then kneaded into it some moisture until it stuck together; then he fashioned from this a form with curves and joints, limbs and parts. He compacted it until it held tightly together, solidified it until it became as sounding clay,[20] assigning to it a measured duration and a known consummation.

Then He breathed into it of His spirit, and it stood up as a human being, endowed with intellectual powers with which to reflect, thoughts by which to conduct himself, limbs to put to service, instruments at his disposal, and knowledge[21] with which to discern between the true and the false, between different tastes and fragrances, and between different colours and categories; having a constitution compounded of different hues, unified forms, contrasting oppositions, and distinct admixtures of heat and cold, moisture and dryness.

And God—glorified be He!—demanded from the angels the fulfilment of that with which He had charged them, and their compliance with His injunction to them,[22] by [ordering] their submissive prostration to him [Adam] and humble reverence of him. So He said, 'Prostrate to Adam', and they prostrated, except Iblīs. Passionate scorn deranged him, wretchedness overwhelmed him;[23] he prided himself upon [his] constitution of fire and disdained the creature made of clay.[24] Then God granted him a respite, that His wrath be fully warranted,[25] that the affliction be consummated, and that the promise be fulfilled. So He said, 'Thou art of those given respite unto a day whose time is appointed'.[26]

Then He—glorified be He!—settled Adam in an abode wherein He made his life comfortable, and his domain secure; and He warned him of Iblīs and his enmity. But his enemy beguiled him, through envious desire for his immortal abode and his intimacy with the righteous. So Adam exchanged certainty for his doubt and resolution for his weakness;[27] and replaced joy with dread and self-esteem with remorse. Then God accepted his repentance, and whelmed him with a word from His Mercy and promised him a return to His Garden. Then He made him descend to the abode of tribulations and to the begetting of progeny. And from his offspring He chose prophets, taking from them a pledge in respect of the Revelation, entrusting to them the conveyance of His Message; this, at a time when most of His creatures had deviated from their covenant with God, so that they ignored His due and set up peers alongside Him, and the demons distracted them from knowledge of Him and sundered them from worship of Him. So He sent amongst them His messengers, dispatching prophets in succession, in order to claim from them [His creatures] the fulfilment of the covenant of His creation;[28] to remind them of His forgotten graces; to remonstrate with them through communication [of His Revelation]; to unearth for them the buried treasures of the intellects;[29] and to show them signs of omnipotence: the outspread earth laid low beneath them, provisions which give them life, finalities which mete out death; ailments hastening their decrepitude, and a succession of events that flow over them.

And God never deprived His creation of a prophet sent forth, a revealed scripture, an imperative proof or a clear path; messengers who were not diminished by the paucity of their number, nor by the multitude of their deniers. Amongst them, those who came before were told the names of those who would follow them, and those who came after were informed of those who came before.

Thus, generations were begotten and ages elapsed, fathers passing away and sons succeeding them, until God sent forth Muḥammad, Messenger of God, in fulfilment of His promise and completion of His [cycle of] prophecy; he regarding whom a pledge was taken from the prophets,[30] renowned through signs, of noble birth. At this time the people on earth were split up into different religious communities; caprice was widespread, pathways were disordered: among them [such paths as] likening God to His creation, distorting His Name, alluding to other than Him. So God guided them through him [the Prophet] out of error and, through his presence, delivered them from their ignorance.

Then He chose for Muḥammad the meeting with Him and desired for him what was with Himself, and removed him with dignity from the abode of the lower world and took him away from any link with [the domain of] trial; so He drew him to Himself honourably. He left behind amongst you that which the prophets leave for their communities, lest they abandon them to stray as they will, without a clear path and a visible beacon: the scripture of your Lord, [the Prophet] clarifying what is lawful and unlawful according to it, the obligatory and the recommended, [verses that] abrogate and [others that are] abrogated therein, the conditionally permissible and the unconditionally compulsory,[31] the specific and the general,[32] His admonitions and analogies, undelimited and delimited [ordinances],[33] unambiguous and equivocal [verses];[34] elucidating what is condense and clarifying what is obscure therein.

In it are things knowledge of which is binding upon His slaves, and others, ignorance of which is overlooked; injunctions affirmed as obligatory in the scripture, and known to be abrogated by the *Sunna*; and actions made obligatory by the *Sunna* but abstention from which has been permitted by the scripture; duties incumbent at their prescribed time, but which cease to be so at a later time; [and in it is] the distinction between different forbidden acts, the major ones which He has threatened to punish with His fires, and the minor ones for which He has prepared His forgiveness; [and in it are described] acts that are acceptable when performed to a modest extent, and to a higher degree, without being obligatory.

NOTES

1. As noted in Chapter 1, note 1, this translation of Sermon no.1 is by the present author, based on the critical edition of the *Nahj al-balāgha* by Shaykh ʿAzīzullāh al-ʿUtārdī. The final paragraph of the sermon on the subject of pilgrimage, while important in itself, has not been included, as it is not directly related to our discussion in this book.

2. *Alladhī lā yudrikuhu buʿd al-himam, wa lā yanāluhu ghawṣ al-fiṭan.* The term *himam*, the plural of *himma,* comprises all kinds of effort, ardour, concentration and intensity in pursuit of a sought after goal. The word *ghawṣ* means depth, *ghāṣa* means to dive deeply into the sea, and *fiṭan* is the plural of *fiṭna*, meaning intelligence, astuteness, sagacity.

3. *Riyāḥ* (sing. *rīḥ).* As Lane notes, the singular form is often used to signify wind in a negative sense, one which brings no good, whereas the plural form often refers to good winds, those that bring rain. The Arabs said that clouds produce rain through diverse winds being blown together. A *ḥadīth* states, 'O God, make it to be winds and not a wind.' See Lane, *Lexicon*, vol.1, p.1181.

4. *Awwalu'l-dīn maʿrifatuhu.* The word *awwal* literally means 'the first' and can be understood as the starting-point, the foundation and hence the foremost element of religion. As for the word *maʿrifa*, as discussed throughout this book, the word denotes not simply knowledge but also 'recognition': one comes to know, once again, that which one knew as a seed of consciousness at the dawn of creation: 'And when thy Lord brought forth from the children of Adam, from their loins, their seed, and made them testify of themselves, "Am I not your Lord?" They said, "Yea, we testify." [This was] lest ye say on the Day of Resurrection, "Truly of this we were unaware"' (7: 172).

5. *Kamālu maʿrifatihi al-taṣdīqu bihi.* The word *taṣdīq* is the verbal noun of *ṣaddaqa*, which means to confirm something as true, to give one's consent or affirmation to it, hence to believe it to be true. The 'belief' in question has a dynamic quality about it, connoting the sense of affirming that which one believes—or knows, through the *maʿrifa* referred to as the starting point of religion—to be true.

6. *Kamālu'l-taṣdīq bihi tawḥīduhu.* As noted in Chapter 1, the word *tawḥīd*, all too often translated into English as 'unity' literally means 'making one', and acquires the meaning of affirming or declaring the oneness of God, in theological terms, and realizing ('making real') that oneness within one's consciousness, in spiritual terms.

7. *Kamālu tawḥīdihi al-ikhlāṣu lahu.*

8. This negation of the attributes should be understood in the light of the earlier phrase, 'He Whose attribute has no binding limitation (*alladhī laysa li-ṣifatihi ḥadd maḥdūd*).' So when the Imam says that pure devotion to God (*ikhlāṣ*) requires divesting God of all attributes (*nafyu al-ṣifāti ʿanhu*), the negation here is not of the divine attributes or Names as such, but a negation of them as separate, autonomous or super-added realities, conceived of as being substantially 'other than' or ontologically distinct from, the essence of God. This type of apophatic discourse is clearly intended to highlight the utter incommensurability between human *conceptions* of the divine Reality and that Reality *in itself*. See Chapter 1 for discussion of the apophasis here expressed; and Chapter 3 for discussion of the divine attributes in relation to spiritual realization.

9. *Man ashāra ilayhi faqad ḥaddahu; wa man ḥaddahu faqad ʿaddahu.* Having pointed to Him, one confines Him to a particular place, marking it off from all other places, thus denying His omnipresence; and having so confined Him, one is able to distinguish between Him and 'others' so numbering Him as one among others, and this is a denial of the full ontological meaning of His oneness. See our discussion of this point in Chapter 1.

10. That is, one isolates or removes Him from that which He is not 'upon'.

11. *Kāʾinun lā ʿan ḥadathin, mawjūdun lā ʿan ʿadamin.* Every existent entity comes into being as the result of a *ḥadath,* that is, a contingent event situated in time and space, on the one hand, and enters into being from a previous state of non-existence, *ʿadam*; on the other hand, God indeed 'is', but His Being cannot be compared with the being of anything that 'comes to be', having once not been. The phrase *ʿan ʿadam* might be read as an Arabic foreshadowing of the *creatio ex nihilo,* 'creation from nothing', of scholastic theology in the Christian Middle Ages.

12. *Maʿa kulli shayʾ, lā bi-muqārana; ghayr kulli shayʾ, lā bi-muzāyala.* As noted in Chapter 3, this sentence can be read as a prefiguration and summary of the doctrine of the 'oneness of being' (*waḥdat al-wujūd*), associated with the school of Ibn al-ʿArabī.

13. Ibn Abiʾl-Ḥadīd comments that the word *thumma*, 'then', here should not be read as if it implied a chronological sequence in creation; for what the Imam goes on to describe—the origin of the cosmos—precedes what has been described before—the creation of creatures and forms. It should instead be understood as 'Now I shall say, after what I have said before… ' *Sharḥ Nahj al-balāgha*, vol.1, p.84.

14. *Anshaʾa subḥānahu fatqaʾl-ajwāʾ, wa shaqqaʾl-arjāʾ wa sakāʾik al-hawāʾ.* The word *ajwāʾ* is the plural of *jaww*, which means air, environment, milieu.

The word *arjā'* is the plural of *rajan*, which means the side or direction of a thing, as well as a region or an expanse of space. The image evoked here is that of a cleaving up of the very directions and dimensions of space, dimensions of a vast compass. Thus one finds Ibn Maytham writing that these words refer to the void (*al-khalā'*) out of which an existential space is created, the space within which the primeval water is made to flow, as the Imam goes on to describe. *Sharḥ Ibn Maytham* (Beirut, 1999), vol.1, p.181. Likewise, in the commentary of 'Allāma al-Khu'ī, one finds a possible meaning of *al-jaww* as 'a conceivable dimension' (*al-bu'd al-mawhūm*). This is given in the context of his citation of Majlisī's comment on these words in his *Biḥār al-anwār*: 'What is intended by the words, "He created a fissure in the atmospheres", is the production of forms within empty spaces.' Khu'ī, *Minhāj*, vol.1, p.373.

15. That is, a wind that does not raise rain-producing clouds, nor does it carry pollen; such a wind is called *'aqīm*.

16. The image evoked here may be seen as a commentary on the words in the Qur'ān, 'Then He turned to the heaven when it was smoke...' (41: 11). Ibn Abi'l-Ḥadīd cites this and other verses in his commentary on this part of the sermon. *Sharḥ Nahj al-balāgha*, vol.1, pp.85–87.

17. The word 'firmament' translates *raqīm* which literally refers to an inscription or a tablet; 'Allāma al-Khu'ī writes that this is given as a name of the heavenly spheres, because their orbits are 'flattened out' like a written inscription, and the stars are, as it were, 'inscribed' upon the 'tablet' of the firmament. Khu'ī, *Minhāj*, vol.1, p.371.

18. The mention of a plurality of 'worlds' in the phrase 'lowest worlds' (*al-arḍīn al-suflā*) adds to the mystery of the Qur'ānic verse: 'God it is Who hath created seven heavens and of the earth the like thereof' (65: 12).

19. 'Pure' translates *khalaṣat*. The edition of Muḥammad 'Abduh has the word *khaḍalat*, meaning 'to become moist', but our reading would appear to make more sense in the context.

20. The word here is *ṣalṣāl*, which Lane, citing the *Tāj al-'arūs*, renders as 'dry clay that makes a sound by reason of its dryness'. Cf. Qur'ān, 55: 14: 'He created man of sounding clay (*ṣalṣāl*) like that of the potter', and 15: 26: 'And We created man of sounding clay (*ṣalṣāl*), of black mud altered'.

21. The word here is, again, *ma'rifa*. One can deduce important cognitive and spiritual principles from the use here of the same word for both knowledge of the Absolute and knowledge of relativities.

22. According to Ibn Abi'l-Ḥadīd, the prior injunction referred to here is the one indicated in the verse cited above: 'When thy Lord said unto the angels, "Lo, I am about to create a mortal out of clay, and when I have fashioned him

and breathed into him of My spirit, fall down prostrate before him'" (38: 71–72). *Sharḥ Nahj al-balāgha*, vol.1, p.99.

23. Ibn Abi'l-Ḥadīd refers to the words in the Qur'ān, 'O our Lord, our evil fortune (*shiqwatunā*) overcame us, and we were folk in error' (23: 106), to explain the meaning of the word *shaqwa*. Ibid., vol.1, p.97.

24. The words of Iblīs are given as follows in the verse: 'He said, I am better than him. Thou createdst me of fire, whilst him Thou didst create of clay' (38: 76). In this connection 'Allāma al-Khu'ī cites the following interesting comments by Ṣadr al-Dīn al-Shīrāzī, from the latter's *Mafātīḥ al-ghayb*, which we summarize as follows: Only from an extrinsic point of view can fire be said to be superior to clay. The mystery hidden within clay, that which makes it capable of receiving the influx of the Spirit, is that clay retains and develops what is placed within it, whilst fire, on the contrary, destroys whatever is placed in it. The Spirit of God, being breathed into the clay of Adam, renders him receptive to the divine theophany; the angels then rightly prostrate to him because 'his heart has become, as it were, a veritable Ka'ba (*ṣāra qalbuhu ka-ka'ba ḥaqīqiyya*).' Khu'ī, *Minhāj*, vol.2, p.57. Also of significance in connection with the false analogy made by Iblīs are the comments of Ibn Maytham. The pride of Iblīs arose out of a comparison of material elements alone, his error consisting in seeing in man nothing but the formal substance of which he is made. Ibn Maytham relates this superficial way of looking at things to the nature of vain thought (*al-wahm*) as such, which perceives 'only partial meanings, those attached to objects of the senses, so that its judgement and its effectiveness can be confirmed only in relation to sense-perceptions'. *Sharḥ Ibn Maytham,* vol.1, p.242.

25. 'Allāma al-Khu'ī comments on the relationship between the divine respite and the divine wrath by referring to the Qur'ānic verse, 'Let not the disbelievers imagine that the respite We give them bodeth well for their souls; We only grant them respite that they may increase in sinfulness. And theirs will be a shameful punishment' (3: 178). Later on in his commentary upon these words of the sermon, he nuances the notion of divine wrath: 'As for the punishments of the Hereafter that come from God—they are not brought about through wrath and vengeance, and [brought to an end by] the subsiding of anger—far exalted be God above such things! They are but necessary concomitants and consequences of interior causes pertaining to the soul and inward spiritual states ...' Khu'ī, *Minhāj,* vol.2, pp.62, 81. This accords, we might add, with the Qur'ānic verse, 'Read thy book; thy soul is sufficient this day as reckoner against thee' (17: 14).

26. Qur'ān, 38: 80–81.

27. *Fa-bāʿaʾl-yaqīn bi-shakkihi waʾl-ʿaẓīma bi-wahnihi.* One feels that the Imam's use of the definite article for the positive elements—certainty and resolution—and the possessive pronoun for the negative elements in Adam—*his* doubt and *his* weakness—may be a subtle allusion to the spiritual principle enunciated by the well-known prophetic *ḥadīth* and so clearly expressed throughout the Imam's discourses: 'There is no strength or power save through God (*lā ḥawla wa lā quwwata illā biʾLlāh*).' All goodness, truth, beauty, virtue are rooted in the divine Reality, and thus cannot be said to be the 'possessions' of man, rather they 'belong' to God and are bestowed upon man; they are therefore qualities to which man has access, and in which he can participate, but cannot 'possess'. It is only their opposites that man comes to possess as his own, and this appropriation of negative properties—the 'fall from grace'—takes place in the very measure of man's dereliction of the obligations attendant upon being the recipient of these divine gifts: *noblesse oblige*.

28. In his commentary on these words, Ibn Maytham writes that the covenant in question refers to that mentioned in the Qurʾānic verse 7: 172, cited in note 4 above (*Sharḥ Ibn Maytham*, vol.1, p.201). Ibn Abiʾl-Ḥadīd, on the other hand, refers to the prophetic *ḥadīth*, 'Every child is born in accordance with the primordial nature (*fiṭra*)' and writes that the covenant mentioned by the Imam here (*mīthāq fiṭratihi*) should be understood in the light of this primordial nature, which entails the implanting of 'knowledge of God and the evidences of *tawḥīd* and of justice (*ʿadl*)' within the intellects. The function of the prophets is to confirm these intellectual evidences (*Sharḥ Ibn Abiʾl-Ḥadīd*, vol.1, p.115). It is clear that the two explanations offered by the commentators are, in fact, complementary rather than mutually exclusive, insofar as the 'primordial nature' comprises the very element—knowledge of God—to which the whole of humanity is made to bear witness in the primordial pact (*mīthāq*) mentioned in the discourse and in the Qurʾānic verse.

29. Reference has been made throughout this book to this fundamental principle in the Imam's perspective. Divine revelation is intended not to replace or abolish the intellect, but to bring to the surface the treasures contained within it.

30. This pledge (*mīthāq*) is referred to in the Qurʾān: 'And when God took a pledge from the prophets, [saying], "Inasmuch as I have given you of the scripture and wisdom, then there cometh unto you a messenger confirming that which is with you—then ye shall believe in him and help him..."' (3: 81). Some commentators understand this pledge to be taken by the prophets on behalf of their respective communities, so that it is incumbent upon the

followers of these prophets to 'believe in' and 'help' the Prophet when he arose and proclaimed his mission. See, for example, al-Zamakhsharī's comment on this verse in his *Tafsīr al-kashshāf*, vol.1, p.371.

31. The 'conditionally permissible' (*rukhaṣ*, plural of *rukhṣa*) refers, as the commentators explain, to those acts that are permissible in extreme circumstances only, and forbidden outside of those circumstances. Ibn Abi'l-Ḥadīd gives the example of 5: 3, which details all the kinds of food forbidden to Muslims (such as carrion and pork, etc.), and then concludes, 'Whoso is forced by hunger, not through inclination to sin, [unto him] God is forgiving, merciful'. The 'unconditionally compulsory' (*'aẓā'im*, plural of *'aẓīma*) refers to those principles of belief which must be adhered to in an unconditional and absolute manner. The example given here is the fundamental principle of faith enunciated in verse 47: 19, 'So know that there is no god save God ...' Ibn Abi'l-Ḥadīd, *Sharḥ Nahj al-balāgha*, vol.1, p.121.

32. *Khāṣṣahu wa 'āmmahu*. An example of the 'specific' kind of ordinance is, according to Ibn Abi'l-Ḥadīd, that in which the Qur'ān permits the Prophet, alone, certain privileges as regards the formalities of the marriage contract (33: 50); and as regards the 'general' ordinances, these pertain to the injunctions to pray and fast, and so on. Ibid., vol.1, p.121.

33. *Mursalahu wa maḥdūdahu*. The word *mursal* literally means 'the sent forth' but according to the commentators, it is to be understood as undelimited or universally applicable (*muṭlaq*, according to Ibn Abi'l-Ḥadīd), as opposed to being conditional. Ibid., vol.1, p.121.

34. *Muḥkamahu wa mutashābihahu*. The 'unambiguous', clear and decisive verses are those about the meaning of which there is no doubt, such as 'Say: He is God, the One' (112: 1); the example given by Ibn Abi'l-Ḥadīd of an ambiguous equivocal verse is, 'Looking upon their Lord ...' (75: 23). Ibid., vol.1, p.121.

APPENDIX II

The Letter of Imam ʿAlī to Mālik al-Ashtar

(Written when the Imam appointed him as governor of Egypt and its regions, at a time when the rule of its governor, Muḥammad b. Abī Bakr, was unstable; it is the longest of the letters written by the Imam, and the most all-embracing as regards beauty of form and excellence of meaning.)[1]

In the Name of God, the Compassionate, the Merciful.

This is what the servant of God, ʿAlī, Commander of the Faithful, enjoins upon Mālik b. al-Ḥārith al-Ashtar, in his mandate (*ʿahd*) to him, appointing him as governor of Egypt: to collect its revenues; to fight its enemies; to establish the welfare of its inhabitants; and to bring prosperity to its lands.

He enjoins him to have fear of God; to prefer obedience to God [above all things]; and to abide by what He has commanded in His Book—acts both obligatory and recommended—for no one prospers except through abiding by them, and no one is wretched except through repudiating and neglecting them. [He further enjoins him] to assist God with his heart, his hand and his tongue: for truly He—majestic is His Name—has undertaken to grant victory to him who assists Him, and to elevate him who exalts Him.[2] He enjoins him to break the passionate desires of his soul, and to restrain it when it is beset with whim and caprice, for truly the soul incites to evil, unless God has mercy.

And be aware, Mālik, that I am directing you to a land which has been ruled by states—just and unjust—before you; and that the people will evaluate your conduct, just as you have evaluated the conduct of governors before you. They will speak about you just as you spoke about them; and the righteous are proven such only through what God has caused to flow from the tongues of His servants. So let your most beloved treasure be the treasure of virtuous acts. Dominate your inclinations, and exercise self-restraint in the face of that which is unlawful for you—for indeed self-restraint engenders within the soul a proper balance as regards what it likes and what it dislikes.

Infuse your heart with mercy for the subjects, love for them and kindness towards them. Be not like a ravenous beast of prey above them, seeking to devour them. For they are of two types: either your brother in religion or your like in creation.[3] Mistakes slip from them, defects emerge from them, deliberately or accidentally. So bestow upon them your forgiveness and your pardon, just as you would have God bestow upon you His forgiveness and pardon; for you are above them, and the one who has authority over you is above you, and God is above him who appointed you. He expects you to satisfy their needs; and through them He tests you.

Do not set your soul up for war with God. For before His retribution you have no resistance, and in the face of His forgiveness and mercy, no independence. So feel no regret when you pardon, and do not rejoice when you punish. Do not let an impulse propel you rashly towards any course of action, if you can see an alternative to it. Do not say, 'I have been given authority, I order and am obeyed', for this leads to corruption in the heart and the erosion of religion; and it brings closer the adversities of fate. If the authority of your position engenders vanity and arrogance, then look at the grandeur of God's dominion above you, and at His power to do for you that which you have no power to do for yourself. This will calm your ambition, restrain you from your own vehemence, and restore to you what had strayed from your intellect. Beware of comparing [yourself] with God in greatness and likening [yourself] to Him in might, for God abases every tyrant and disgraces every braggart. Be just with God and be just with people [giving them what is their due] from yourself, from your close relatives, and from those of your subjects towards whom you are most affectionate. If you fail to do this, you will be an oppressor. And he who oppresses the servants of God will find that God, as well as His servants, will oppose him. God refutes the argument of whomever He opposes. He [the oppressor] remains at war with God until he desists and repents. Nothing so surely induces the removal of God's grace and hastens His retribution as persistence in oppression. For God hears the cry of the oppressed and keeps a vigilant watch over the oppressors.

Let the most beloved of affairs to you be those most centred upon the right, the most comprehensive in justice, and the most inclusive of popular contentment, for the discontent of the common folk (*al-ʿāmma*) undermines the contentment of the elite (*al-khāssa*); while the discontent of the elite is compensated by the contentment of the common folk. In times of prosperity no subjects are more of a burden to the ruler as regards seeking his favour than the elite, and none who are less helpful to him in times of trial; none more repelled than they by justice, more importunate in making demands, less grateful when granted favour, slower to pardon when deprived, less patient in the face of the vicissitudes of time. By contrast, the pillar of the religion, the cohesion of the Muslims, and the implement [for fighting] the enemies are constituted by the common folk, so be well disposed to them and incline towards them.

Let those of your subjects who most keenly seek out the faults of others be the ones furthest away from you and the most despicable in your eyes. For people do have faults which it behoves the governor—above all others—to conceal. So do not disclose those faults which remain hidden from you. Your duty is but to purify that which has become apparent and obvious to you; God will judge concerning those things which remain hidden from you. So try and veil deficiencies as much as you can, so that God may veil from your subjects that in yourself which you wish to be veiled. Untie the knot of all resentment amongst the people, and cut from yourself the rope of all rancour. Ignore everything which is obscure to you. Never be quick to believe a slanderer, for a slanderer is a deceiver, even if he appear in the guise of a good adviser.

Do not allow into your sphere of consultation any misers, for they would deflect you from generosity and threaten you with poverty; nor any cowards, who would weaken you in your affairs; nor those who are avaricious, for they would adorn avidity for you with injustice.[4]

Truly, miserliness, cowardice and avarice are so many diverse inclinations comprised within a bad opinion of God. The worst of your ministers is he who ministered to evil [rulers] before you, participating in their sins. So do not allow them to enter your inner circle, for they are assistants to sinners, brothers of tyrants. The best alternatives to them will be found among those who are as intelligent and capable as they are, but who are not saddled with their burden of sin, and have not assisted any tyrant in his tyranny nor any sinner in his sin. Such people will be less of a burden for you as regards provision, most helpful to you as regards succour, most deeply inclined towards you in affection, and least attached to people other than you. So choose such people as intimate companions, to be with you in private and in public. Within this group, give preference to the one who most sincerely speaks the truth, however bitter it may be to you, and who supports you least in doing that which God dislikes for His friends, however painfully this may strike at your desires.

Attach yourself to those who are known for their piety and sincerity, and train them in such a manner that they do not flatter you or lavish praise upon you for doing something which you have not in fact done. For excessive praise breeds pride and carries one headlong towards vainglory. Do not place the virtuous and the wicked in the same rank before you, for this would result in the virtuous belittling the virtues and the wicked entrenching their vices. Impose upon them [the appropriate reward or punishment for] what they have imposed on themselves. Be aware that nothing so effectively engenders the governor's confidence[5] in his subjects than his virtuous behaviour towards them, his relieving of their hardship, and his refraining from compelling them to do what is beyond their power.

Let there thus arise a situation in which you can enjoy confidence in your subjects, for such an attitude will spare you much trouble. He who is most worthy of your confidence is he by whom your trial was deemed good, while he who is most deserving of your distrust is he by whom your trial was deemed bad.[6]

Do not rupture any beneficial tradition established by the leaders of this community, as a result of which unity has been harmoniously established, and from which the subjects have prospered. Do not set up some new practice which is detrimental to the already established traditions; if you do so, the reward for their observance will redound to him who established them, while the onus of their destruction will be upon you.

Study much with the scholars (*al-ʿulamāʾ*) and hold much discourse with the sages (*al-ḥukamāʾ*), in order to consolidate that which brings well-being to your lands, and to further entrench that which has already been established by your predecessors. Be aware that the subjects consist of various classes, none of which can be sound without the others being so, and none can function independently of the others. Among these classes are the soldiers of God (*junūd Allāh*); the scribes (*kuttāb*, sing. *kātib*) administering to the common people and the elite; the judges (*quḍāt al-ʿadl*); officials responsible for upholding fairness, and establishing the right of redress (*rifq*);[7] those who pay the *jizya* (poll-tax) and the *kharāj* (land-tax) from among the 'protected people' (*ahl al-dhimma*)[8] and the Muslims; the merchants and artisans; and the lowest class, comprising the needy and destitute. God has prescribed to each [class] its share and has ordained—as a binding covenant (*ʿahdan*) with us from Him—for each its limits and its duties, according to His Book or the *Sunna* of the Prophet—God bless him and his family.

So as regards the soldiers, they are—by the grace of God—the fortresses of the subjects, the adornment of the governors, the power of religion, and the pathways to security (*subul al-amn*). The subjects cannot maintain themselves except by means of the soldiers, and the soldiers for their part cannot be maintained except by means of the [revenues of the] *kharāj* which God extracts for them; with this, they have the wherewithal to wage war on their enemies, establish their welfare, and fulfill their needs.

These two classes [the soldiers and the peasants] cannot be maintained except through the third: the judges, administrators and scribes, inasmuch as they uphold all contracts, harmonize and organize all interests and benefits, being charged with the maintenance of the specific and general affairs [of state and society]. All of these classes need for their proper functioning the merchants and artisans, who gather the requisite goods, and establish the appropriate markets. They fulfill [the needs of the other classes] by procuring through their specific functions those resources which cannot be obtained by the work of others. Finally, there is the lowest class, consisting of the needy and the destitute—those deserving assistance and favour. For each [class] there is plenitude with God; and each has, in relation to the governor, a right proportioned to the needs of its welfare. The governor cannot fully accomplish the tasks imposed upon him by God without resolute determination and resorting to God's help (*al-ihtimām wa'l-istiʿāna*), galvanizing himself for the prerogatives of rectitude, and manifesting patience in the face of ease and difficulty.

Appoint as the commander of your soldiers the person whom you feel deeply is the most sincere in relation to God, the Prophet and your Imam, the purest of heart, the one most excellent in forbearance (*ḥilm*); who is slow to anger, happy to pardon, kind to the weak, severe with the strong; one who is neither moved by violence, nor held back by weakness. Cleave to those of noble descent, belonging to pious families of established name and repute, and to men known for their bravery, courage, generosity (*al-sakhāʾ*) and tolerance (*al-samāḥa*)—for they constitute a group formed by nobility, and a party made of honour. Then supervise their affairs as parents would supervise their child. Let no act by which you strengthen them appear too great in your eyes. Do not belittle any kindness—however slight—which you have promised them, for such kindness is as a summoner (*dāʿiya*) unto them, calling them to dispense good advice to you, and to enjoy trust in you. Do not abandon a close inspection of their affairs in favour of [ostensibly more] weighty matters, for there is a situation in which they benefit from even a small act of kindness, and one in which they cannot dispense with the weighty matters.

Let the most preferred of your commanders be one who is benevolent to the people, and most generous to them with his bounty, such that they have ample means, they and those among their relatives who succeed them. Let their concern be integrated within one resolve: to fight the enemy. Truly, your kindness towards them will cause their hearts to incline towards you.

The greatest source of joy for the governors is the establishment of justice in the land, and the emanation of love from his subjects. Such love will not be manifest unless their hearts be secure. And their advice will not be sound except through the governors' supervision of those in charge of the subjects' affairs, and their ensuring that they find the burden of rule light and easy to bear, and that they no longer anxiously hope that the rule of the governor will be terminated. So raise their hopes, keep up your continuous praise of them, and your enumeration of the brave deeds of those who have been brave—for truly, abundant praise of their noble acts rouse the brave, and spur on the lazy, if God wills. Acknowledge the courageous deeds of every man, and do not ascribe the deeds of one to someone else, or fall short in granting due acknowledgement. Do not let the nobility of a man cause you to reckon a small accomplishment great; and do not allow the lowliness of a man cause you to reckon a great one small.

Refer to God and His Messenger any matter which weighs heavily on you, or which is unclear to you, for God the Exalted has declared to a folk whom He loved to guide: 'O ye who believe, obey God and obey the Messenger and those in authority among you. And if ye dispute with one another over anything, then refer it to God and the Messenger' (Qur'ān, 4: 59). To 'refer to God' means following that which is clear and unequivocal in His Book; and 'refer to the Messenger' means following that part of his Sunna which unites, rather than that which divides.

Choose as judges those whom you consider the most excellent of your subjects—those who are not confused by complex matters, nor angered by disputants; who do not persist in error, and are not reticent about turning to the truth when they perceive it; whose souls are not susceptible to avarice; who, dissatisfied with a superficial understanding, will probe deeply; who are most circumspect in the face of ambiguities; most consequent in argumentation; least perturbed by the appeals of litigants; most patient in efforts to disclose the true state of affairs; most resolute when the right judgement is clear; who are not beguiled by praise nor misled by blandishment. Such people are indeed rare!

Then examine carefully and frequently the execution of the judge's verdicts, and be generous in paying him, so that any deficiency [in terms of livelihood] will be removed, thus diminishing his need for help from people. And bestow upon him a rank of proximity to yourself, one which nobody else from among your close companions might hope to attain. He should be made safe in your presence, protected against the attacks of other influential men. Scrutinize them with a piercing scrutiny, for this religion had been held captive in the hands of evil people, abused by them and their caprice, exploited by them for the sake of this world.

Then consider your administrators. Employ them after due examination, and do not appoint them out any partiality or favouritism, for such indulgence will engender various forms of injustice and treachery. Look for men of proven experience and modesty from among the righteous households, families enjoying precedence in Islam,[9] for they are the most noble in character, most rooted in dignity, least susceptible to greedy desires, and most acutely conscious of the consequences of all things. Provide them with a generous stipend, for this will be a source of strength for them, enabling them to establish their welfare, obviating any need to appropriate for themselves what that have power over, and providing an argument against them should they disobey your orders or betray your trust. Examine carefully their actions, by appointing supervisors known for their sincerity and reliability to watch over them. Your secret observation of their affairs will motivate them to fulfil their trust, and to be considerate towards the subjects. Pay attention also to your assistants: should any one of them stretch his hand towards some treacherous deed—and your observers are unanimous in their report, which you deem sufficient evidence of the act—then impose corporal punishment upon him. Let him be chastised on account of the affliction effected by his act. Let him be disgraced, brand him a traitor, and gird him with the ignominy of accusation.

Carefully examine the question of the *kharāj* land-tax, so that those subject to it are maintained in a proper state of well-being, for it is from their welfare, and the proper collection of the tax itself, that the benefit of others is derived. There can be no welfare of others except through them [the peasants], for all without exception are dependent on the [revenues of the] *kharāj* and those subject to it. Let your concern with the cultivation of the land outweigh your concern with the collection of the tax, for no tax will be collected if there be no cultivation. And whoever exacts the tax, without cultivating the land, ruins the land and destroys the people. His rule will not endure for long.

So if they complain of a heavy burden—or of some deficiency, or the cutting of irrigation supplies, or lack of rain, or a change in the condition of the soil as a result of flooding or drought—then lighten their burden, inasmuch as your hope is that their situation be set right. Do not let any favour you bestow upon them—by way of lightening their burden—weigh heavily upon you; for this will be an investment,[10] which will yield a return for you in terms of the prosperity of your land and the adornment of your rule, through your reaping the finest praise from them, and taking pride in dispensing justice among them. You can then depend upon an increase in their potential as a result of what you have invested in them when you gave them respite; and you can trust them inasmuch as you have accustomed them to receiving your justice and kindness.

It is possible that a situation might arise in which you depend upon them: they would then bear this responsibility gladly, for a prosperous land can bear a burden which you place upon it. The devastation of the land only comes about through the destitution of its inhabitants; and the destitution of its inhabitants only comes about when the desire to amass wealth rules the souls of the governors, when they have doubts about what endures, and when they profit little from exemplary teachings.

Now consider with care the situation of your scribes, appointing the best of them in charge of your affairs. Assign those letters containing the most sensitive strategies and secrets to the scribe in whom you find the most comprehensive moral qualities; one who will not be emboldened by his elevated status to contradict you in the presence of others at a public assembly; one who is not negligent in delivering to you the correspondence of your officials, and properly despatching your replies, regarding what he takes and gives on your behalf. He must not weaken any agreement contracted for you, nor be incapable of repudiating that which has been contracted to your detriment. He must not be ignorant of the value of his own capabilities; for one who is unaware of the value of his own capabilities will be even more ignorant of the value of others. Do not allow yourself to make your selection only on the basis of your own discrimination, confidence and trust, for men know how to present themselves to the discrimination of rulers through pretence and good service, behind which there is no sincerity or fidelity. Rather, investigate them carefully, doing so in relation to that with which they were entrusted by good people before you; and trust him whose virtue left the deepest impression upon the common people, and whose reputation for integrity is most widespread. This will be proof of your sincerity towards God and towards the one who appointed you.

Appoint for each of your affairs a head-officer among your officials, one who will not be daunted by the magnitude of affairs nor dispersed by their multiplicity. Any fault of your scribes which you have ignored will be ascribed to yourself.

Then attend to the merchants and artisans. Treat them well, urging the same on others. [Among them are] those of fixed abode, those who travel with their goods, and those who earn their livelihood with their hands. They are sources of benefit and the means by which conveniences are obtained. By them are procured goods from distant and remote places, brought by land and sea, from plains and mountains, and from places where men do not settle nor even dare to venture. They are in a state of reconciliation (*silm*), and from them no calamity need be feared; and they are in a state of peace (*ṣulḥ*), from them no disturbance need be feared. Examine their affairs attentively, both those which are close to you and those in all corners of your land. Be aware that, despite what has been said, there is in many of them a despicable stinginess, a repugnant greed, a propensity to hoard goods, and to arbitrarily fix prices. All of this brings about loss for the populace, and is a source of shame for the governors. So prohibit hoarding, for the Messenger of God—God bless him and his family—prohibited it. Let trading be carried out with propriety and fairness, according to prices which do not harm either of the two parties, the buyers or the sellers. So if any one of them succumbs to the temptation to hoard, after you have prohibited it, inflict upon him an exemplary—but not excessive—punishment.

Then—O God, O God!—[pay particular attention to] the lowest class, those who have no wherewithal, the destitute, the needy, the afflicted, the disabled. Within this class are those who beg, and those whose wretchedness calls out to be alleviated but do not beg.[11] Be mindful of God in regard to their rights, for He has entrusted these rights to your care. Assign to them a portion from your public treasury (*bayt al-māl*), and a portion of the produce of what is taken as booty by the Muslims in every region, for those who are furthest have the same rights as those nearest. Upholding the right of each of them is incumbent upon you. Do not let any haughtiness on your part cause you to neglect them, for you will not be pardoned even the slightest shortcoming [in fulfilling your obligations towards them] as a result of attending to some important matter. So do not turn your concern away from them, nor assume a contemptuous attitude towards them. Keep a watchful eye over the affairs of those who have no access to you, and who are disdained by men of high standing. Appoint from among those you trust a God-fearing and humble person to be responsible for bringing their affairs to your attention. Treat these people in a manner such that God may excuse you on the day you meet Him, for they are more in need of justice from you than any others among your subjects. In regard to each of them, offer your excuse to God[12] in respect of fulfilling his right. Assume responsibility for the orphans and the elderly, those who have no resources yet cannot being themselves to beg. This is onerous for the governors, and [the fulfilment of] all rights is onerous, but God makes it light for those who aspire to the Hereafter, who restrain their souls in patience, and trust in the truth of that which is promised them by God.

Apportion a part of your time to those who have special needs, making yourself free to attend to them personally, sitting with them in a public assembly with all due humility before God, your Creator. Keep your soldiers, guards and officers away from them, so that they can speak to you in an uninhibited manner[13] for I heard the Messenger of God say—God bless him and his family—on more than one occasion: 'A nation in which the rights of the weak are not wrested in an uninhibited manner from the strong will never be blessed.'

Bear patiently any coarseness or inarticulate expression that they might manifest; do not show any irritation or disdain towards them—God will thereby extend the most extensive dimensions of His compassion to you and make incumbent the reward for your obedience to Him. Give whatever you give with beneficence, and withhold [if this be unavoidable] with grace and apology.

There are certain affairs which you must take care of personally—among which are replying to your officers if your scribes are incapable of so doing; issuing [responses to] the requests of people when they are brought to you in person because your aides find their hearts constricted on their account.

Perform each day the task proper to it, for to each day belongs a particular task. Set apart the most excellent of your available time, and the greatest portions thereof, for your soul, for what is between you and God, even though all times [and actions performed therein] are for God, if the intention underlying them is good, and if your subjects derive security as a consequence. Let your observance of those duties (*farāʾiḍ*, sing. *farīḍa*) relating exclusively to God be the special means by which you purify your religion for God.[14] Give unto God of your vital energy[15] in your nights and your days, and perform fully that by which you draw near to God, doing so perfectly, without becoming dull or deficient, taking your body to its limits.[16]

When you lead the people in prayer, do so without repelling [them] or squandering [it],[17] for there are people with infirmities or special needs. Indeed, I asked the Messenger of God—God bless him and his family—when he sent me [as his representative] to Yemen, 'How should I lead them in prayer?' He replied, 'Lead them according to the prayer performed by the weakest among them; and be merciful to the believers.'

In addition to all of this, do not prolong any period of absence from your subjects, for the isolation of the governors from their subjects is a kind of constriction and causes deficiency in awareness of their affairs. Such isolation cuts rulers off from acquiring knowledge about things hidden from them, so that which is great will appear small, and that which is small, great; the beautiful will appear ugly, and the ugly, beautiful; the true will be mixed with the false. The governor is but a human being: he cannot know what people hide from him. There are no visible signs on the truth, by virtue of which apparent expressions of veracity can be distinguished from falsehood.

You can only be one of two types: either a man who gives himself generously for the sake of the truth—in which case why seclude yourself [thereby preventing yourself] from bestowing a necessary right or performing an honourable deed? Or else you are a man afflicted with refusal [to give of oneself] in which case, how quickly people will refrain from making requests of you, despairing of your generosity!

This, despite the fact that [fulfilling] most of the needs which people present to you is not burdensome, whether they be complaints against injustice or demands for fairness in transactions.

The governor has favourites and intimate friends, among whom some are prone to presumptuousness, arrogance and unfairness in transactions. Sever the root of these people by eliminating the causes of these vices, by not allotting any landed estates to anyone among your entourage or friends. Do not let them entertain any hope that you may grant them some estate; [were they to receive such an estate] it would be detrimental to those living adjacent to it, as regards [their access to] water resources, or any common undertaking, the burden of which would doubtless fall on them, while the profit therefrom would redound to those acquiring the estate, and not upon you. Upon you will fall only the resulting blame (*'ayb*), both in this world and the next.

Impose what is right upon whomsoever it is incumbent, whether he be close to you or distant. Be steadfast and vigilant in this matter, regardless of how it may affect your close ones and favourites. Always desire the consequences of [this principle], however heavily it may weigh upon you, for its outcome will be laudable.

If any of your subjects suspect you of an injustice, present your case such that you may be exonerated,[18] thus deflecting their suspicions away from you through your clear explanations. Such conduct is a means of self-discipline, it is a form of kindness towards your subjects, and a way of presenting your plea which will help you to fulfill your need to keep them upright in accordance with the truth.

Never reject any call to peace made to you by your enemy, if there be divine acceptance of his call,[19] for truly in peace lies repose for your soldiers, relaxation of your concerns, and security for your lands. But maintain all due vigilance regarding your enemies once you have contracted peace with them, for it is possible that the enemy is only making peace with you in order to lull you into a false sense of security.[20] So proceed with all due precaution, and be wary of having too trusting an opinion in such circumstances. But if you and your enemy enter into a solemn agreement, or if he obtain from you the right of protection (*dhimma*), then faithfully abide by what you have promised, and honourably uphold your obligation of protection. Make your very life a shield for what you have promised, for there is no divine obligation which so strongly unites people—despite having diverse inclinations and multifarious opinions—as that of honouring the principle of fulfilling one's pledge. The polytheists had observed this amongst themselves—even apart from their dealings with the Muslims—such was their dread of the consequences of treachery. So do not violate your pledge of protection, do not break your promises, and do not be treacherous towards your enemy—for only an ignorant wretch (*jāhil shaqiyy*) dares to oppose God.[21] God has indeed made His pledge and His protection a means of security, spreading it over His servants by His mercy, a sanctuary in the impregnability of which they find peace, and towards the protective power of which they make haste. So let there be no corruption, no treachery, and no deception. Do not enter into any agreement which contains defects, nor fall back on ambiguous connotations once the agreement has been confirmed and solemnized. Do not let any difficult matter lead you to break unfairly an agreement which God has made binding upon you. For indeed, your patience in the face of a difficulty—hoping for its resolution and its positive outcome—is far better than acting treacherously and then fearing its consequence: being overwhelmed by an exacting demand (*ṭilba*) from God, from which you will not be able to seek exemption in this life or the next.

Beware of unlawfully shedding blood: nothing is more conducive to retribution, more momentous in consequence, more deserving of the cessation of blessings and the severance of one's term [of life] than the unjust shedding of blood. On the Day of Resurrection, God—glorified be He—commences judgement of His servants by [calling them to account over] the blood they have shed. So do not try and strengthen your authority by unlawful bloodshed, for such action in fact weakens and debilitates it, indeed, brings it to an end and removes it.

You have no excuse before God or before me if you intentionally murder anyone, for this calls forth capital punishment. If you fall prey to some error, and your tongue or your hand goes too far in inflicting punishment—for even a punch, and other such assaults, can be a cause of death—do not allow pride in your power to make you seek a way of avoiding payment of what is rightfully due as recompense to the relatives of the person killed.

Beware of being self-satisfied, of being over-confident in what you find impressive about yourself, and of loving to be flattered, for these are among Satan's most reliable opportunities to efface the virtue (*iḥsān*) of the virtuous (*al-muḥsinīn*). Beware of making your subjects beholden to you for your virtue towards them; of exaggerating your deeds; and of making promises to them which you break. For making people beholden ruins virtue; exaggeration removes the light of the truth; and breaking promises imposes upon you the hatred of God and men. God the Exalted has said: 'It is indeed hateful to God that ye say that which ye do not' (61:3). Beware of rushing your affairs before their proper time, of squandering the possibility of dealing with them, of obstinacy when they prove intractable, of feebleness in dealing with them when they become manifestly clear. Put every affair in its proper place, and deal with it in its proper time. Beware of appropriating that in which all men have an equal share, and of negligence in regard to what is urgent and has become self-evident, for this will be to the detriment of yourself, and to the benefit of others. Soon, the veil covering all affairs will be lifted for you, and justice will be sought from you by those who have been wronged.

Dominate the zeal of your pride, the vehemence of your castigation, the power of your hand, and the sharpness of your tongue. Guard against these vices by restraining all impulsiveness, and putting off all resort to force until your anger subsides, and you regain self-control. But you cannot attain such self-domination without increasing your pre-occupation with remembrance of your return to your Lord.

It is incumbent upon you to remember what transpired in earlier times as regards just rule and virtuous customs, the practices of the Prophet—God bless him and his family—and the obligations enshrined in the Book of God. So faithfully follow that which you have witnessed us performing in these respects, and strive with all your soul to act in accordance with the injunctions contained in this mandate of mine. I am confident that this [mandate] will furnish an argument for myself against you, so you have no excuse if your soul hastens instead to gratify its caprice.

I beseech God by the abundance of His compassion, and the magnitude of His power, to fulfill every desire, to cause me and you to do that which will please Him, to present a clear justification to Him and His creatures, to earn the fairest praise amongst the servants [of God], and leave behind us the most beautiful vestiges in the land. [I beseech him to grant us] perfect blessings and ever-increasing honour, and that He seal [the lives of] myself and yourself with felicity (*al-saʿāda*) and the testimony (*al-shahāda*).[22] 'Truly unto him we are returning' (2: 156).[23]

And peace be with the Messenger of God—God bless him and his good and pure progeny.

NOTES

1. These are the words of the compiler of the *Nahj*, al-Sharīf al-Raḍī.

2. *Takaffala bi-naṣri man naṣarahu, wa iʿzāzi man aʿazzahu.*

3. *Immā akhun laka fi'l-dīn, wa immā naẓīrun laka fi'l-khalq.*

4. *Yuzayyinu laka'l-sharaha bi'l-jawr.* The meaning here appears to be this: an avaricious person will make greed for things of this world appear pleasing and good through disguising the means to obtain them—misappropriation, oppression, injustice; these vices will be presented as virtues inasmuch as they are means to the gratification of one's desires, this being the only 'virtue' which the avaricious recognise as such.

5. Literally, 'good opinion', *ḥusn al-ẓann.*

6. *Inna aḥaqqa man ḥasuna ẓannuka bihi laman ḥasuna balā'uka ʿindahu; wa inna aḥaqqa man sā'a ẓannuka bihi laman sā'a balā'uka ʿindahu.* This subtle point can be understood in the light of the statement of the Imam in his discourse to Kumayl, studied in chapter 1 of this work: the sage, or 'lordly knower' (*ʿālim rabbānī*) is he who 'befriends that by which the ignorant are estranged'. One thing that the sages befriend and embrace (as a purification) is a trial (*balā'*), while those who are 'ignorant' are 'estranged' by trials, deeming them to be negative, seeing them only from a flat, horizontal and worldly point of view. (I am grateful to Shaykh Hamza Yusuf for helping me to understand the Arabic meaning of this difficult sentence in the Letter of the Imam.)

7. The primary meaning of *rifq* is 'gentleness, tenderness', but it can also refer to 'a thing by means of which one seeks help or assistance' (Lane, *Lexicon*, I, 1126); thus, it can be translated in this context as 'redress' given that the officer in question is chiefly responsible for establishing 'fairness' (*inṣaf*).

8. That is, 'the People of the Book', those recipients of earlier revelations (principally Christians and Jews but the category was also extended in practice to other faith-communities) who were granted protection by the Muslim authorities upon due payment of the *jizya* tax.

9. That is, those who embraced Islam earliest, at a time when doing so promised no earthly reward, quite the contrary. This willingness to sacrifice is a key criterion of what the Imam refers to as nobility (*karam*) of character.

10. *Dhukhr*, literally, 'treasure'.

11. The translation given here of the two types—*al-qāniʿ* and *al-muʿtarr*—is based on ʿAbduh's gloss. See his edition of the *Nahj*, p.639.

12. That is, be prepared to justify your conduct before God.

13. *Ghayr mutataʿtiʿ*, literally, 'without stammering', implicitly, through fear.

14. This could also be translated as 'that by which your religion is rendered sincere for God' (*mā tukhliṣu li'Llāhi bihi dīnaka*).

15. Literally, 'of your body' (*min badanika*).

16. *Bālighan min badanika mā balagha.*

17. *Lā takūnanna munaffiran wa lā muḍayyiʿan.* The meaning here seems to be: do not repel the people by making the prayers too lengthy; but do not make the opposite mistake either, that of making the prayers too short, and thus squandering the blessings and the solidarity generated by congregational prayer.

18. *Fa'ṣḥir lahum bi-ʿudhrik*, literally: present your excuse to them. The primary meaning of the word *ʿudhr* is indeed 'excuse', but it can also mean 'a plea whereby one excuses oneself' (Lane, *Lexicon*, II, 1984), thus, a means of exonerating oneself of any misconduct, and not just asking to be excused for misconduct. In this context, to translate the word as 'excuse' would carry the implication that an injustice had indeed been committed, and that one was seeking to be excused for it. It is clear, however, that the Imam expects Mālik to act justly in all circumstances, and thus never need to be 'excused' for acting unjustly. The governor may, however, be required to explain the circumstances pertaining to an apparent act of injustice on his part, the exigencies and ambiguities of political life being what they are.

19. That is, in legal terms: if it conforms outwardly to the conditions laid down in the sources of the divine revelation; and in spiritual terms: if it conforms with your innate sense of what accords with the principle of justice, which is at one with the divine nature itself, as discussed in Chapter 2 of this work.

20. *Rubbamā qāraba li-yataghaffala.*

21. In other words, any breaking of a promise—even to an enemy—is tantamount to daring 'to oppose God'.

22. The word *shahāda* means testimony, witness, and also martyrdom, as in the Greek origin of the word, the martyr being the one who bears testimony to his faith by sacrificing his life for it.

23. *Innā ilayhi rāji'ūn.* Most editions of the *Nahj* have this phrase from the Qur'ān, but the Persian critical edition has the word *rāghibūn* instead of *rāji'ūn*, which would mean: 'truly unto Him we make our request'. The editor notes that two manuscripts consulted for the edition do contain these words from the Qur'ān, which seem the most fitting way to seal the Imam's mandate. See *Nahj*, p.383.

Bibliography

ʿAbd al-Zahrāʾ al-Ḥusaynī al-Khaṭīb. *Maṣādir Nahj al-balāgha wa asānīduh*. Beirut, 1988.

ʿAbduh, Muḥammad. *Nahj al-balāgha*. Beirut, 1996, pp.67–74.

Addas, Claude. *Ibn ʿArabī ou La quête du Soufre Rouge*. Paris, 1989; tr. Peter Kingsley, *Quest for the Red Sulphur*. Cambridge, 1993.

Ajmal, M. 'Sufi Science of the Soul', in S.H. Nasr, ed., *Islamic Spirituality*. London, 1987, vol.1, pp.294–307.

Amir-Moezzi, Mohammad Ali. *The Divine Guide in Early Shiʿism: The Sources of Esotericism in Islam*, tr. David Streight. New York, 1994.

——'Le combattant du *ta'wīl*: Un poème de Mollā Ṣadrā sur ʿAlī,' in Todd Lawson, ed. *Reason and Inspiration in Islam: Theology, Philosophy and Mysticism in Muslim Thought*. London, 2005, pp.432–454.

ʿAlī b. Abī Ṭālib. *Nahj al-balāgha*, ed. Shaykh ʿAzīzullāh al-ʿUtārdī. Tehran, 1993; ed. Muḥammad ʿAbduh. Beirut, 1996; Persian tr. Jaʿfar Shahīdī. Tehran, 1378 Sh./1999; English tr. Sayed Ali Reza. *Peak of Eloquence*. New York, 1996.

——*Duʿāʾ Kumayl*, tr. W.C. Chittick in *Supplications: Amīr al-Muʾminīn*. London, 1995.

——*Ghurar al-ḥikam wa durar al-kalim*, compiled by ʿAbd al-Wāḥid Āmidī, with Persian tr. Sayyid Ḥusayn Shaykhul-Islāmī, in *Guftār-i Amīr al-muʾminīn ʿAlī*. Qom, 2000; ed. with Persian tr. Muḥammad ʿAlī Anṣārī. Qom, 2001.

Āmulī, Sayyid Ḥaydar. *Jāmiʿ al-asrār*, ed. H. Corbin and O. Yahya, in *La philosophie shiʿite*. Tehran–Paris, 1969.

——*al-Muḥīṭ al-aʿẓam wa'l-baḥr al-khiḍamm fī ta'wīl kitāb Allāh al-ʿazīz al-muḥkam*, ed. Muḥsin al-Mūsawī al-Tabrīzī. Qom, 2001.

Āmulī, Ḥasanzādah. *Insān-i kāmil az dīdgāh-i Nahj al-balāgha*. Qom, 1379 Sh./2000.

Āshtiyānī, Jalāl al-Dīn. *Sharḥ-i muqaddam-i Qayṣarī bar Fuṣūṣ al-ḥikam*. Qom, 1372/1953.

'Aṭṭār, Farīd al-Dīn. *Tadhkiratu'l-awliyā'*, ed. R.A. Nicholson. London, 1905–1907; abridged tr. A.J. Arberry, *Muslim Saints and Mystics*. London, 1966.

Bābulī, Abu'l-Faḍl Ḥāfiẓiyān. 'Nahj al-balāgha', in A.A. Rashād, ed., *Dānish-nāmah*. Tehran, 2001, vol.12, pp.9–92.

——'Mashāriq anwār al-yaqīn', in A.A. Rashād, ed., *Dānish-nāmah*. Tehran, 2001, vol.12, pp.483–495.

al-Bayḍāwī, Nāṣir al-Din. *Anwār al-tanzīl wa asrār al-ta'wīl*. Beirut, 1996.

The Bhagavadgītā in the Mahābhārata, ed. and tr. J.A.B van Buitenen. Chicago, 1981.

Boethius. *The Consolation of Philosophy*, tr. V.E. Watts. London, 1969.

al-Bukhārī. *Ṣaḥīḥ al-Bukhārī* (summarized). Riyad, 1996/1417.

Chirri, Mohammad Jawad. *The Brother of the Prophet Mohammad*. Detroit, 1982.

Chittick, William. *A Shi'ite Anthology*. London, 1980.

—— *The Self-Disclosure of God: Principles of Ibn al-'Arabī's Cosmology*. Albany, NY, 1998.

—— *The Sufi Path of Knowledge: Ibn al-'Arabī and the Metaphysics of the Imagination*. Albany, NY, 1989.

Chodkiewicz, Michel. *Seal of the Saints: Prophethood and Sainthood in the Doctrine of Ibn 'Arabī*, tr. Liadain Sherrard. Cambridge, 1993.

——'Une Introduction à la Lecture des *Futūḥāt Makkiyya*,' in M. Chodkiewicz et al., ed., *Les Illuminations de La Mecque: The Meccan Illuminations. Textes Choisis/Selected Texts*. Paris, 1988, pp.21–73.

Corbin, Henry. *Cyclical Time and Ismaili Gnosis*, trs. R. Manheim, J. Morris. London, 1983.

—— *En Islam iranien*. Paris, 1971–1973.

—— *History of Islamic Philosophy*, tr. Philip Sherrard. London, 1993.

Dakake, David. 'The Practice of *Dhikr* in the Early Islamic Community', in Zailan Moris, ed., *Knowledge is Light: Essays in Honor of Seyyed Hossein Nasr*. Chicago, 1999, pp.169–193.

Daylamī, Aḥmad. 'Mabānī wa niẓām-i akhlāq', in A.A. Rashad, ed., *Dānish-nāmah*. Tehran, 2001, vol.4, pp.97–160.

Djebli, Moktar, 'Encore à propos de l'authenticité du *Nahj al-balāgha*!', *Studia Islamica*, 75 (1992), pp.33–56.

——'*Nahdj al-Balāgha*', *EI2*, vol.7, p.904.

Ernst, Carl W. *Words of Ecstasy in Sufism*. Albany, NY, 1985.

Fakhry, Majid. *Ethical Theories in Islam*. Leiden, 1994.
al-Farābī, Abū Naṣr Muḥammad. *al-Madīnat al-fāḍila*, tr. Richard Walzer, in *Al-Farabi on the Perfect State*. Oxford, 1985.
Gardet, L. 'Dhikr', *EI2*, vol.2, pp.223–227.
al-Ghazālī, Abū Ḥāmid. *Iḥyā' 'ulūm al-dīn*, 5 vols. Beirut, 1992.
——*Freedom and Fulfillment: An Annotated Translation of al-Ghazālī's* al-Munqidh min al-Ḍalāl *and other relevant works of al-Ghazālī*, tr. R.J. McCarthy. Boston, 1980.
——*Al-Ghazālī on Disciplining the Soul, and Breaking the Two Desires* (Books 22 and 23 of the *Iḥyā'*), tr. T.J. Winter. Cambridge, 1995.
——*Invocations and Supplications* (Book 9 of the *Iḥyā'*), tr. K. Nakamura. Cambridge, 1990.
——*Kīmiyā-yi sa'ādat*, tr. Claud Field, *The Alchemy of Happiness*. Lahore, 1987.
——*Mishkāt al-Anwār*, tr. W.H.T. Gairdner, *The Niche for Lights*. New Delhi, 1988.
——*The Remembrance of Death and the Afterlife* (Book 40 of the *Iḥyā'*), tr. T.J. Winter. Cambridge, 1989.
Gimaret, D. '*Ṣifa*', *EI2*, vol.9, pp.316–323.
Guillaume, Alfred. *The Life of Muhammad: A Translation of Ibn Ishaq's* Sirat Rasul Allah. London, 1955.
al-Ḥallāj, Manṣūr. *Dīwān al-Ḥallāj*, ed. S. Ḍannāwī. Beirut, 1988.
al-Ḥamawī, Yāqūt. *Mu'jam al-buldān*. Beirut, 1388/1968.
al-Harawī, 'Alī b. Abī Bakr. *Kitāb al-ishārāt ilā ma'rifat al-ziyārāt*. Damascus, 1953.
Hujwīrī, 'Alī. *Kashf al-maḥjūb*. Tehran, 1376 Sh./1997; tr. R.A. Nicholson. London, 1936.
Ibn Abi'l-Ḥadīd. *Sharḥ Nahj al-balāgha li-Ibn Abi'l-Ḥadīd*. Beirut, 1965.
Ibn 'Ajība. *Īqāẓ al-himam fī sharḥ kitāb al-ḥikam*. Cairo, 1983.
Ibn al-'Arabī. *al-Futūḥāt al-makkiyya*. Cairo, 1911; French tr. M. Chodkiewicz et al., *Les Illuminations de La Mecque: The Meccan Illuminations. Textes Choisis/Selected Texts*. Paris, 1988.
——*Fuṣūṣ al-ḥikam*, tr. R. Austin, *The Bezels of Wisdom*. New York, 1980.
——*Kitāb al-fanā' fi'l-mushāhada*, in *Rasā'il Ibn al-'Arabī*. Damascus, 1998; French tr. M. Valsan, *Le Livre de l'Extinction dans la Contemplation*. Paris, 1984.
——*Kitāb al-jalāla wa huwa kalimatu'Llāh*, in *Rasā'il Ibn al-'Arabī*. Damascus, 1998; French tr. M. Valsan, 'Le Livre du Nom de Majesté,' in *Études Traditionelles*, no. 268, July-Aug (1948), pp.206–215.

——*Tarjumān al-ashwāq*, tr. R.A. Nicholson. London, 1978.
Ibn ʿAṭā'illāh al-Iskandarī, *Kitāb al-ḥikam*, tr. Victor Danner, *Sufi Aphorisms*. Leiden, 1973.
——*Miftāḥ al-falāḥ wa miṣbāḥ al-arwāḥ*, tr. Mary A.K. Danner, *The Key to Salvation: A Sufi Manual of Invocation*. Cambridge, 1996.
Ibn Ḥanbal, Aḥmad. *al-Musnad*, ed. A.M. Shākir. Cairo, 1949.
Ibn Kathīr, Ismāʿīl. *al-Bidāya wa'l-nihāya*. Beirut, 1974.
Ibn Mardawayh, Abū Bakr Aḥmad. *Manāqib ʿAlī b. Abī Ṭālib wa mā nazala min al-Qur'ān fī ʿAlī*. Qom, 2001.
Ibn Maytham al-Baḥrānī. *Sharḥ Ibn Maytham*. Beirut, 1999.
al-Iṣfahānī, al-Rāghib. *Muʿjam mufradāt alfāẓ al-Qur'ān*. Beirut, n.d.
Izutsu, Toshihiko. *Ethico-Religious Concepts in the Qur'ān*. Montreal, 1966.
Jabre, F. *La Notion de la* Ma'rifa *chez Ghazālī*. Paris, 1958.
Jaʿfariyān, Rasūl. *Tārīkh wa sīrah-i siyāsī-yi amīr al-mu'minīn ʿAlī b. Abī Ṭālib*. Qom, 1380 Sh./2001.
Jafri, S. Husain M. *Origins and Early Development of Shiʿa Islam*. London—New York, 1979.
——*Political and Moral Vision of Islam*. Lahore, 2000.
al-Jāḥiẓ, Abū ʿUthmān ʿAmr b. Baḥr. *al-Bayān wa'l-tabyīn*. Beirut, 1968.
Jordac, George. *The Voice of Human Justice*, tr. M. Fazal Haqq. Qom, 1990.
al-Kalābādhī, Abū Bakr. *Kitab al-Taʿarruf li-madhhab ahl al-taṣawwuf*. Cairo, 1960; tr. A.J. Arberry as *The Doctrine of the Sufis*. Cambridge, 1953.
al-Kāshānī, ʿAbd al-Razzāq. *al-Iṣṭilāḥāt al-ṣūfiyya*. Cairo, 1992.
——*Majmūʿ-i rasā'il wa muṣannafāt*, ed. M. Hādīzādah. Tehran, 2000.
——*Laṭā'if al-iʿlām fī ishārāt ahl al-ilhām*, ed. M. Hādīzādah. Tehran, 2000.
——*Tafsīr Ibn al-ʿArabī*. Cairo, n.d.
Kāẓimī, Bahrām. 'Barrisī-yi taṭbīqī-yi mafhūm-i ʿadālat dar andīshi-yi Imām ʿAlī wa Aflāṭūn,' in Mehdi Golshani, ed., *Proceedings of the International Congress on Imām ʿAlī* (Persian articles). Tehran, 2001, pp.165–187.
al-Khānī, ʿAbd al-Majīd b. Muḥammad. *al-Ḥadā'iq al-wardiyya fī ḥaqā'iq ajilla al-Naqshabandiyya*. Damascus, 1306/1889.
al-Kharrāz, Abū Saʿīd. *Kitāb al-ṣidq*, tr. A.J. Arberry, *The Book of Truthfulness*. Oxford, 1937.
al-Khu'ī, Abu'l-Qāsim. *Muʿjam rijāl al-ḥadīth*. Qom, 1983.
Khu'ī, ʿAlī Ṣadrā'ī. '*Mi'a kalima*', in A.A. Rashād, ed., *Dānish-nāmah*. Tehran, 2001, vol.12, pp.471–476.
al-Khu'ī, Mīrzā Ḥabību'Llāh. *Minhāj al-barāʿa fī sharḥ Nahj al-balāgha*. Tehran, n.d.

Kingsley, Peter. *Ancient Philosophy, Mystery and Magic: Empedocles and Pythagorean Tradition*. Oxford, 1995.

Knysh, Alexander. *Ibn 'Arabi in the Later Islamic Tradition: The Making of a Polemical Image in Medieval Islam*. Albany, NY, 1999.

al-Kulaynī, Muḥammad b. Ya'qūb. *al-Uṣūl min al-kāfī*. Tehran, 1418/1997–8.

Landolt, Hermann. 'Walāyah', in *The Encyclopedia of Religion*, 1st ed., vol.15, pp.316–323.

Lane, E.W. *Arabic-English Lexicon*. Cambridge, 1984.

Lawson, Todd. 'The Dawning Places of the Lights of Certainty in the Divine Secrets Connected with the Commander of the Faithful', in L. Lewisohn, ed., *The Heritage of Persian Sufism*. Oxford, 1999, vol.2, pp.261–276.

Lewisohn, Leonard. 'Alī b. Abī Ṭālib's Ethics of Mercy in the Mirror of the Persian Sufi Tradition,' in Ali Lakhani. ed., *The Sacred Foundations of Justice in Islam*. Vancouver, forthcoming.

Lings, Martin. *A Sufi Saint of the Twentieth Century: Shaikh Aḥmad al-'Alawī*. London, 1971.

——*Muhammad: His Life Based on the Earliest Sources*. London, 1986.

——*Sufi Poems*. Cambridge, 2004.

——*The Book of Certainty*. Cambridge, 1992 (under the name Abū Bakr Sirāj ad-Dīn).

Lumbard, Joseph. 'The Decline of Knowledge and the Rise of Ideology in the Modern Islamic World', in J. Lumbard, ed., *Islam, Fundamentalism and the Betrayal of Tradition*. Bloomington, IN, 2004, pp.39–77.

MacIntyre, Alasdair. *After Virtue: A Study in Moral Theory*. London, 1981.

Madelung, Wilferd. *The Succession to Muḥammad: A Study of the Early Caliphate*. Cambridge, 1997.

Mahdi, Muhsin S. *Alfarabi and the Foundation of Islamic Political Philosophy*. Chicago-London, 2001.

Mahjub, Muhammad Ja'far. 'Chivalry and Early Persian Sufism', in L. Lewisohn, ed., *The Heritage of Persian Sufism*. Oxford, 1999, vol.1, pp.549–581.

al-Majlisī, Muḥammad Bāqir. *Biḥār al-anwār*. Tehran. 1397/1977.

Meri, Josef. *A Lonely Wayfarer's Guide to Pilgrimage: 'Alī ibn Abī Bakr al-Harawī's* Kitāb al-Ishārāt ilā Ma'rifat al-Ziyārāt. Princeton, 2004.

Michon, J.-L. *Le Soufi Marocain Aḥmad Ibn 'Ajība* (1746–1809) *et son* Mi'rāj. Paris, 1973.

——'The Spiritual Practices of Sufism,' in S.H. Nasr, ed., *Islamic Spirituality*. vol.1, pp.265–293.

Moosa, Matti. *Extremist Shiites: The* Ghulāt *Sects*. Syracuse, 1988.

Morris, James. 'Ibn Arabī and his Interpreters,' *Journal of the American Oriental Society*, 106 (1986) pp.539–551, pp.733–756; 107 (1987), pp.101–119.

——'The Spiritual Ascension: Ibn 'Arabī and the *Mi'rāj*,' *Journal of the American Oriental Society*, 107 (1987), pp.629–652 and 108 (1988), pp.63–77.

——'Ibn 'Arabī's Spiritual Ascension,' in M. Chodkiewicz et al., eds., *Les Illuminations de La Mecque*, pp.351–381.

Morris, Zailan. ed. *K nowledge is Light: Essays in Honor of Seyyed Hossein Nasr*. Chicago, 1999.

Mottahedeh, Roy. *The Mantle of the Prophet*. Harmondsworth, UK, 1987.

Muir, William, *The Caliphate: Its Rise, Decline and Fall*. Edinburgh, 1924.

Murādī, Muḥammad. 'Rawish-i tafsīr-i Qur'ān,' in A.A. Rashād, ed., *Dānish-nāmah*. Tehran, 2001, vol.1, pp.229–284.

Murata, Sachiko and W. Chittick. *The Vision of Islam*. New York, 1994.

Muṭahharī, Murtaḍā. "Irfān: Islamic Mysticism,' in Murtaḍā Muṭahharī, *Understanding Islamic Sciences*. London, 2002, pp.89–141.

——*'Adl-i ilāhī*. Tehran, 2001.

Muslim. *Ṣaḥīḥ*, 2 vols. Cairo, 1349/1930.

——*Ṣaḥīḥ Muslim*, English translation, 'Abdul Ḥamīd Ṣiddīqī. Lahore, 1976.

al-Najāshī, Abu'l-'Abbās. *Rijāl al-Najāshī*. Qom, 1407/1986.

Nanji, Azim. 'The Ethical Tradition in Islam,' in A. Nanji, ed., *The Muslim Almanac*. New York, 1996, pp.205–211.

al-Nasā'ī, Aḥmad b. Shu'ayb. *Khaṣā'iṣ amīr al-mu'minīn 'Alī b. Abī Ṭālib*. Tehran, 1419/1998.

Nasr, Seyyed Hossein, 'An Intellectual Autobiography,' in L.E. Hahn et al., eds., *The Philosophy of Seyyed Hossein Nasr*. Carbondale, IL, 2001, pp.3–85.

——'Introduction' in S.H. Nasr, ed., *Islamic Spirituality*, vol.1, *Foundations*. New York, 1987, pp.xv–xxix.

——*Islamic Art and Spirituality*. Ipswich, UK, 1987.

——ed., *Islamic Spirituality*, vol.2, *Manifestations*. New York, 1991.

——*Knowledge and the Sacred*. New York, 1981.

——*Man and Nature: The Spiritual Crisis of Modern Man*. London, 1968.

——'Reply to Zailan Moris,' in Hahn et al., ed., *The Philosophy of Seyyed Hossein Nasr*, pp.632–638.

——*Science and Civilization in Islam*. Cambridge, 1987.

——'Spiritual Chivalry', in S.H. Nasr, ed., *Islamic Spirituality*. New York, 1991, vol.2, pp.304–315.

——*Sufi Essays*. London, 1972.

al-Nawawī, Yaḥyā b. Sharaf. *An-Nawawī's Forty Hadith*, tr. E. Ibrahim and D. Johnson-Davies. Damascus, 1976.

Niʿma, ʿAbd Allāh. *Madārik Nahj al-balāgha*. Beirut, 1972.

al-Nīsābūrī, al-Ḥākim. *al-Mustadrak ʿalāʾl-ṣaḥīḥayn*. Beirut, 2002.

Nūrī Hamadānī, Shaykh Ḥusayn. 'Uṣūl wa mabānī-yi ḥukūmat-i Islāmī az manẓar-i Imām ʿAlī', in Mehdi Golshani, ed., *Proceedings of the International Congress on Imām ʿAlī*, pp.3–32.

Paketchy, Ahmad. *Mawlid Amīr al-muʾminīn: Nuṣūṣ mustakhrija min al-turāth al-Islāmī*. Tehran, 2004.

Parens, Joshua. *Metaphysics as Rhetoric. Alfarabi's Summary of Plato's Laws*. Albany, NY, 1995.

Perry, Whitall. *Treasury of Traditional Wisdom*. London, 1971.

Plato. *Plato. The Collected Dialogues*, ed. and tr. E. Hamilton and H. Cairns, Bollingen Series 71. Princeton, 1999.

——*Protagoras and Meno*, tr. W.K.C. Guthrie. London, 1979.

——*Phaedrus and Letters VII and VIII*, tr. R. Hackforth in *Plato. The Collected Dialogues*, ed. and tr. E. Hamilton and H. Cairns, Bollingen Series 71. Princeton, 1999.

al-Qāḍī al-Nuʿmān, Abū Ḥanīfa. *Sharḥ al-akhbār fi faḍāʾil al-aʾimmat al-aṭhār*, ed. M. al-Ḥusaynī al-Jalālī. Qom, 1409–12/1988–92.

al-Qāḍī, Wadād. 'An Early Fāṭimid Political Document', *Studia Islamica*, 48 (1978), pp.71–108.

al-Qummī, Shaykh ʿAbbās. *Kulliyyāt mafātīḥ al-janān*. Qom, n.d.

Qummī, Nāṣir al-Dīn Anṣārī. 'Ghurar al-ḥikam wa durar al-kalim', in A.A. Rashād, ed., *Dānish-nāmah*. Tehran, 2001, vol.12, pp.243–260.

al-Qushayrī, Abu'l-Qāsim. *al-Risāla al-Qushayriyya*. Cairo, 1995; tr. R.T. Harris as *Sufi Book of Spiritual Ascent*. Chicago, 1997.

——*Laṭāʾif al-ishārāt*. Cairo, n.d.

Rajabī, Muḥammad Ḥusayn. '*Sabb*', in A.A. Rashād, ed., *Dānish-nāmah*. Tehran, 2001, vol.9, pp.295–365.

Rappe, Sara. *Reading Neoplatonism: Non-discursive Thinking in the Texts of Plotinus, Proclus, and Damascius*. Cambridge, 2000.

Rashād, ʿAlī-Akbar, ed., *Dānish-nāmah-i Imām ʿAlī*. Tehran, 2001.

Rāstgū, Sayyid Muḥammad. 'Faṣāḥat wa balāghat-i Imām ʿAlī', in A.A. Rashād ed., *Dānish-nāmah*. Tehran, 2001, vol.11, pp.11–76.

Rayshahrī, Muḥammad. *Ahl al-bayt dar Qurʾān wa ḥadīth*, tr. Ḥamīd Riḍā

Shaykhī and Ḥamīd Riḍā Āzhīr. Qom, 1379 Sh./2000.

——ed. *Mawsū'at al-Imām 'Alī ibn Abī Ṭālib fi'l-kitāb wa'l-sunna wa'l-ta'rīkh.* Qom, 1421/2000.

——ed. *Mīzān al-ḥikma.* Qom—Tehran, 1403/1983.

al-Rāzī, Fakhr al-Dīn. *al-Tafsīr al-kabīr.* Beirut, 2001.

Rūmī, Jalāl al-Dīn. *Fīhi mā fīhi.* Tehran, 1369 Sh./1990; tr. A.J. Arberry as *The Discourses of Rūmī.* London, 1961.

——*Mathnawī-yi ma'nawī*, ed. R.A. Nicholson. Tehran, 1984; tr. R.A. Nicholson, *The* Mathnawī *of Jalāluddīn Rūmī.* London, 1926–1934.

al-Ṣadūq, Abū Ja'far Muḥammad b. 'Alī b. Bābawayh. *al-Tawḥīd.* Beirut, 1967.

Sajoo, Amyn B. *Muslim Ethics: Emerging Vistas.* London, 2004.

Schuon, Frithjof. *Light on the Ancient Worlds.* Bloomington, IN, 1984.

——*Stations of Wisdom.* Bloomington, IN, 1995.

Shah-Kazemi, Reza. "'Alī b. Abī Ṭālib', in *The Encyclopedia of Religion*, 2nd ed., vol.1, pp.256–261.

——'From the Spirituality of Jihad to the Ideology of Jihadism,' in *Seasons: Semiannual Journal of Zaytuna Institute*, vol.2, no.2 (2005), pp.44–68.

——*Paths to Transcendence: According to Shankara, Ibn Arabi and Meister Eckhart.* Bloomington, IN, 2006.

——*The Other in the Light of the One: The Universality of the Qur'ān and Interfaith Dialogue.* Cambridge, 2006.

——'Tradition as Spiritual Function', *Sacred Web*, 7 (2001), pp.37–58.

Shankaracharya (Śaṃkara). *A Śaṃkara Source Book*, tr. and compiled by A.J Alston, vol.1, *Śaṃkara on the Absolute.* London, 1981; vol.2, *Śaṃkara on the Creation.* London, 1983.

al-Sha'rānī, 'Abd al-Wahhāb. *al-Anwār al-qudsiyya fī ma'rifa qawā'id al-ṣūfiyya.* Cairo, 1987.

Shaykhul-Islāmī, Sayyid Ḥusayn. *Guftār-i amīr al-mu'minīn 'Alī.* Qom, 2000.

Shūshtari, 'Allāma. *Qaḍā' Amīr al-mu'minīn 'Alī ibn Abī Ṭālib.* Tehran, 2001.

al-Suyūṭī, Jalāl al-Dīn. *al-Durr al-manthūr fi'l-tafsīr bi'l-ma'thūr.* Beirut, 1314/1896.

——*al-Itqān fī 'ulūm al-Qur'ān.* Beirut, 1987.

——*Ta'rīkh al-khulafā'*, tr. H.S. Jarrett, *History of the Caliphs.* Amsterdam, 1970.

al-Ṭūsī, Abū Ja'far. *al-Fihrist.* Mashhad, 1351/1932.

al-Ṭabarī, Abū Ja'far Muḥammad b. Jarīr. *Jāmi' al-bayān.* Beirut, 2001.

——*Ta'rīkh al-rusul wa'l-mulūk*. Leiden, 1964.

Ṭabāṭabā'ī, 'Allāma. *Kernel of the Kernel Concerning the Wayfaring and Spiritual Journey of the People of Intellect* (Risāla-yi lubāb dar sayr wa sulūk-i ulu'l-albāb)*: A Shī'ī Approach to Sufism*, ed. Sayyid M.H.H. Ḥusaynī Tihrānī, tr. M.H. Faghfoory. Albany, NY, 2003.

——*Shi'ite Islam*, ed. and tr., S.H. Nasr. Albany, NY, 1975.

Trimingham, Spencer. *The Sufi Orders in Islam*. Oxford, 1971.

Unno Taitetsu. 'The Practice of *Jodo-shinshu*,' in Alfred Bloom, ed., *Living in Amida's Universal Vow: Essays in Shin Buddhism*. Bloomington, IN, 2004, pp.63–73.

Uždavinys, Algis. *Philosophy as a Rite of Rebirth*. London, 2006 (forthcoming).

Voll, John O. 'Sufi Orders' in John L. Esposito, ed., *The Oxford Encyclopedia of the Modern Islamic World*. New York—Oxford, 1994, vol.4, pp.109–117.

Waley, M.I. 'Contemplative Disciplines in Early Persian Sufism,' in Leonard Lewisohn, ed., *The Heritage of Sufism*. Oxford, 1999, vol.1, pp.497–548.

Wannell, Bruce and Hermann Landolt. *A Tradition of Esoteric Commentary: Imam 'Alī's* Ḥadīth al-ḥaqīqa (London, forthcoming).

Wensinck, A.J., et al. *Concordance et indices de la tradition musulmane*. Leiden, 1936–1969.

Whelan, Estelle. 'Forgotten Witness: Evidence for the Early Codification of the Qur'ān', *Journal of the American Oriental Society*, 118 (1998), pp.1–14.

Winter, T.J. 'Preface' to *Al-Ghazali on Disciplining the Soul, and Breaking the Two Desires*. Cambridge, 1995.

Wu, John C.U. *The Golden Age of Zen: Zen Masters of the T'ang Dynasty*. Bloomington, IN, 2003.

al-Yaman, Ja'far b. Manṣūr. *Kitāb al-'ālim wa'l-ghulām*, ed. and tr. James Morris, *The Master and the Disciple: An Early Islamic Spiritual Dialogue*. London, 2001.

Yazdi, Mehdi Ha'iri. *The Principles of Epistemology in Islamic Philosophy*. Albany, NY, 1992.

Yūsufiyān, Ḥasan and Sharīfī, Aḥmad Ḥusayn. 'Imām 'Alī wa mukhālifān' in A.A. Rashād, ed., *Dānish-nāmah*. Tehran, 2001, vol.6, pp.193–252.

al-Zamakhsharī, Abu'l-Qāsim Maḥmūd. *Tafsīr al-Kashshāf*. Beirut, 1995.

General Index

Aaron 20, 63
'Abbāsids 1
'Abd Allāh b. al-'Abbās 83, 84, 100–101, 198
'Abd Allāh b. Busr 158
'Abd al-Muṭṭalib 14
Abraham 17, 61
al-abrār (the righteous) 112
Abu'l-Dardā' 167
Abū Bakr 14, 19, 62, 63, 190, 241
Abū Dharr al-Ghifārī 21, 206
Abū Sa'īd al-Kharrāz 156, 200
Abū Ṭālib al-Makkī 146
Adam 20, 91, 96, 150, 210, 211, 217
Advaita Vedanta 66, 67
Ahl al-Bayt 16, 17, 22, 135
Aḥmad al-'Alawī 139, 241
Aḥmad b. Ḥanbal 18
a'immat al-ḥaqq (true leaders) 7, 98
'Ā'isha 20
Akbarī 170, 180
akhlāq 74, 80, 238
alchemy 12
'Alī b. Abī Ṭālib
and *Ahl al-Bayt*, 16–17
and *balāgha* (eloquence, rhetoric) 1–3, 12, 68, 141–142, 196
and battle of Khaybar 15–16
and Ghadīr Khumm 21–22
and Mu'āwiya 82, 83, 84, 126
as *quṭb* (spiritual pole) 22, 136, 139
attitude to political power 83–85, 89–93, 102, 219 ff
biographical sketch 13–22
early partisans (*shī'a*) of 21–22
on beauty 47–48
on compassion 46–47, 99–103, 109–110, 208, 211, 220, 229
on *dhikr* (remembrance/invocation) 33, 44, 116, 138, 141–168, 162–164, 168–169, 177, 199
on joy 45–47, 49, 50, 54–55, 110, 211, 224
on justice 77–137, 82–114, 117, 221, 224, 227, 229, 233, 235
on knowledge 11, 19, 24, 31, 35–72, 87, 129, 140, 149–151, 177, 182, 184, 186–188, 208, 210, 213, *et passim*
on *mujāhadat al-nafs* (spiritual struggle against the soul) 40–42, 96–97
on prayer 20, 43–44, 50, 80–81, 111, 114–117, 122, 160–161, 230, *et passim*
on *taqwā* (piety) 52, 114
on *ta'wīl* (spiritual/esoteric interpretation) 23–28
on the creation of Adam 34, 210

on the heart 29–30, 32–33, 36–37, 44–45, 52, 55, 57, 76, 93, 101, 116 ff, 138, 141 ff, 219, 220
on the Hereafter 52–59, 94, 107, 109, 111–112, 142–143, 167, 189, 229
on the intellect 12, 22–59, 68, 78, 87–88, 93, 103, 116–117, 142–143, 149–152, 195, 210, 211, 220
on the Khārijites 50, 70–71, 131
on the veil (*al-ḥijāb*) 151–156
on the vision of God 29–32, 59, 76, 119, 145–146, 156
on *zuhd* (asceticism, detachment) 52–53, 98
prophetic sayings concerning 18–21
proximity to the Prophet 11–13, 15, 19–20
ʿAlids 2
ʿālim rabbānī (lordly knower) 36, 37, 234
ʿAllāma Ṭabāṭabāʾī 4–5
ʿAmmār b. Yāsir 21, 126
Āmidī, ʿAbd al-Wāḥid 4, 237
Anamnesis 78, 119, 123
ʿāqil (intellectual) 35, 39, 46, 50
ʿAqīl b. Abī Ṭālib 100
ʿaql (intellect; see also ʿintellectʾ) 22, 35, 40, 42, 48, 195
Āshtiyānī, Jalāl al-Dīn 181, 238
ʿĀṣim b. Ziyād 98
al-asmāʾ al-ḥusnā (the most beautiful [divine] Names) 143, 171, 171, 181–182, 189
ʿAṭṭār, Farīd al-Dīn 184, 238
Awliyāʾ (friends [of God], saints) 135, 167, 182, 205

baqāʾ (subsistence) 107, 177, 200
Baṣra 100
Al-bāṭin (the inward) 153, 190, 206
Bāyazīd al-Basṭāmī 182, 206
bayt al-māl (public treasury) 102, 229
beauty 47–48, 50, 53, 58, 70, 79, 159, 177, 217, 219
al-Bukhārī 18, 238

Camel, (al-Jamal) battle of 24, 65
Christendom 22
compassion 31, 40, 46–47, 54, 97, 99-103, 104, 106, 109-110, 199, 208, 211, 220, 229
Corbin, Henry 4–5, 6, 9, 190, 238

Deconstructionism 30–31
dhawq (mystical taste) 176
dhikr (remembrance; see also under ʿAlī b. Abī Ṭālib, ʿon *dhikr*ʾ) 33, 44, 78, 116, 117, 134–186, 200, 204, *et passim*
Dhiʿlib al-Yamānī 119
Djebli. Moktar 3, 238
Duʿāʾ Kumayl 146, 158, 237
Duʿāʾ Mashlūl 173
Dustūr maʿālim al-ḥikam (al-Qāḍī Abū ʿAbd Allāh Quḍāʿī) 4

Eckhart, Meister 69
Elijah 187
Enoch (Idrīs) 62

fanāʾ (extinction) 34, 52, 55, 162–166, 174–175, 177, 200, 204, 239
faqīh (jurist) 46–47, 124
al-Fārābī, Abū Naṣr 80, 132
al-fātiḥa (the opening [chapter of the Qurʾān]) 25
Fāṭima bt. Asad 14 16, 20, 167
Fāṭima bt. Muḥammad 16, 20, 60–61, 63, 167
fikr (reflection, meditation) 159
fiṭra (primordial nature) 86–89, 150, 163, 197, 217

Fuṣūṣ al-ḥikam (Ibn al-ʿArabī) 180, 239
Futūḥāt al-makkiyya (Ibn al-ʿArabī) 169, 170, 239
futūwwa 134, 190

Ghadīr Khumm 21
Ghafla (heedlessness) 151, 158, 162, 178, 199
al-Ghazālī, Abū Ḥāmid Aḥmad 80, 139, 175, 176, 178, 240
al-Ghazālī, Aḥmad 4
Ghurar al-ḥikam wa durar al-kalim (ʿAbd al-Wāḥid Āmidī) 3, 140, 243, *et passim*

ḥadīth 2, 3, 4, 17, 18, 50, 78, 115, 145, 158, 164, 170, 182, 243
ḥadīth al-ḥaqīqa (the saying on ultimate reality) 170
al-Ḥākim al-Nīsābūrī 18, 59
al-Ḥallāj 178, 182, 187, 239
ḥaqāʾiq al-īmān (verities of faith) 29, 32, 59, 76, 119, 145–146, 156
ḥaqīqa (truth, reality) 38, 162–164, 170, 174–175, 177, 190
al-Ḥaqq (the Real, the True) 25, 43, 75, 77, 81, 87, 90, 98, 117, 121, 156, 164, 182
al-Ḥasan b. ʿAlī b. Abi Ṭalib, Shiʿi Imam 16, 101, 245
Hashimites 14
hawā (whim, caprice) 40, 41, 49
Ḥaydar Āmulī 135
heart 29–30, 32–33, 36–37, 39, 42, 44–45, 48–49, 50, 52, 53–55, 57, 76, 93, 101, 116 ff, 137–139, 141–156, 159, 162–163, 166, 171–172, 177, 178, 181, 186, 187, 189, 194, 195, 196, 197, 204, 206, 216, 219, 220
Hell 57, 101, 111
Hereafter 41, 45, 52–59, 94–95, 107–109, 111–112, 142–143, 167, 189, 229
ḥilm (wise forbearance) 48, 106, 224
ḥujja bāṭina (inner proof) 66
ḥujja ẓāhira (outer proof) 66
Hujwīrī, ʿAlī 135, 194, 239
ḥulūl (incarnation) 207
al-Ḥusayn b. ʿAli b. Abi Ṭalib, Shiʿi Imam 2, 16, 101, 245
al-Ḥusaynī al-Khaṭīb, ʿAbd al-Zahrā' 3, 237

Iblīs 91, 92, 93, 211, 216
Ibn Abi'l-Ḥadīd 2, 239
Ibn al-ʿAbbās *see* ʿAbd Allāh b. al-ʿAbbās
Ibn ʿAjība 178, 241
Ibn al-ʿArabī 136, 146, 155, 164, 165, 166, 169, 170, 171, 172, 174, 175, 179, 180, 183, 184, 240
Ibn ʿAṭā'illāh 152–153, 177, 205
Ibn Bābawayh (al-Shaykh al-Ṣadūq) 4
Ibn Khallikān 2
Ibn Muljam 189
Ibn Shahrāshūb 4
Ibn Shuʿba 4
Ibn Ziyād 2
iḥsān (spiritual virtue) 47, 58, 75, 78, 79, 80, 121, 122, 165, 233
Iḥyāʾ ʿulūm al-dīn (al-Ghazālī) 80
ikhlāṣ (sincerity, purity) 31, 32, 42–49, 116, 162, 163, 183, 214
ʿilm (knowledge) 11, 31, 36–38, 65, 67, 72, 132, 135, 139, *et passim*
al-ʿilm al-ḥuṣūlī (representational knowledge) 67
al-ʿilm al-ḥuḍūrī (knowledge by presence) 67
intellect 12, 22–59, 64, 66, 67, 68, 70, 78, 87–88, 93, 103, 116–117, 142–143,

149–152, 156, 163, 195, 197, 210, 211, 220
'irfān (spiritual knowledge) 134, 135, 140, 181, 242
isnāds 2, 3
istidrāj 94

Ja'far al-Ṣādiq, Shi'i Imam 138, 160, 178, 180, 184
al-Jāḥiẓ, Abū 'Uthmān 'Amr b. Baḥr 3, 4, 9, 240
Jesus 19, 61, 71, 113, 166, 196
al-jihād al-akbar (the greater holy war) 40–42, 163
joy 45–47, 49, 50, 54–55, 110, 178, 211, 224
justice i, 35, 43, 58, 73, 74, 77, 81 ff, 137, 156, 221, 224, 227, 229, 233, 235

Ka'ba 14, 23, 216
Kāfūr (fountain of) 185–186
al-Kalābādhī, Abū Bakr 174, 240
Karbalā' 2
al-Kāshānī, 'Abd al-Razzāq 146, 170, 177, 180, 185, 186, 240
Kashf al-maḥjūb (Hujwīrī) 135, 239
Khadīja 13, 14, 16
khalwa (spiritual retreat) 138
Khārijites 50, 71
Khaybar, battle of 15, 63
al-Khu'ī, 'Allāma 150, 241
Khuṭbat al-bayān (sermon of clarifying expression) 187, 206
knowledge 11, 19, 24, 31, 35–72, 87, 129, 140, 149–151, 177, 182, 184, 186–188, 197, 198, 205, 206, 208, 210, 213, *et passim*
Krishna 65
Kūfa 2, 23, 36, 127
al-Kulaynī, Muḥammad b. Ya'qūb 4, 241
Kumayl b. Ziyād vii, 23, 36, 37, 45, 146, 158, 170, 237
Lings, Martin 60, 197
lubb (inner substance) 132, 159, 199, 200

MacIntyre, Alisdair 74, 241
Madārik Nahj al-balāgha ('Abd Allāh Ni'ma) 3, 243
makhīla (arrogance) 93
Mālik al-Ashtar 73, 77, 81, 82, 84, 85, 86, 88, 97, 100, 103, 105, 106, 107, 108, 114, 115, 120, 126, 130, 199, 219 ff
Manāqib āl Abī Ṭālib (Ibn Shahrāshūb) 4
ma'rifa (gnosis) 54, 135, 137, 149–150, 152, 163, 198, 213, 244
Maṣādir Nahj al-balāgha wa asānīduh (al-Ḥusaynī al-Khaṭīb) 3, 237
Mathnawī (Rūmī) 145, 175, 244
Mecca 14, 15, 21, 63
Medina 15, 20, 21, 81, 83, 167
Miqdād b. 'Amr 21
Mi'a kalima (al-Jāḥiẓ) 4, 240
Morris, James 64
Moses 20, 165, 166, 200
Mu'āwiya 82, 83, 84, 126
mubāhila (mutual imprecation) 16
Muḥammad al-Bāqir, Shi'i Imam 150, 160
Muḥammad b. Abī Bakr 97, 125, 219
al-Murtaḍā, al-Sayyid 2, 123
Mūsā al-Kāẓim, Shi'i Imam 66
al-Mustadrak (al-Ḥākim al-Nīsābūrī) 18–21, *et passim*

al-nafs al-ammāra (the commanding/inciting soul) 86, 88, 96, 219
al-nafs al-lawwāma (the upbraiding soul) 127
al-nafs al-muṭma'inna (the soul at

peace) 57, 127–128
Nahj al-balāgha 1–6, 23, 31, 34, 52, 56, 81, 87, 140, 141, 147, 149, 154, 182, 243, *et passim*
Naqshabandī, Sufi order 190
al-Nasā'ī, Aḥmad 18
Nasr, Seyyed Hossein 9, 59, 64, 124, 125, 135, 189–190, 245
Neoplatonism 77
Niʿma, ʿAbd Allāh 3

Paketchy, Ahmad 60
Paradise 41, 45, 53–58, 111, 112, 167, 206
Plato, Platonism 77, 78, 85, 102, 106, 118, 119, 120, 243
Platonic 77, 80, 133
polytheism 49, 90, 92, 93
prayer 17, 20, 43–44, 49–50, 53, 55, 80–81, 111, 114-117, 122, 132, 136, 138, 157-162, 168, 230, 235, *et passim*
Prophet Muḥammad 6, 7, 12, 13, 14, 15, 16, 17, 18, 19, 20, 21, 22, 23, 24, 25, 40, 41, 47, 48, 50, 58, 73, 78, 79, 81, 85, 86, 92, 101, 105, 106, 115, 134, 135, 136, 138, 139, 140, 144, 145, 157, 158, 161, 165, 167, 168, 182, 212, 223, 224, 233, 242

al-Qāṣiʿa (sermon) 91–92
al-Qayṣarī, Dā'ūd 180, 181, 238
Quḍāʿī, al-Qāḍī Abū ʿAbd Allāh 4
al-Qushayrī, Abu'l-Qāsim 176, 243
quṭb (spiritual pole) 22, 135, 136, 139, 190

al-Raḍī, al-Sharīf 1, 2, 3, 234
al-Rāghib al-Iṣfahānī 137, 192
riḍwān (beatitude) 45
riyā' (pretension) 92
rūḥ (spirit) 22, 45, 177
Rūmī, Jalāl al-Dīn 145, 175, 244

Sabziwārī 182
Ṣadr al-Dīn al-Shīrāzī (Mullā Ṣadrā) 216
Sajoo, Amyn 75, 244
Salmān al-Fārisī 21, 206
al-Shāfiʿī 4, 17
Shankara (Ṣamkara) 67–68, 69, 205
al-Shiqshiqiyya (sermon) 10, 102
shirk (polytheism, idolatry) 41, 49, 92, 148, 154, 182, 186
Shiʿism 21, 22, 134, 135, 207
al-Shūshtarī, ʿAllāma 178
ṣifa (attribute [of God]) pl. *ṣifāt* 31, 67, 181–183, 208, 214
Ṣiffīn, battle of 83, 126
silsila (spiritual chain of affiliation) 22, 134, 190
Sufis 79, 80, 135, 136, 138, 139, 145, 153, 176, 180, 182, 184, 240
Sufism 4, 12, 18, 22, 25, 78, 80, 134, 135, 136, 137, 139, 140, 141, 152, 154, 156, 162, 167, 173, 174, 177, 178, 180, 245
Sunna 7, 11, 27, 105, 136, 141, 212, 223, 225, 244
Sunnis, Sunnism 21, 134, 190

al-Ṭabarī, Abū Jaʿfar Muḥammad b. Jarīr 3, 21, 82, 244
Tabula secreta 187
Tadhkiratu'l-awliyā' (ʿAṭṭār) 184, 238
tafsīr (exegesis) 12, 25, 244
taḥqīq (realization) 27, 90, 161
tajallī (divine manifestation) 143–147, 153, 166, 170, 195, 200, 207
tanzīh (incomparability) 154–155
tanzīl (descent, revelation) 19, 24, 238
taqarrub (drawing near) 115–116, 145, 164, 185
taqlīd (imitation) 27
taqwā (piety) 52, 114

Tarjumān al-ashwāq (Ibn al-ʿArabī) 166, 240
taṣawwuf see Sufism, Sufis, Sufi
tashbīh (analogy) 155
tawaddud (assimilation of love) 48, 70
al-Tawḥīd (Ibn Bābawayh) 4
tawḥīd (integration) 24, 26, 39–42, 48, 54, 73, 75, 87, 88, 122, 135, 150, 154, 155, 156, 162, 168, 170, 181, 182, 185, 186, 217
ta'wīl (spiritual, esoteric interpretation) 19, 23–28
al-thaqalayn (the two weighty things) 17
Tuḥaf al-ʿuqūl (Ibn Shuʿba) 4

ʿUbayd Allāh b. Ziyād 2
Uḥud, battle of 15
ʿUmar 19, 21, 62
al-Uṣūl min al-kāfī (al-Kulaynī) 4
ʿUthmān b. ʿAffān 84, 176, 240

walāya (sanctity) 16, 21, 22, 59–60, 135, 190, 205
walī (saint, patron, master) 18, 20–21, 56, 135, 139
Whelan, Estelle 194

Yazdi, Mehdi Ha'eri 67
Yūsuf (prophet Joseph) 53, 86–88, 127–128

al-Ẓāhir (the Apparent, the Manifest) 152–153, 190, 196
Zaynab bt. ʿAlī 2
Ziyād b. Abīhi 100
zuhd (asceticism, detachment) 52, 53, 98
Zulaykhā 88, 128

Index of Qur'ānic Verses

2: 10 'In their hearts is a disease and God increased them in disease.' 49
2: 25 'And give good tidings to those who believe ...' 58
2: 31 'And He taught Adam the names, all of them ...' 150
2: 115 'Wherever ye turn, there is the Face of God.' 47, 187
2: 152 'Remember Me, I will remember you.' 159
2: 155 'And We shall try you with something of fear and hunger ...' 51
2: 198 'Remember Him as He hath guided you.' 177
2: 285 'We make no distinction between any of His messengers.' 7
3: 31 'Say: O ye who believe, if ye love God, follow me ...' 47
3: 190–191 'Truly in the creation of the heavens and the earth ...' 60, 159
4: 59 'O ye who believe, obey God and obey the Messenger ...' 225
4: 135 'O ye who believe, be staunch in justice ...' 101
6: 54 'Thy Lord has prescribed for Himself mercy.' 99
6: 162 'Say: Truly my worship and my sacrifice ...' 43
7: 55 'Call upon thy Lord in humility and in secret.' 156
7: 143 '... fell down stunned.' 165, 166, 200
7: 156 'My mercy encompasseth all things.' 47, 99
7: 172 'Truly, of this we were unaware.' 96, 150
7: 179 'They have hearts with which they understand not ...' 143
7: 180 'Unto God belong the most beautiful Names, so call Him by them.' 143
7: 181–182 'Of those We have created are people who guide with truth ...' 95
7: 205 'And invoke thy Lord within thyself ...' 156
8: 2 'Those are true believers whose hearts quake with awe ...' 144
8: 17 '... thou didst not throw when thou threwest ...' 88, 164
8: 24 'O ye who believe, respond to God and His Messenger ...' 35
9: 85 'Let not their wealth nor their children please thee ...' 95
9: 118 'There is no refuge from God except [fleeing] to Him.' 167
13: 7 'Verily thou art a warner, and for

every people there is a guide.' 20
13: 19–20 'Is one who knoweth that what is revealed to thee …' 105
13: 28 '...Those who believe and whose hearts are at peace …' 144
15: 56 '… and who despaireth of the mercy of his Lord …' 47
15: 99 'Worship thy Lord until certainty cometh to thee.' 44
17: 18 'Whoso desireth that [life of the world]…' 52
17: 34 'Approach not the wealth of the orphan…' 105
17: 44 'And there is nothing that does not hymn His glory with praise …' 53
17: 81 'The Truth hath come and falsehood hath passed away …' 94
17: 110 'Call upon *Allāh* or call upon *al-Raḥmān* …' 171
20: 14 'Establish the prayer for the sake of My remembrance.' 160
21: 25 'And We sent no Messenger before thee …' 7
22: 37 'It is not their [sacrificed] flesh nor their blood …' 50
22:46 'Have they not travelled in the land …' 49, 143
23: 91 'Glorified be God above what they describe.' 33
24: 35 'God is the light of the heavens and the earth …' 142
24: 36–37 'In houses which God has allowed to be elevated …' 142
24: 41 '... whosoever is in the Heavens and the earth praises God …' 53, 187
25: 43 'Hast thou seen him who maketh his desire his god?' 41
26: 214 'Warn thy nearest kin.' 14
28: 88 'Everything perisheth except His Face.' 53, 94, 176
29: 45 'Truly, prayer keepeth [one] away from lewdness…' 138, 161
29: 64 'And the life of this world is naught but sport …' 52
30: 30 'So set thy purpose for religion with unswerving devotion…' 86, 150
32: 7–9 'He began the creation of man with clay…' 34
32: 9 'He fashioned him and breathed into him of His spirit.' 150
33: 6 'The Prophet is closer to the believers than they are to themselves.' 11
33: 33 'God only wisheth to remove from you all impurity …' 16
33: 41–43 'O ye who believe, invoke God with much invocation …' 156, 158, 160
33: 56 'Truly, God and His angels bless the Prophet …' 17
35: 15 'O mankind, ye are the poor before God …' 98
37: 96 'God hath created you and what ye do.' 164
38: 46 'Assuredly, We purify them with a pure quality …' 57
39: 22 'Is he whose breast God hath opened up to submission …' 144
39: 23 'God hath revealed the most beautiful saying …' 144
40: 16 'To whom belongeth the dominion this day …' 91
41: 53 'We shall show them Our signs …' 25, 147
42: 23 'Say: I ask you for no reward, save love of the near of kin.' 16
45: 23 '… taketh his own desire as his god …' 41, 97
48: 29 '… severe against the disbe-

lievers, compassionate amongst themselves.' 106
50: 16 'We are closer to man than the neck-artery.' 148
50: 37 'Truly, therein is a reminder ...' 144
53: 3–4 'It is naught but a revelation revealed.' 40
53: 23 'They are but names ...' 171
55: 26 'Everything thereon perisheth ...' 94, 175
55: 60 'Is the reward of goodness aught but goodness?' 58
57: 3 'He is the First and the Last, the Outward and the Inward' 25, 146, 147
57: 16 'Hath not the moment come for the believers ...' 151
58: 19 'The devil hath overcome them ...' 157
61: 3 'It is indeed hateful to God ...' 233
63: 9 'O ye who believe, let not your wealth ...' 157
68: 4 'Verily, thou art of a tremendous nature.' 11
70: 23 '... perpetually at prayer.' 160
73: 8 'And invoke the Name of thy Lord ...' 156, 157
73: 20 'Whatever good ye send before for your souls ...' 58, 157
76: 8–9 'They feed, out of love for God ...' 112
76: 25 'And invoke the Name of thy Lord morning and evening.' 156
79: 40–41 'But whoso feareth the station of his Lord...' 41, 167
83: 14 'Nay, their hearts have become rusted by that which they have done.' 39
85: 3 'By a witnesser and that which is witnessed.' 146
87: 1 'Glorify the Name of thy Lord, the Exalted.' 157
87: 6–7 'thou wilst not forget ...' 174
87: 17 '... the Hereafter is better and more lasting.' 57
89: 27 '... soul at peace in absolute certainty.' 57
91: 3 'By the day, as it bringeth to light ...' 143
91: 7–8 'And the soul and that which perfected it ...' 95
92: 1–2 '... by the night when it enshroudeth ...' 143
92: 17–21 '... the most pious will be far removed from it ...' 112
94: 5–6 'Verily, with hardship cometh ease ...' 51
96: 6–7 'Truly man is rebellious ...' 97
98: 7 'Those who have faith and do righteous deeds ...' 21
103: 1–3 'By the Age, truly man is in a state of loss ...' 51
104: 1–4 'Woe be to every slandering backbiter...' 108
107: 1–7 'Hast thou seen the one who belieth religion ...' 49
107: 4–6 'Woe to those who pray ...' 162
108: 1–2 'We have given thee al-Kawthar ...' 111
112: 1 'Say: He, God is One.' 148, 218
112: 4 '...there is none comparable unto Him.' 148
113: 2 '... the evil of that which He created.' 76